The Bank Recovery and Resolution Directive

ILFS

Institute for Law and Finance Series

Edited by
Theodor Baums
Andreas Cahn

Volume 13

The Bank Recovery and Resolution Directive

Europe's Solution for "Too Big To Fail"?

Edited by
Andreas Dombret
Patrick S. Kenadjian

DE GRUYTER

ISBN 978-3-11-032107-4
e-ISBN 978-3-11-032140-1

Bibliographic information published by the Deutsche Nationalbibliothek
The Deutsche Nationalbibliothek lists this publication in the Deutsche Nationalbibliografie; detailed bibliographic data are available in the Internet at http://dnb.d-nb.de.

Cover image: Medioimages/Photodisc
Data Conversion: Werksatz Schmidt & Schulz GmbH, Gräfenhainichen
Printing and Binding: Hubert & Co. GmbH & Co. KG, Göttingen
♾ Printed on acid-free paper
Printed in Germany

www.degruyter.com

Preface

Since the beginning of the financial crisis in 2008, legislators and scholars alike have identified the potential repercussions of the failure of a major banking institution within the global financial system as a key regulatory issue. On November 5, 2010, the Institute for Law and Finance of Goethe University hosted a conference focusing on issues related to the "too big to fail" problem. Papers based on the presentations given at this first "too big to fail" conference have been published in volume 9 of the ILF Series. The current volume contains articles based on presentations given at a follow-up conference entitled "The Crisis Management Directive – Europe's Solution for Too Big to Fail?" hosted by the Institute for Law and Finance of Goethe University on May 3, 2012. The range of topics discussed in both conferences reflects the progress made in the field of bank resolution between fall of 2010 and spring of 2012. While the first conference dealt with basic conceptual issues, such as whether special rules for bank resolution are needed, what the appropriate triggers and tools of bank resolution should be, and how a creditor protection regime should be designed, the second conference focused on more specific issues. The papers by *Dombret* and *Tucker* review the development of the new regulatory approach to bank resolution. In part 2 of the volume, *Gleeson* and *Randell* highlight the importance of group rather than single company resolution. Parts 3 and 4 deal with specific new instruments of bank resolution. In part 3, *Hüpkes*, *Otto* and *Guynn* explore the potential and the limitations of living wills, while in part 4, *Huertas*, *Bliesener* and *Kenadjian* analyse key aspects of bail-ins as a resolution tool.

The organizers are particularly pleased that eminent experts from the United States, the United Kingdom, Switzerland and Germany agreed to participate in the event and to share their views on and experiences with the new regulatory approach on bank resolution. The presentations given at the conference of May 3, 2012 have been updated in 2012 to reflect recent developments.

Andreas Cahn

Table of Contents

The Authors

Prof. Dr. Andreas Cahn

Andreas Cahn studied law at the Johann Wolfgang Goethe-University Frankfurt/Main and at the University of California at Berkeley, where he earned an LL.M. After his Second State Examination in Frankfurt he worked for 6 years as a research assistant at the University of Frankfurt. During this period of time he wrote his doctoral thesis on problems of managers' liability (published in 1996) as well as his post-doctoral thesis on legal aspects of intra-group financing (published in 1998).

In 1996 he took up the Chair of Civil Law, Commerce Law and Corporate Law at the University of Mannheim. Since October 2002 he is Director of the Institute for Law and Finance at Goethe-University in Frankfurt. He has published extensively on corporate law, capital markets law, the law of products liability, general civil law as well as on civil procedure. He is co-publisher of "Der Konzern", a law journal focusing on company law, taxation and accounting of corporate groups, of "Corporate Finance law", a journal with a focus on current legal issues corporate finance, co-editor of the Institute for Law and Finance Series and member of the editorial board of the law journal "European Company Law".

Dr. Dirk H. Bliesener

Dirk H. Bliesener is a partner of Hengeler Mueller in Frankfurt am Main, Germany. Admitted to the New York and Frankfurt bars, Dirk Bliesener acted for Hypo Real Estate in setting up the bad bank FMS Wertmanagement (2009–2010) and was legal adviser to WestLB during their restructuring and transformation (2007–2012) which included state-guaranteed securitizations, two successive portfolio transfers to the bad bank Erste Abwicklungsanstalt and the transfer of banking activities to Helaba. Since 2010, Dr. Bliesener has been counsel to the German Federal Ministry of Finance on the European Financial Stability Facility (EFSF). He also frequently advises on debt capital markets, banking and securitization matters.

Dirk Bliesener speaks frequently on topics related to bank restructuring and resolution. He is a co-editor and co-author of the recent commentary on German banking law (Bankrechts-Kommentar, 2013) and author of various publications on banking and securities laws. Previously a research associate of Hamburg-based Max Planck Institute for Foreign and Private International Law, Dirk Bliesener holds a doctorate of Hamburg University and is an alumnus of Yale Law School (LL.M.), University of Paris 1 (Maîtrise en Droit) and Institut d'Etudes Politiques de Paris (Sciences Po, C.E.P.).

Dr. Andreas Dombret

Andreas Dombret was born on 16 January 1960 in the USA to German parents. After completing his "Abitur" (senior school-leaving certificate) at the Neusprachliches Gymnasium in Ahlen, North Rhine-Westphalia, he trained as a bank clerk with Dresdner Bank before studying business management at the Westfälische Wilhelms University in Münster. He was awarded his PhD by the Friedrich-Alexander University in Erlangen-Nuremberg. From 1987 to 1991, he worked at Deutsche Bank's Head Office in Frankfurt as a manager with the power of procuration. From 1992 to 2002, he worked at JP Morgan in Frankfurt and London, from 1999 as a Managing Director. From 2002 to 2005, he was the Co-Head of Rothschild Germany located in Frankfurt and London, before serving Bank of America as Vice Chairman for Europe and Head for Germany, Austria and Switzerland between 2005 and 2009. He was awarded an honorary professorship from the European Business School in Oestrich-Winkel in 2009. Since May 2010, he has been a member of the Executive Board of the Deutsche Bundesbank with responsibility for Financial Stability, Statistics and Risk Control.

Dr Andreas Dombret holds several other positions outside the Deutsche Bundesbank. He sits on the Board of Trustees of the Center for Financial Studies (CFS) in Frankfurt, the Österreichische Bankwissenschaftliche Gesellschaft (Austrian Society for Bank Research) in Vienna, the Westfälische Wilhelms University in Münster, the Schirn Kunsthalle art exhibition centre and the Städel Museum in Frankfurt, and the Museum Wiesbaden. In addition, he is a member of the Board of the International Center for Monetary and Banking Studies (ICMB) in Geneva and the Exchange Experts Commission (BSK), as well as the treasurer of the Verein für Socialpolitik and the Atlantik-Brücke. He is also a co-editor.

Simon Gleeson

Simon Gleeson joined Clifford Chance in 2007 as a partner in the firm's Financial Regulation group, where he specialises in financial markets law and regulation. He has advised Governments, regulators and public bodies as well as banks, investment firms, fund managers and other financial institutions on a wide range of regulatory issues. He advised the World Economic Forum on their report on their 2009 Report on The New Global Financial Architecture, and has worked with regulators and governments around the world on the establishment of regulatory regimes. He has been a member of the Financial Markets Law Committee, chairs the Institute of International Finance's Committee on Cross-Border Bank Resolution, has written numerous books and articles on financial regulation, and is the author of "International Regulation of Banking", recently published by Oxford University Press.

Randall D. Guynn

Mr. Guynn is the head of Davis Polk & Wardwell LLP's Financial Institutions Group. He has advised the Securities Industry and Financial Markets Association, the principal trade organization for U.S. banks, securities firms and asset managers, all six of the U.S.'s largest banks and many non-U.S. banks on the Dodd-Frank Act and its regulatory implementation. His practice focuses on providing strategic bank regulatory advice and advising on M&A and capital markets transactions when the target or issuer is a banking organization or other financial institution. He also advises on regulatory enforcement actions and white collar criminal defense, bank failures and recapitalizations, corporate governance and internal controls, cross-border collateral transactions, credit risk management, securities settlement systems and payment systems. Mr. Guynn has been considered a thought leader on bank regulatory matters for many years. He has been listed in numerous guides to the world's leading business lawyers since 1996, most recently Chambers Global 2012, Chambers USA 2012, and the IFLR1000 2013. He has been a guest lecturer on bank regulation at the Harvard, Pennsylvania, Virginia and Yale Law Schools and frequently speaks on panels at bank regulatory conferences.

Dr. Eva Hüpkes

Dr. Hüpkes is Adviser on Regulatory Policy and Cooperation at the Financial Stability (FSB) Board. Prior to assuming her position with the FSB in September 2009 she served as Head of Policy and Regulation with the Swiss Financial Market Supervisory Authority FINMA and FINMA's predecessor organization, the Swiss Federal Banking Commission (SFBC), which she joined in 1999. Before that she worked at the Legal Department of the International Monetary Fund in Washington D.C.

Dr Hüpkes is a member of the New York Bar and holds degrees in law and international relations from the University of Geneva, the Graduate Institute of International Studies, Geneva, and Georgetown University (LLM. with distinction), and a doctorate in law (magna cum laude) from the University of Berne.

She played a pivotal role in promoting effective resolution of financial institutions as Secretary to the FSB's groups working on resolution, as Co-Chair of the Basel Committee Working Group on Cross-Border Bank Resolution and as member of the Advisory Panel of the International Association of Deposit Insurers. She also served as Consulting Counsel to the IMF advising national authorities on the implementation of international standards relating to banking regulation and supervision and crisis management and is a Member of the Committee on International Monetary Law of the International Law Association. She is a Lecturer in international financial regulation at the University of Zurich and Frankfurt Goethe University.

Thomas F. Huertas

Thomas F. Huertas is currently a partner in the risk practice at Ernst & Young LLP where he advises major financial institutions on regulatory and strategic issues. He is also an Adjunct Professor at the Institute of Law and Finance in the Goethe University Frankfurt where he teaches a course on financial intermediation and risk management. He has published extensively on finance, including his recent book Crisis: Cause, Containment and Cure. He holds a Ph.D. in Economics from the University of Chicago.

Prior to joining Ernst & Young at the start of 2012 Dr. Huertas was a Member of the Executive Committee at the UK Financial Services Authority and Alternate Chair of the European Banking Authority. He also served as a member of the Basel Committee on Banking Supervision and as a member of the Resolution Steering Committee at the Financial Stability Board. Prior to joining the FSA in 2004, Dr. Huertas held a number of senior positions at Citigroup, including Chairman and Chief Executive of Citibank AG (Germany) in the years 1999 to 2001.

Patrick S. Kenadjian

Patrick S. Kenadjian is currently an Adjunct Professor at the Goethe University in Frankfurt am Main, Germany, where he teaches courses on the financial crisis and financial reform and comparative public mergers and acquisitions at the Institute for Law and Finance. He speaks frequently on topics related to financial reform, including too big to fail, the architecture of financial supervision and the new regulatory environment in the US and the EU.

Mr. Kenadjian is also Senior Counsel at Davis Polk & Wardwell, LLP in their London office. He was a partner of the firm from 1994 to 2010, during which time he opened the firm's Tokyo and Frankfurt offices in 1987 and 1991, respectively and spent over 25 years in their European and Asian offices. His practice includes cross-border securities offerings, especially for financial institutions, mergers and acquisitions, privatizations and international investments and joint ventures, as well as general corporate advice, with an emphasis on representing European clients. He has been active in securities transactions for issuers in Asia and Europe, particularly on initial public offerings and privatizations in Germany, Austria, Italy and Switzerland. He has represented bidders and targets in cross-border acquisitions throughout Europe, in particular in France, Germany, Italy, Switzerland, the United Kingdom and the United States. Mr. Kenadjian has also represented European and Asian issuers in U.S. debt private placements. He speaks French, German and Italian.

Dr. Mathias Otto

Mathias Otto is Deutsche Bank's Deputy General Counsel for Germany, Central & Eastern Europe. He also serves as global co-head of the Governance, Regulation and Litigation practice group. Based in Frankfurt, his responsibilities include bank and securities regulatory matters, the agenda on regulatory reform, governance aspects, group investments and restructurings and capital markets transactions. In his over 20 years of experience, Dr. Otto was involved in numerous strategic initiatives of Deutsche Bank, securities issuances, hybrid capital, Deutsche Bank's listing on the New York Stock Exchange, licensings, acquisitions, restructurings and disposals. Dr. Otto received his legal education at the Augsburg University which awarded him his PhD for a thesis on comparative procedural law.

Charles Randell

Charles Randell joined Slaughter and May in 1980 and became a partner in 1989. In the field of restructuring of financial institutions, he advised the UK Treasury on a range of assignments arising from the financial crisis, including the resolutions of Northern Rock, Bradford & Bingley and the UK operations of Landsbanki and Kaupthing; the recapitalisation of the UK banking sector, including the Government investment in RBS and the merged Lloyds/HBOS; and the £280 billion Asset Protection Scheme. He also advised the Portuguese Ministry of Finance on the €8 billion recapitalisations of the Portuguese banks BCP, BPI, CGD and Banif. His practice also included other major insolvencies and restructurings and a variety of mergers and acquisitions work. In March 2013, he became a director of the Prudential Regulation Authority and he will cease to be a Partner of Slaughter and May at the end of August 2013. Charles graduated from Oxford University and holds an MA in jurisprudence. He is a Visiting Fellow at Queen Mary University of London.

Paul Tucker

Paul Tucker was appointed as Deputy Governor, Financial Stability in March 2009. He is a member of the Bank of England's Monetary Policy Committee, Financial Policy Committee, Court of Directors and of the Board of the Prudential Regulation Authority. He was appointed chair of the Committee for Payment and Settlement Systems in April 2012. He is a member of the G20 Financial Stability Board Steering Committee, and chairs the Financial Stability Board's group on resolving large and complex banks. From June 2002 until Paul's current appointment, Paul was Executive Director for Markets.

Andreas Dombret, Patrick S. Kenadjian

Introduction

On May 3, 2012, the Institute for Law and Finance ("ILF") at the Johann Wolfgang Goethe University in Frankfurt am Main hosted its second symposium on bank resolution. The first session, held on November 5, 2010, in which we both participated, took place at a time when the consensus that special bank resolution laws were necessary to combat the phenomenon known as "too big to fail" was still forming and Germany was preparing to adopt its law on bank resolution. Eighteen months later the ILF held a follow up conference as the European Commission was preparing to publish its long awaited directive establishing a framework for the recovery and resolution of credit institutions and investment firms which was finally issued on June 6, 2012 (the "Bank Recovery and Resolution Directive", or "RRD").

In those eighteen months the consensus that bank resolution laws are an essential element in resolving "too big to fail" has become quasi-universal. The G20 endorsed the 'Key Attributes of Effective Resolution Regimes for Financial Institutions' issued by the Financial Stability Board as a new international standard and national laws have been adopted in numerous countries, but the twin problems of international coordination and uniformity of approach which the RRD attempts to tackle within the European Union still remain largely unresolved.

"Too big to fail" refers to the conundrum that large, complex financial institutions, especially those active internationally, present regulators and public authorities in the countries in which they operate. On the one hand, classical insolvency proceedings, designed for commercial and industrial firms, have proven too slow and not appropriate for complex financial institutions, which lose going concern value very quickly and are so interconnected with other similar institutions that contagion is an incalculable risk. On the other hand, bailing out their shareholders and creditors places undue burdens on the public sector and encourages the kind of reckless behavior, known as "moral hazard," which makes failure more likely. Bank resolution regimes are meant to provide a "third way" between a disorderly value destroying and contagion spreading insolvency such as that which Lehman Brothers experienced in September 2008 and a moral hazard generating bail-out of shareholders and creditors of large, complex financial institutions, of which the financial crisis provided many examples in 2008 and 2009.

The effort to develop bank resolution regimes is taking place as controversy continues to surround financial institutions, leading to a variety of alternative proposals to deal with "too big to fail," such as those to divide up financial institutions by function so that insured deposits and essential commercial banking services are insulated from losses generated by trading activities or to cap their size. The motivation for such proposals is understandable and we are open to considering their pros and cons. However, these proposals raise complex collateral questions and they cannot be a substitute for developing the tools necessary to allow large, complex financial groups to be resolved.

The history of the financial crisis and of the subsequent sovereign debt and banking crisis in Europe does not provide any conclusive evidence that a functional division of financial institutions into commercial banking and investment banking activities would have removed a significant cause of the crisis nor any practical help in drawing a line as to the optimal or maximum size of financial institutions. Both investment banks and commercial banks, as well as other financial institutions, such as insurance companies and money market mutual funds, failed or had to be rescued and many of the rescues were not motivated by the preservation of insured retail deposits within the institutions involved, but rather by the need to prevent contagion to other financial institutions and even the collapse of the financial system. Furthermore, absolute size alone has not proven a reliable indicator of whether at a specific point in time a specific institution would need to be bailed out.

Thus attempts to identify *ex ante* which kinds of activities should be banned or which kinds of institutions should be broken up are not a substitute for the urgent task of ensuring that, sooner rather than later, a set of tools is uniformly available to banking supervisors worldwide to allow large, complex financial groups to be dismantled in a crisis in a way which does not endanger the provision of essential banking services or the stability of the financial systems in which they operate. We are now in year five of the financial crisis and have been relatively lucky that, since the end of 2008, we have not had to face the collapse of a "too big to fail" financial institution, but we cannot continue running for luck. Whatever other solutions to "too big to fail" may be proposed, explored and eventually adopted, the kinds of procedures and tools proposed by the RRD will have to be available if these solutions prove not to be effective at preventing the failure of a large, complex financial institution. Only a credible resolution system is a long term as well as a short term solution to "too big to fail."

The RRD provides a comprehensive catalogue of what these tools need to include and while neither we nor the other authors of this volume agree totally with all elements of the proposed Directive, we believe it is essential that we focus on the issues it raises and that the Directive is finalized, adopted and implemented as soon as possible. In this connection we think it is very important that the RRD become effective as a whole on a single date and that the currently proposed effective date for the "bail-in tool" be brought forward from January 2008 to January 2005, when the rest of the Directive is to take effect. That tool is central to the effectiveness of cross-border resolutions. Deferring it would deprive the RRD of much of its effect. This should, however, be just the next step, as European integration continues to progress. We welcome the EU Commission's intention to go even further, namely to propose a single resolution mechanism for member states participating in the single supervisory mechanism for financial institutions within the Euro zone as soon as the RRD has been adopted.

This volume contains some of the speeches delivered at the conference on May 3 as well as a number of more extensive essays which reflect the contents of the RRD and some of the other relevant developments within the European Union between May 3 and the end of 2012, including proposals to create a Banking Union. The authors' contributions follow the design of the conference and focus on three main themes, the complexities involved in the resolution of financial groups, the theory and practice of recovery and resolutions plans, colloquially known as "living wills" and the controversy generated by one particular resolution "tool", the "bail-in".

Frankfurt, April 2013

From G-20 to FSB to EU Directive

Andreas Dombret

Solving the Too-Big-To-Fail-Problem for Financial Institutions[1]

Contents

1. A special insolvency law for financial institutions – context and objectives

In the light of the financial crisis the G20 leaders agreed at the London summit in April 2009 that, in future, they will supervise and regulate "all systemically important financial institutions, financial instruments and financial markets". Since then, a bulk of measures has been adopted at subsequent summits in Pittsburgh, Seoul, Cannes and most recently in Los Cabos. One focal point referred to rules on systemically important financial institutions (SIFIs) designed to contain the "Too-Big-To-Fail" problem. One overarching aim was to put an end to bail-outs of such institutions using taxpayers' money. Such bail-outs and the implicit guarantees for SIFIs connected to them give rise to misguided incentives, thus encouraging SIFIs to take excessive risk. Economists call this phenomenon "moral hazard". The scale of this problem is vast.

This is borne out by the fact that, faced with the financial crisis, the governments within the European Union provided banks with assistance equiva-

1 Based on a speech, held at the Institute for Law and Finance Goethe University, Frankfurt am Main on 3 May 2012.

lent to 30% of the EU GDP.[2] However, the economic implications of the crisis go far beyond the fiscal burdens. They affect the real economy and therefore, for instance, every entrepreneur who relies on a bank loan to finance his investment decision. Thus, the process of adjustment within the euro-area banking sector is not over yet, particularly as the sovereign debt crisis has presented new challenges. Essentially, banks have got to remove problematic assets from their balance sheets, devise sustainable balance sheet structures and develop resilient business models. In its recent Global Financial Stability Report,[3] the IMF estimates that 58 major banks in the EU could reduce their aggregate balance sheet total by €2 trillion, or around 7%, by the end of 2013. The IMF fears that this deleveraging process could have a negative impact on the credit supply within the euro area and pose a potential danger to economic development throughout Europe and beyond.

The IMF's estimate needs to be evaluated in finer detail. Nevertheless, it does illustrate the sheer scale of the problem. The point is, not least, that it must be possible in a market economy for financial institutions to withdraw from competition for economic reasons without casting the financial system into turmoil. This underlines how important it is to find a sound preventive solution for dealing with big banks.

What does the G20's solution proposal entail? The new SIFI rules are built on two pillars. First, the likelihood of a SIFI failing has to be reduced, meaning that SIFIs are to be more resilient, mainly through specific capital surcharges that go beyond the requirements of Basel III. Second, the restructuring or resolution of a SIFI is to be made possible in future without jeopardising financial stability and without having to resort to taxpayers' money.

---

2 European Commission, Framework for crisis management in the financial sector, 10 January 2011 http://europa.eu/legislation_summaries/internal_market/single_market_services/financial_services_banking/mi0062_en.htm.

3 IMF, Global Financial Stability Report – The Quest for Lasting Stability, April 2012.

2. A new international standard for resolution regimes

2.1. Basics of the FSB Key Attributes of Effective Resolution Regimes for Financial Institutions

For this purpose, the Financial Stability Board (FSB), has developed, and the G20 have adopted, a new international standard for resolution regimes: the *FSB Key Attributes of Effective Resolution Regimes for Financial Institutions* (*'Key Attributes'*)[4]. This is the first time that the main features that national resolution regimes should include have been stipulated at the global level. For example, in future each of the G20 jurisdictions will have to set up a designated resolution authority for financial institutions. Moreover, specific requirements fostering cooperation between national authorities will promote crisis prevention and crisis management. Finally, institutions and supervisors alike will have to become very concrete in their planning of possible responses to an upcoming crisis.

These Key Attributes were urgently needed, even if some financial sector commentators would have preferred a globally uniform insolvency law. It goes without saying that this would have been an optimal solution. At the same time, however, it would have been a target that was not realistic to be achieved on a global level within a reasonable time-horizon. The scope and complexity of the individual and mutually dependent issues which have had to be, and still remain to be, solved in an overall package are sometimes like a Gordian knot. Unlike Alexander the Great in the legend, however, the G20 states have no magic sword to cut through the knot, and a reasonably timely approach that can be implemented at the global level is perhaps only a first step that may be followed by others at a later point in time.

2.2. Establishment of a designated resolution authority for financial institutions

One end of the rope forming the Gordian knot involves the institutional set-up for national resolution regimes. In adopting the Key Attributes, the G20 states committed to establish a designated resolution authority for financial institutions so that the particularities of crisis situations in the financial sector, such as the

4 FSB, Key Attributes of Effective Resolution Regimes for Financial Institutions, October 2011.

danger of runs on banks, can be taken into consideration. This new authority will be given a strong mandate. In particular, its tasks will be to

- promote financial stability,
- ensure continuity of systemically important financial services,
- protect depositors, although this could be done – as in Germany – in coordination with the deposit guarantee schemes,
- seek to minimise the overall costs of resolution in home and host jurisdictions and
- duly consider the potential impact of resolution actions on financial stability in other countries.

To fulfil its role, the resolution authority will be equipped with far-reaching instruments. For example, it will be able to

- remove senior management and replace it with an administrator to take control of the firm,
- transfer or sell assets and liabilities to a third party or a bridge bank and
- impose a moratorium with a suspension of payments to unsecured creditors.

Implementing the Key Attributes will lead to a gradual alignment of the national legal frameworks for resolution regimes. I am convinced that this will most certainly have a positive impact on financial stability.

2.3. Strengthening international cooperation between national supervisory and resolution authorities

A further cluster of problems – the other end of the rope forming the Gordian knot – concerns the handling of crisis situations at large complex financial institutions. Insolvency proceedings are currently carried out on a national and territorial level. However, the 30 largest systemically important banks hold on average 53% of their total assets abroad, according to data from a study carried out in 2010.[5] 68% of their subsidiaries are located abroad, and they generate 56% of their pre-tax earnings from cross-border operations. In the past, if institutions like these became distressed, national supervisors regularly ring-fenced their assets. The banking groups were broken up according to national boundaries or were rescued by the respective home states as separate national entities. This meant systemic distortions and considerable cost for the taxpayer. Mervyn King

5 *S Claessens, R J Herring and D Schoenmaker* A Safer World Financial System: Improving the Resolution of Systemic Institutions, 2010.

once summed this up succinctly with the words: *"Global banking institutions are global in life but national in death"*.[6]

Nobody today has Alexander the Great's sword, but there are two magic words which will help deal with these challenges. These words are "cooperation" and "planning". In order to systematically enhance cooperation between home and host countries, thereby improving crisis prevention, the Key Attributes contain a wide range of requirements which seek to promote cooperation. First, the competent authorities of the home jurisdictions of a SIFI are required to conclude institution-specific cooperation agreements with their counterparts in the respective key host countries. Second, Crisis Management Groups are to be set up for each SIFI; within these groups, all responsible national bodies[7] will come together at regular intervals to discuss crisis planning and crisis management. Third, in order to lay the necessary foundations for this, all impediments to sharing confidential information must be removed. This last point is especially important.

Although some progress has been made in the European context for supervisory authorities an effective exchange of information between relevant bodies in crisis situations is still hampered by the lack of or an inadequate legal basis. Incidentally, this particular impediment not only obstructs resolution regimes but also affects many different areas of the G20 financial sector reform agenda. The necessary legislative changes will have to be made when the requirements resulting from the Key Attributes are transposed into European and, later, German law such as the German Banking Act. The European Commission is already aware of this problem.

2.4. Recovery and resolution planning

Recovery and resolution planning will facilitate cooperation between the authorities. This planning process consists of three mutually dependent components. First, the responsible authorities agree on an assessment on the banking group's resolvability, the aim being to examine the practicability and credibility of a resolution strategy. Any impediments to resolution should be identified and removed. As a second component, the institutions themselves must submit plans describ-

6 Quoted from *A Turner* The Turner Review: A regulatory response to the banking crisis, March 2009.

7 The FSB Key Attributes specifically mention the supervisory and resolution authorities, the central banks, the finance ministries and the bodies responsible for statutory deposit protection.

ing how they envisage a potential restructuring and discuss them with supervisors. Ideally, the supervisory authority would be able to take these plans out of the drawer in the early stages of a crisis and restructure the institution in cooperation with the resolution authority. This planning process is useful for the institutions as well. According to a survey involving 19 big financial institutions, 40% of those questioned claimed to have drawn up complete recovery plans. Despite the costs involved, the majority of the surveyed institutions see benefits in this planning process, for example in that they provide a better operational understanding of the business structures.[8]

If restructuring is not possible or fails, the third component comes into play, namely that of resolution planning, which is to be developed by the authorities. The purpose of this is to prepare for the effective use of the resolution tools. The resolution of an institution has to be planned in such a way that

- systemically important functions performed by the institution are continued,
- the stability of the financial system is not jeopardised, and
- the use of taxpayers' money is avoided.

3. From standard-setting to the application of the new rules

3.1. The European Commission's proposal for a directive

These and other standards from the Key Attributes are a milestone on the road to containing the Too-Big-To-Fail problem. On the one hand, the fact that international consensus has been reached with the backing of top G20 policymakers can be considered a success. On the other hand, a great deal of detailed work remains to be done since the Key Attributes still have to be transposed into legal texts which, by necessity, have to be much more concrete than the international standard. Just how difficult this is may be seen from the fact that an EU legislative proposal originally planned to be published in 'summer of 2011'[9] has been

8 Ernst & Young, Planning for all terrains – Global Banking Recovery and Resolution Planning, Survey 2012, [Interviews conducted during September and October 2011].

9 European Commission, Commission seeks views on possible EU framework to deal with future bank failures, press release 6 January 2011.

postponed for one year. It was finally published only as of 6th June 2012[10] after a further period of consultation, namely on the the bail-in tool, had been carried out. Currently all European jurisdiction are in the process of assessing this legislative proposal and evaluating its impact on their national resolution regimes.

3.2. Germany: the Bank Restructuring Act

Notwithstanding international initiatives, German legislators responded to the financial crisis early on. On 1 January 2011, the Bank Restructuring Act[11] entered into force, aiming to facilitate dealing with a distressed systemically important bank without jeopardising financial stability and, as far as possible, without using taxpayers' money. Moreover, the Act is intended to enable coordinated action with other responsible authorities at the European level if a cross-border banking group becomes distressed. This is why, when drawing up the Act, care was taken to ensure that the new instruments, such as stronger powers of intervention for BaFin, fitted into the already recognisable contours of the expected EU legislative proposal.[12] In addition, with all banks contributing to a Restructuring Fund by paying a bank levy introduced in 2011, the banking industry is for the first time being made to participate in the costs of overcoming future crises – even though the amount accumulated in the fund is still far too small. The basic idea is that the money paid into the Restructuring Fund will be saved over many years until the target amount of €70 billion has been reached. Admittedly, this leaves us with a problem in the interim. However, the act in itself was a step in the right direction since it heightens what the IMF, in its last Article IV Consultation,[13] called the "level of preparedness". This does not contradict the fact that – similar to other European jurisdictions – Germany will have to check a further need for legislative changes in order to fully implement the Key Attributes and the EU directive.

---

10 European Commission, Proposal for a directive of the European Parliament and the Council establishing a framework for the recovery and resolution of credit institutions and investment firms and amending Council directives ... [COM(2012) 280/3], published on 6 June 2012.

11 Act on the restructuring and orderly resolution of credit institutions, on the establishment of a restructuring fund for credit institutions and on the extension of the limitation period of management liability under the German Stock Corporation Act (Gesetz zur Restrukturierung und geordneten Abwicklung von Kreditinstituten, zur Errichtung eines Restrukturierungsfonds für Kreditinstitute und zur Verlängerung der Verjährungsfrist der aktienrechtlichen Organhaftung).

12 Deutsche Bundesbank, Monthly Report, June 2011, Fundamental features of the German Bank Restructuring Act, pp 59–75.

13 IMF Country Report No 11/168, Germany: 2011 Article IV Consultation – Staff Report, July 2011.

3.3. Rigorous monitoring of the implementation of the new international standard

Experience over the past few years has shown that international standards can sometimes be futile if they are not implemented and applied in a consistent and timely manner. For this reason, the FSB wants to rigorously monitor the progress made in implementing the Key Attributes in its member states. What makes this all the more important is the fact that the Key Attributes take us into uncharted waters. Moreover, implementation will require legislative and institutional changes – some of them extensive – in all G20 jurisdictions. Last but not least, monitoring of consistent implementation is crucial for overcoming obstacles to cross-border cooperation which play such an outstanding role for the project's success. To facilitate the monitoring process, work is currently underway, as a matter of urgency, on an assessment methodology that will make it easier to objectively assess the level of implementation in individual countries. This instrument is to be used by various bodies: a) countries will be able to perform a self-assessment in order to identify any gaps in implementation; b) the IMF/the World Bank will use this methodology when carrying out their FSAP assessments; c) the FSB is already planning a first review for 2012 as part of its peer review process. Countries with a below-average performance in these assessments will be required to provide an explanation, and can expect the results to be published. It is of utmost importance to rigorously monitor implementation because the new standard closes a serious gap in the regulatory framework.

4. Conclusion

Broadly spelling out a brand-new international standard on resolution regimes for financial institutions has not been an easy task for the Financial Stability Board and the G20 leaders. However, consistently transforming these new rules into concrete legislative texts in various jurisdictions can turn out to become as difficult as to unravel the Gordian knot. According to ancient Greek mythology, the gods tied this intricate knot to the chariot of King Gordius to secure the drawbar of the chariot to the yoke. There was actually no need to cut the knot. If the peg had been pulled from the drawbar, the knot would have fallen apart on its own. When comparing that image with the Gordian knot as represented by the resolution regime, neither a brute force solution nor a brilliantly simple one seems to be at hand. In fact jurisdictions will have to get on with the painstaking work of untangling the knot and working out the details of the legal contribution to solving the economic problem of Too-Big-To-Fail.

Paul Tucker

Resolution: a Progress Report

Thank you very much for inviting me to join this important conference. The EU have made a massive contribution to global planning for resolution regimes to address the fundamental problem of Too Big To Fail, inputting very significantly to the G20 Financial Stability Board's Key Attributes for Resolution Regimes. It comes as no surprise, therefore, that the EU is committed to implementing that International Standard, via a Directive.

As Chair of the FSB's Resolution Steering Group, I thought the most useful thing I could do this morning is to give a brief progress report, and also to air some emerging thoughts on how to operationalise the FSB's high policy.

Preliminaries: what this is about

For those who hesitate to grasp the nettle of implementing resolution regimes, I want to stress that the genie is out of the bottle. While myopia gripped the financial markets in the years leading up to the crisis, they are now seized of the risks on bank balance sheets. That will be reflected in the prices of the debt of those who bear that risk. If the risk in banking is not incorporated into the yields of bonds issued by banks themselves, then it will be reflected in higher sovereign borrowing costs. There is nowhere to hide. Quietly maintaining a policy of bailing out banks is not a free option for governments and their taxpayers. Anyone tempted to argue against pursuing the resolution policy agenda would effectively be wanting to increase the (contingent) burden on the taxpayer. That would be liable to increase the pressure for fiscal austerity.

As well as avoiding bailout by taxpayers, we must avoid liquidation – putting a failed bank through a standard bankruptcy procedure. That brings chaos. Resolution regimes are a way for the authorities to avoid the direct hit to the public finances while at the same time containing disorder in the financial system. That can lead to a much better financial system, with stronger market discipline and so less stability-threatening imprudence.

Contemplating this, some commentators are concerned that one particular resolution tool – commonly known as bail-in – entails losses for bond holders. That is a misthink. ***All*** resolution tools put losses on to debt holders and creditors. Because that is the only place they can go. Bail-in is just one technique for delivering that. Its distinguishing characteristic is that it applies losses up front based upon a valuation rather than at the end of a liquidation of assets. As such, it prospectively avoids an unnecessary destruction of value.

But there is no silver bullet. We need resolution tools that work in different contexts for different types of bank/dealer. That means having a rich set of tools but with a common trigger for going into resolution. I will say something first about the trigger, and then about different resolution tools and strategies.

The trigger for resolution

Not a few people worry about the trigger for putting a firm into resolution – not too early, not too late. It is obviously important to get that trigger right.

To my mind, the best way of thinking about it is that a firm should go into resolution when its time is up – when Recovery strategies are exhausted, and the firm just will not be able to reverse its decline into insolvency or lack of viability. How to frame that thought more precisely? Every country has criteria for authorising/licensing a bank. A sensible trigger for resolution would be when a bank no longer meets the criteria for being authorised and, crucially, when there is no reasonable prospect of its doing so again. That does not give a damaging degree of flexibility to the authorities; it is a demanding test.

Some resolution strategies

In the banking field, many resolution tools entail separating out a distressed firm into different parts. Separating bad from good assets; and separating essential from non-essential functions. The good and critical functions are sold and transferred to another bank (often known as 'Purchase & Assumption'); or to a bridge bank pending such a transfer. The rump goes into administration, run down and disposal.

That is achievable for relatively simple commercial banks operating in a single jurisdiction, and all of whose contracts are under the law of that jurisdiction. It is harder for so-called Systemically Important Financial Institutions (SIFIs), spanning many markets, jurisdictions, and currencies, with complex counterparty relationships. As one international colleague put it, the standard toolkit would face an 'exponentially greater challenge'.

Top-down capital restructuring: bail-in

That is why resolution authorities in a number of countries are exploring how to execute 'top down' resolutions of complex groups, employing bail-in of debt issued by the holding company or top-level operating company. The US and UK have been working together very constructively in planning how to operationalise that strategy; and if we continue to make progress I hope that we will be able to say more about it over the next few months.

Imagine that a large, complex, global firm – just one legal entity for the moment – has 20 lines of business, each the same size, which is to say using the same amount of balance sheet and capital. Imagine it is 50 times levered. Now imagine that one of those lines of business is completely toxic, worthless. The firm is insolvent, bankrupt. Unless it can be resolved, it must cease trading and go into insolvent liquidation.

But, in this stylized example, only a single line of business is toxic; the other 19 are fine. In other words, the franchise has value. In the non-financial corporate sector, there are established tools for this. The remedy would be a negotiated reconstruction of the firm's capital structure, writing off the equity and partially converting debt claims into new equity. In the US, that goes by the name of Chapter XI. In banking, which is subject to depositor and counterparty runs, there is not time for a process involving negotiations between the different classes of creditors and shareholders under the jurisdiction of the courts. And the public policy priority is the stability of the system, not only the welfare of creditors. An administrative agency needs to make and execute some rapid judgments. That is precisely what so-called bail-in via resolution is about. The essential difference from other resolution tools is, as I have said, that losses are applied ex ante, up front rather than at the end of a process of running down the assets associated with 'non-critical' functions.

I have been making a simplifying assumption: one legal entity. Now imagine a cross-border group with subsidiaries in many jurisdictions and with a holding company. Under the provisions of the FSB Resolution Standard, recapitalisation through reconstruction of liabilities can also prospectively cut through a number of the long-standing impediments to resolution stemming from conflicts between home and host country insolvency laws; in other words, the cross-border problem. If the bail-in I have described were executed at the level of such a banking group's holding company, there should in principle be no need to trigger default clauses in subsidiaries around the world that are not themselves affected by the problem causing the group's losses. The bail-in changes the ownership of the group but it does not affect the balance sheets of the subsidiaries. Contrast Lehmann.

That doesn't mean there is nothing to do. Far from it. For example, firms (legal entities) issue bonds not only in their home county but in a host of other jurisdictions. We shall need the documentation of bond issues by banks and by their holding companies to make clear in terms that they may be bailed in or subjected to another type of resolution operation by the firm's home authorities; at the consequent change of ownership does not trigger 'default' or 'control' clauses. That should not be a high hurdle. It is equivalent to incorporating Collective Action Clauses (CACs) in sovereign bond documentation.

There is also a debate about which particular kinds of creditor claim should be subject to bail-in via resolution. Indeed, this is one of the key questions in the Commission's consultation. One thought on this. It seems to me that the approach to putting losses on to different types of creditor should probably be the same whatever the resolution tool used and, indeed, the same as in a standard insolvent liquidation. That would suggest that one way of addressing proposals to 'exempt' some types of claim from bail in, and to establish a hierarchy amongst other types of claim subject to bail-in, would be to alter the creditor hierarchy in insolvency law. While that could be useful in the longer run, I don't think that is essential to make this resolution tool work. Moreover, operating on the capital structure of a holding company can cut through some of the complexity, since topco debt is structurally subordinated to the debt and other obligations of the bank operating companies it owns.

A final thought before moving on to a possible resolution strategy for a different type of SIFI. What I have been describing is not a matter of designing new instruments with terms that automatically trigger a pre-determined write down or conversion into equity, which would essentially be a putative form of 'Tier 3' capital. Today's topic is rather the toolkit the authorities need, in a statutory resolution regime, to maintain order when all such instruments have converted, all other options are exhausted and liquidation beckons. But whether via contractual terms or under resolution, debt can add to a bank's loss absorbing capacity.

The resolution of deposit-funded international commercial banking groups

We should not assume a monolithic approach to resolution. It is not a case of one size fits all. What I have described could work for banking groups that issue plenty of debt. It would not work so easily for groups operating commercial banks around the world that are funded pretty well entirely from insured deposits. If they haven't issued bonds, then there would be no bond holders to bail in.

It has become fairly common to say that such groups should be resolved on a regional basis, ie broken up. Maybe. But, even if that is correct, it is obvious that 'break it up' is an incomplete resolution plan. What happens to the broken-up parts? Under a 'breakup' strategy, one needs a plan for each of the parts, both the distressed and the undistressed parts of the group. Under the FSB Standard (KA 11.8), it is clearly the responsibility of the home authorities of the group to ensure that a group wide resolution plan exists. There is no ducking that. It removes an ambiguity that has quietly haunted banking authorities for decades.

Imagine that some of such a group's regional/local commercial banks are smallish and simple, but that others are very large and complex. (Contrary to what is sometimes imagined, commercial banking can be complex!)

To the extent that the group's problems are in a bank(s) that is relatively small and simple, standard 'Purchase & Assumption' techniques can be employed. Ie break up that bank into a good and bad bit; and effect a sale of the good and economically critical parts, aided by an injection of resources, in the usual way, by the Deposit Insurance Scheme, up to but not beyond what it would have had to pay out to insured depositors in a liquidation. The critical services are thereby maintained, and the DIS becomes a creditor in the administration and realisation of the rump. At the end of that process of realising the assets in the rump, the Deposit Insurer learns how much it has lost. I want to stress that the DI typically incurs losses but discovers how much ex post.

Now imagine that the commercial bank subsidiary in question is big and complex. The realisation of the assets via a standard rump-administration is liable to destroy a lot of value, increasing the Deposit Insurer's losses. And in any case that strategy may not be consistent with maintaining stability (or containing disorder). A way of cutting through that would be to bail in the Deposit Insurer. Rather than the Deposit Insurer waiting until the end of the process of a potentially destructive realisation of the assets, it would hear up front how much it had lost. In the scenarios I have described, its losses should be smaller that way. That approach could, if necessary, be applied in different regions to different distressed subsidiaries of the group.

In the world of real banks, the firms have uninsured as well as insured deposit liabilities, and they typically combine deposit taking with some bond issuance. That means that, after equity and subordinated debt holders were extinguished, losses would be shared amongst the DIS and those bonds etc that could be bailed-in. Whether they got bailed-in together or in sequence (bonds first) would depend on whether a jurisdiction operated depositor preference in its insolvency regime.

But I must stress that in no way does any of this dilute the protection assured to insured deposits.

It does transfer losses to the surviving parts of the local banking system. But so do other resolution techniques, and liquidation would entail much bigger losses for the Deposit Insurer and thus for other banks.

There is much work to be done on planning how to operationalise that kind of resolution strategy, but it is worth doing.

The FSB work programme

This brings me, briefly, to the FSB work programme for 2012 and into 2013. There will be a preliminary peer review of the extent to which jurisdictions' resolution regimes comply with the FSB Standard. That will be followed by more exacting examinations, led by the IMF and World Bank, once an Assessment Methodology for the Resolution Key Attributes is complete.

Meanwhile, authorities are enjoined to produce assessments of resolvability of Global SIFIs and the obstacles in their way; firm-specific agreements for co-operation amongst home and host resolution agencies and supervisors; and resolution plans by the end of this year. Each of those requires a conception of a high-level resolution strategy for individual firms agreed amongst top officials of home and key host authorities. And the development of those strategies will inform the information that the authorities need from firms.

I have sketched in very general terms two broad kinds of resolution strategy, potentially appropriate for different types of global SIFI. In other cases, where a business is rotten through and through, a more 'traditional' break-up of a group may be needed, perhaps using a 'bad bank' in some cases. Planning for that will not be easy, and so for those extreme cases there is a special need somehow to ensure continuity in the provision of absolutely critical services to the economy. In the UK, that is one way that ring-fencing fits into resolution planning.

Implications for supervision

All this has important implications for prudential supervisors.

In the first place, supervisors get some allies: debtholders. The prospect of taking losses will incentivize bondholders (and fellow banks) to monitor the risks taken by banks – pricing or rationing accordingly. This is market discipline: an extra line of defence. Risk being priced into bank bonds will not, as some suggest or threaten, kill the market. It would be uncertainty about the regime governing what happens in the event of distress that would kill the market because that kind of uncertainty could not be priced.

Supervisors won't be idle though. Resolution needs preparation. Hence the international agreement that firms should prepare Recovery Plans and contribute to Resolution Plans. To be clear, while the firms will own the Recovery Plans, the authorities will design and own the Resolution Plans. It has to be that way.

To a much greater extent than ever before, supervisors will need to work backwards from the end game, working with resolution authorities. That work is commencing around the world through dedicated Crisis Management Groups. In this context, Living Wills are effectively, in US parlance, a 'pre-pack'. What I mean by that is that firms and regulators can do a lot of detailed planning for how they would, for example, execute a bail in of their debtholders. That will focus minds. Including on who holds bank paper. This is, therefore, relevant to supervisors of insurance companies – a function that the Bank of England Prudential Regulation Authority will combine with bank supervision.

But I must stress that none of what I have said entails supervisors diluting efforts to reduce the probability of failure, and to ensure plans are in place to enable recovery.

Conclusion: the FSB's planned Peer Reviews

The nations of the G20 have signed up to the FSB's Standard on resolution regimes. But, of course, we need to keep each other honest. That is why the FSB has proposed a Peer Review process, involving top officials, to ensure that this is working. The Bank of England is 100% behind this. Not only would we like an opportunity to vet the existence of viable resolution plans for the current SIFIs from the US, Germany, France, Switzerland and, no doubt, other countries down the road. We also really want other countries to be able to confront us with harsh reality if we don't deliver on having viable resolution plans for UK SIFIs over the next few years.

To all of this, the EU Directive will be crucial in giving us all the tools we need. I really do believe that, with *Dodd Frank* already in place, it will help set the tone for the world.

Group Resolution – the Key European Innovation

Simon Gleeson

The Importance of Group Resolution

This paper considers the complexities which arise where "simple" bank resolution models are flexed to reflect the fact that all globally systemically significant financial institutions ("G-SIFI"s) in fact operate through a group structure, using multiple legal entities in multiple jurisdictions. It notes the tension which exists between the economic concept of the "firm" and the legal structures which form the basis of group resolution. The concept of resolving the group as a single entity using an "insolvency consolidation" model is examined and rejected, and it is concluded that the optimal strategy for accomplishing group resolution is to ensure that national resolution authorities (i) are empowered by their local legislation to act in support of cross-border resolution co-ordinated and administered by the host resolution authority, (ii) are mandated as part of their statutory objectives to ensure the optimal outcome for the business as a whole, and not to prioritise the interests of domestic creditors, and (iii) should enter into public agreements with each other by which they commit themselves to conducting resolution on principles of multi-jurisdictional fair treatment of creditors and preservation of systemic stability.

In order to understand the critical importance of group resolution within the sphere of bank resolution generally, it is necessary to remember only two facts. One is than no globally systemically important institution operates in only one jurisdiction, and the other is that no G-SIFI is a single legal entity.

Once stated, these concepts seem so obvious that it may be asked why they should need to be stated at all. However, it is clear that much of the discussion on bank resolution thus far has disregarded them – or, to be precise, has proceeded on the simplifying assumption that a SIFI is a single homogeneous entity. At first glance, this does appear to be blatantly disregarding reality. However, at this point lawyers in particular need to realize that in many respects it is they who are disregarding reality. When a normal person deals with a bank, the conception which they have in their mind is of a "firm". This conception has more in common with the economist's idea of a firm than with the lawyer's idea of a company. In particular, one thinks of "Barclays" or "J.P. Morgan" as unified concepts. Rapid perusal of the annual reports of these entities, or discussion with those who work for them, will further reveal that that is exactly the idea that these entities generally have of themselves. Like all entities, they are subdivided internally, and an employee may well think of himself as working for "the UK business" or " the far east equities desk". However that employee will in general be utterly indifferent as to whether the sub-division which he thus designates has any identifiable legal existence, or whether it could be said to be a separate thing. The business is, in general, managed as a whole, administered as a whole and serviced as a whole. Thus the easiest way to picture the firm is the "layer cake" model, depicted below:

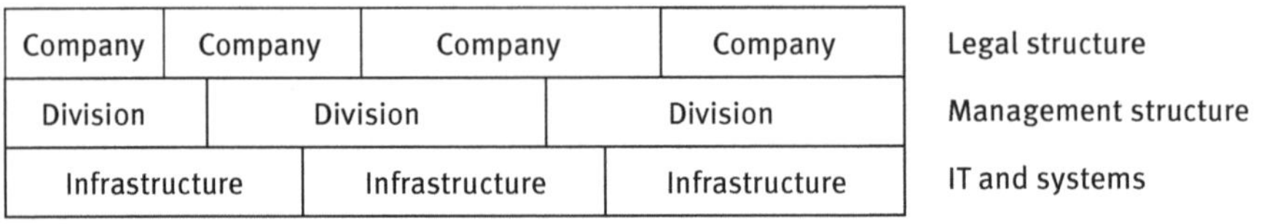

It should be clear that this is in fact a two dimensional drawing of a multi-dimensional reality. Viewed from the perspective of the IT systems, the firm has a clear structure; viewed from a management perspective, the firm has an equally clear structure. However these structures are not congruent and do not interact with each other, and in particular do not necessarily reflect the legal structures which constitute the group in the eyes of lawyers, creditors and bankruptcy judges – indeed anyone familiar with the internal structures of financial institutions would be genuinely surprised to find any very great degree of congruence between any of these aspects of the firm.

Resolution based on legal structures

When a G-SIFI enters resolution, however, it is the legal structure which is king. Since the purpose of resolution is to deliver a better outcome with less destroyed value than a liquidation would deliver, the test of the success of the resolution must be against the outcomes which would result from liquidation. This means that creditors and others will test their rights against a no creditor worse off than in liquidation ("NCWOL") standard. If there had been no resolution of any form, the default treatment for a G-SIFI would be to fall into multiple different national insolvency proceedings. If any creditor finds themselves worse off as a result of the resolution than they would have been had insolvency prevailed, that creditor has a good claim to be compensated by the relevant government, since his fundamental rights have been interfered with. Resolution must therefore use as its sheet-anchor the legal structure of the firm, regardless of how far adrift that structure may be from the reality of the structure.

It may at this point be objected that the legal theoretical architecture of the group is in many ways the least relevant part of it. This is clearly true in some respects – an employee of a firm will certainly know how his reporting lines work, and may well know where his basic IT and systems services are provided from, but is unlikely to know which specific legal entity is notionally responsible for which of his activities. Why not, therefore, abandon the legal structure of the G-SIFI and resolve the firm on the basis of its true internal structures rather than resorting to legal fiction?

This is a proposal which is made more often than might be imagined by insolvency theoreticians, and there are some good arguments in its favour. However, it is subject to the almost overwhelming disadvantage that it does real violence to counterparties' expectations. For those entities who have taken care to identify the legal entity with which they have dealt, and in particular to examine the balance sheet of that entity to discover its solvency, to be told that their claims are to be pitched into a common pot with those of other claimants who have not taken such care is a breach of the legal rights which they have been encouraged to expect. It may be objected that this is clearly the case if such a regime were to be sprung on unsuspecting creditors, but once the regime had been embedded in the relevant insolvency statutes such arguments would lose their force. This is true, and requires a more detailed response.

The starting point is to ask why it is that groups operate using multiple entities. This is sometimes dismissed as an epiphenomenon caused by "tax" which is beyond analysis or understanding. However, in reality tax authorities have never had too much difficulty taxing branches, and although specific tax strategies may require specific legal structures, as a whole the idea that the reasons behind group structures are unknowable does not hold water.

Consider some of the reasons why a G-SIFI might wish to conduct activities through a separate legal entity

- because a local regulator requires it to. If the rules in country X say that you can only do business in country X, or with customers in country X, from a subsidiary established in country X, then the establishment of such a subsidiary is the way to go.[1]
- in order to provide reassurance to local customers. Even where regulators are happy for banks to provide services on a cross-border basis, there may well be local considerations (ranging from membership of the local deposit protection scheme or stock exchange, through to a desire to be able to demonstrate substantial local presence) which mean that a local entity is desirable.
- in order to obtain access to the discount window of the local central bank. If business in country X is done in the currency of country X, any institution

1 The reason that regulators may seek the establishment of such a subsidiary are manifold, but in general boil down to a desire to ensure that deposits taken in the country concerned are matched by assets held there.

wishing to do business in that country should at a minimum be able to access short-term "lender of last resort" liquidity in that currency in order to avoid being at a crippling disadvantage against local competitors. The existence of swap lines between central banks may mitigate this pressure to some extent, but in risk terms there is no substitute for access to the well head.
- in order to separate the liabilities of one part of the business from liabilities of others. This may be either because counterparties require a stronger entity to deal with than the firm as a whole (derivatives products companies fall into this category) or because the firm and the counterparty have agreed that the recourse of the counterparty will be to something less than the balance sheet of the entire firm.

There are many more. However, what is notable is that in all of these cases the selection of multiple legal vehicles is deliberate, and is made specifically because one or more of the persons concerned are indeed seeking to rely on the separation of assets and liabilities which is inherent in the use of a separate legal entity. The existence of a law requiring groups to be resolved without regard to legal entity structure would, in all of these cases, result in further structuring being employed in order to ensure that he subsidiary created was in fact beyond that consolidation and would indeed be fully separate.

It should therefore be clear that the idea that the existence of multiple legal entities within a group is not simply an inconvenient fact which can be brushed aside in order to create an efficient resolution. Legal entities are, in general, used within a group precisely in order to create the segregation which results from entity-by-entity insolvency proceedings, and it is always and in all cases an illegitimate rewriting of the original bargain between the parties if that segregation is disregarded by statute. It therefore appears that the fact that resolution is grounded in legal entity structures is a necessary parameter for the design of G-SIFI resolution policies.

Resolution – the firm

Having established that legal structure must determine the basis of resolution, it is immediately necessary to assert that it is equally important to ensure that legal structure does not determine the path of the resolution. Resolution authorities must take the "cake" as a whole, and resolution itself may become damaging if it loses sight of the fact that although legal structures are relevant and important, the value which they are trying to preserve resides in the economic "firm" and not the legal entities. It is important to reflect the legal rights of specific creditors, but it is also important not to destroy value by futilely attempting to separate activities and services that are indivisible in any practical sense. Resolution is therefore in some respects a harder challenge than insolvency in terms of determining its intellectual infrastructure, in that what it seeks to preserve is not the rights of specific creditors, but the "franchise" value (for want of a better term) which exists within the business unit which is the firm. If franchise value is completely destroyed, then resolution has failed, since the outcome will be no better than that which would have been achieved under insolvency, and the only justification for resolution is that it provides a better outcome than insolvency.

There is one other important point which must be made here, and that is in relation to continuity of service. In general, it is only the firm acting as such which is capable of ensuring complete continuity of service. There are, of course, some G-SIFIs which are specifically structured to be self-standing on a local basis – this is not true for them. However, for most G-SIFIs the disintegration of the firm into legal components would, of itself and without more, significantly impair or terminate its ability to provide services to its clients as a whole. In particular, G-SIFIS are most likely to have global relationships with their clients, providing payment, credit, deposit-taking and transaction processing services in multiple jurisdictions and across multiple boundaries. For such services the preservation of the integrity of the firm during the resolution period may be as important as the preservation of franchise value in terms of the potential damage to business and commercial activity.

Cross-border issues

The major difficulties which arise in respect of G-SIFI group structures arise primarily from the fact that these resolutions will, by definition, be of cross-border entities. For these purposes it is necessary to reflect both on legal structure and on the way in which substantial branches are likely to be dealt with by national insolvency law.

All jurisdictions have some mechanism within which the affairs of a business operating in their jurisdiction may be wound up, even if the entity operating that business is incorporated elsewhere. Regardless of the degree of co-operation which may be suggested or mandated with other relevant authorities (and insolvency is not an area of law notable for sweeping inter-jurisdictional co-operation statutes), the residual power to take unilateral action against the foreign business of an overseas company is one which most counties have had need of on a regular basis.

Translated into bank resolution practice, what this means is that almost every country in which an international bank has a branch has the power to seize the local assets of that branch and distribute them amongst local creditors. This statement must immediately be heavily qualified – over the years most jurisdictions have built up a body of law based in both statute and insolvency practice which requires co-operation with overseas liquidators and discourages, to one degree or another, unilateral local action. However, the fact that these principles have been developed in the field of formal insolvency casts a little doubt, if nothing more, as to how readily they would be followed in the context of a resolution which is *ex hypothesi* not a formal insolvency procedure. In general, when it comes to mutual recognition of overseas resolution measures, we are making the world anew.

This problem is *a fortiori* where the local business is conducted within a subsidiary. The whole point of local subsidiaries, as we have seen above, is that their assets *are* supposed to be got in locally and distributed to creditors of that subsidiary. To ask a bankruptcy court in such a case to consider the greater good of the creditors of the firm as a whole is to ask it to step outside its jurisdiction, and although there are cases where bankruptcy courts have done this (to some extent) in the context of large financial bankruptcies, the position here is even less clear than in the branch case. Again, if we are to ask local resolution authorities to deal with subsidiaries in the interests of preserving maximum value in the group as a whole, we must at least create an intellectually coherent framework which sets out exactly what it is that they are being asked to do.

With this in mind there are a number of issues which need to be addressed in creating a coherent legal and regulatory framework capable of being applied by resolution authorities in cross-border resolutions.

1. Authority to co-operate

The first – and the simplest – of these desiderata is that resolution authorities need – at the very least – to be explicitly authorized under their constitutive legislation to cooperate with other national resolution authorities taking action in relation to other parts of the firm in other jurisdictions. In particular resolution authorities must be permitted to take decisions and exercise their powers in ways which are for the benefit of creditors of the firm as a whole, and not any one national segment of those creditors.

There also needs to be some public acknowledgement by resolution authorities and their sponsor governments of the fact that this is a binding imperative. In the IIF paper "*Making resolution robust—completing the legal and institutional frameworks for effective cross-border resolution of financial institutions*"[2] a non-binding international convention was proposed as a way of making such an acknowledgement. The reason that this is important is that resolution is one of those goods – like life insurance – which the beneficiary by definition does not get to see carried out. Since there can be no meaningful experience of how resolution authorities would behave in the event of a failure of a G-SIFI, the sole commodity to be assessed in practice is the confidence of market participants, customers and clients of a firm that resolution authorities will in fact act in a way which minimizes systemic harm, damage and creditor losses. In this regard the execution by governments and authorities of an instrument setting out that this is indeed their intention is a strong positive as far as creating that confidence is concerned. In this context, it is notable that the IIF proposed draft convention – and, for that matter, any conceivable instrument of that kind –does not commit signatory states to doing anything which they would not normally expect to do anyway.

2. Respect for legal rights

Resolution must operate within the broad framework of insolvency, and insolvency is based on corporate structures. Consequently it is unlikely (except in a very extreme case) that a resolution authority would seek to do anything other than respect the corporate structure of the group concerned. Thus, creditors of a particular group entity should be treated as such. There is no current case for "resolution consolidation". This may well mean treating national creditors differently – if a bank has a branch and a subsidiary in a particular jurisdiction, the resolution authority in that jurisdiction must be prepared to treat the creditors of the branch differently from the creditors of the subsidiary and not – for example – seek to attach assets belonging to the branch in order to satisfy creditors of the subsidiary.

This is an area where there is significant scope for pre-commitment by the public sector. In the abstract, all resolution authorities believe that they both should and will comply with the ordinary legal requirements which rank the claims of individual creditors. However, they are equally uneasily aware that such adherence to general principles can quickly come under intense pressure in particular cases. As a result, a public commitment to rectitude can be of use in supporting individual decisions in a crisis.

2 Institute of International Finance, June 2012.

3. Facilitating Operational Co-operation

The operational infrastructure within a G-SIFI generally involves significant element of service provision including financial, managerial and operational functions across borders. Maintaining the provision of such services cross-border and between banks within a financial group may be essential to the preservation of systemic functions. Where a resolution authority takes action in respect of a group entity which provides such services to other group members, it should commit to use, to its best endeavors, its resolution and other statutory powers to ensure that any bank in which they intervene would continue to provide services to members of its former Group (and other banks).

The reason that this needs to be specified requires a word of explanation. Where resolution authorities in country X discover that the institution which they are resolving is providing services to another legal group legal entity in country Y, their immediate reaction may well be that this is a form of cross-subsidy between the two, in that X is incurring costs which ought to be borne by Y. If (as is likely) there is no formal agreement in place between the two which sets a value on the services, there is a real risk that the provision of the services may simply be terminated. This will generally have disastrous results for continuity of systemic services.

The solution is partly to arrange that the arrangements between different parts of the firm are appropriately documented and valued on an ongoing basis. However even this does not provide a complete solution in circumstances where the receiver of the service is effectively insolvent – a commercial service provider generally does not continue to provide services after it has become clear that the client will be unable to pay for them, so why should a subsidiary of a bank deal any differently with another subsidiary?

The answer to this is that within a firm some degree of cross-supply is inevitable and unobjectionable, and to maintain otherwise would be to require the service arrangements within the firm to be segmented to match the legal structure – a stricture as inconvenient in practice as it would be useless in resolution. Consequently, in practice it is necessary for resolution authorities to accept the existence of these arrangements to the extent of being prepared to pre-commit to maintain the provision of services in these circumstances.

This argument must, however, be qualified by the fact that these arrangements should not in practice be permitted to constitute a cross-subsidy. Such a cross-subsidy, if continued after the point of commencement of resolution, would constitute an interference with the rights of creditors, reducing the claims of some in order to increase the claims of others, in a way which is not consistent with the overall aims of resolution or with the rights of creditors. Consequently, any such arrangement should be subject to three conditions:

(i) the receiving bank must continue to pay for the services;
(ii) the requirements for the services and the standards to which they are provided must remain broadly unchanged; and
(iii) a minimum period to transition to alternative provision must be agreed.

A public commitment by resolution authorities to such a course of action would provide substantial reassurance as to the resolvability of cross-border groups with significant pooled services.

4. Non-discrimination between different classes of creditors

The discrimination which is envisaged here is between types of claimants (e.g. retail vs bank creditors), geographical constituencies of claimants (e.g. domestic depositors vs overseas depositors) or different product types (derivative creditors vs loan creditors). Equality in such cases is very easy for resolution authorities to commit to where there are no specific issue in existence. It is an extremely difficult thing to deliver in circumstances where there may be strong domestic political pressures to benefit domestic creditors. Consequently, the stronger and more binding the commitment that the relevant government and resolution authority is able to make in times of "peace", the easier it will be to deliver this in times of "war".

There are, of course, certain types of creditors which are explicitly protected by legislation – for example payment, clearing and settlement systems are protected in the EU by the Settlement Finality Directive, and certain other types of creditors way be explicitly protected under the EU resolution directive itself. Where such creditors are specifically identified as protected under pre-existing legislation, this protection should be respected in resolution.

5. Ring-fencing

It is almost certain that national ring-fencing of branch national assets in a cross-border resolution will result in sub-optimal outcomes for creditors as a whole. This is another area where national resolution authorities, if they are able to address the issue in the abstract, are likely to be able to agree that national ring-fencing is undesirable.

This is a specific example of the general point that resolution authorities should act to minimise overall harm. However, in order to mitigate the concerns of national resolution authorities, the group resolution framework should allow home country supervisors to downstream equity and/or liquidity created in a recapitalization. A host country should have, at a minimum, a duty to consult with the home supervisor prior to instigating resolution in their jurisdiction.

6. Recognition of bail-in/debt restructuring

Where a resolution in one country involves the restructuring of debt due by the entity in that country, the risk arises of challenge to that restructuring under the laws of other countries. In circumstances where the restructuring is pursuant to a resolution regime which was in place or was prefigured when the relevant debt was incurred (i.e. excluding issues of retrospectivity), governments and resolution authorities ought to be able to commit themselves to recognizing such restructuring in their local laws – or at least to removing obstacles to such recognition.

Recognition of other countries bail-in regimes should extend to recognition of stays imposed in those countries as part of their resolution regimes. This is automatic where hybrid bail-in structures, incorporating explicit bail-in provisions of the term of the relevant instrument, are used.

7. Discrimination between creditors

It is acknowledged that certain creditors (for these purposes "Operating Liabilities") should be given better treatment (full protection) than "Funded Capital" in resolution, even where these exposures would be in the same legal bankruptcy class. However any such discrimination should only be permitted based on the nature of the liability, and based on clearly expressed ex ante principles. Resolution authorities should seek to harmonize the distinction between these two classes of exposure, and in particular should not apply approaches based on nationality, type or identity of an individual holder

8. No Creditor Worse Off than in Liquidation

NCWOL provides a clear minimum standard for fairness and is accepted in both the US and the EU. It has some important implications:

- If a resolution can be credibly effected by only converting capital securities, then other debt obligations should be untouched. There should be no right to force these other creditors into liquidation at such a time.

- It should be impossible to bail-in the debt of solvent "sister" subsidiaries of the failed institution for the same reason unless there are explicit cross guarantees or cross defaults.
- If the amount of Capital Structure debt is small as regards Operating Liabilities in a given bank, then the NCWOL test will become increasingly hard to satisfy, and deposit resolution funds will be involved at an early stage.

9. Mechanisms

Most of the propositions above can be easily accepted by any government in the abstract, but will come under pressure in the face of specific facts. Consequently the establishment of these principles in the form of a public non-binding compact, such as a convention or multilateral MOU, would be beneficial both for public sector entities who may be called upon to defend their activities in crisis, and for private entities to enable them to have confidence in efficient and effective resolution. Such recognition, if acknowledged in a public presumptive path by both home and host regulators, would be a powerful positive force for market stability.

10. Legal recognition across jurisdictions

Home country restructuring (including bail-in at the holding company level, stays on enforcement, suspension of cross-default rights and a number of other features) should be recognized in the courts of other relevant countries. This is, of course, not in the gift of domestic resolution agencies. The question of whether, for example, an English law governed bond issued by a German issuer is affected by a change of German law is a matter for the UK courts, not the UK resolution authority. It would be undesirable – even if it were permissible – to eliminate the jurisdiction of the courts in such a matter. As a broad principle, courts are the correct forum to settle legal disputes, and pre-empting the courts power to decide by removing their jurisdiction and placing it in the hands of an administrative body is constitutionally undesirable and itself potentially subject to legal challenge. As a result, the implementation of resolution on a cross-border basis must be embedded in national legislation as well as being a mandate issued to national resolution authorities. In particular, care must be taken to ensure that the mandate for national resolution authorities includes a positive obligation to act co-operatively with the resolution authorities of other (particularly host) countries, and to ensure that such mandates are not expressed in a way which could be argued to require them to prioritise domestic over foreign creditors in cross-border situations.

In particular, such mandates should acknowledge that authorities have an overriding duty to consider the overall systemic risk impacts of their decisions, and to act so as to minimise overall economic and social harm resulting from the failure. Maximization of the overall value of the franchise post resolution is likely to be the best starting point for this analysis. However this should be accompanied by a recognition that when this value is realized, those immediately disadvantaged should be subsequently compensated with these proceeds.

A host country should have, at a minimum, a duty to consult with the home supervisor prior to instigating resolution in their jurisdiction.

A proposed principle

The majority of the above can be distilled into a relatively simple principle. This can be articulated roughly as follows:

> "Resolution legislation should authorize and direct regulators, resolution authorities and bodies having insolvency jurisdiction, through appropriate local processes, to co-operate with resolution authorities in other jurisdictions where that co-operation maintains systemic stability and ensures fair treatment of creditors in connection with the resolution of multi-jurisdictional institutions."

As with any simple articulation of a complex proposition, there is scope for discussion about what the generalizations in the above actually mean. For these purposes we can say that "*maintenance of systemic stability*" means that the assets of the entities in resolution are dealt with in accordance with the expected resolution approach of the home country resolution authority, in particular where market participants, host countries and other counterparties have relied on their expectations of the resolution being conducted in this particular way. Also, "*fair treatment of creditors*" means treatment based on the following principles

- Non-discrimination on the basis of nationality and physical location (including agreement not to "ring-fence" local assets for the undue benefit of local creditors:
- Appropriate protection of secured creditors:
- Respect for legal structure of the group and the specific legal entity which is indebted to the creditor: and

- Substantive assurance that no creditor will be left worse off than if there had been a liquidation
- Due process of law

The principle that resolution powers should not be exercised so as to leave any creditor worse off than it would be in a liquidation is a key principle of fairness.

It is appropriate to conclude by considering the extent to which the issues raised above are addressed within the framework of the proposed European Recovery and Resolution Directive. It should be pointed out that these comments relate to the draft of the Resolution and recovery Directive published by the Commission as COM (2012) 280/3. As is the way of these things, further drafts with differing provisions may well have been published by the time the reader encounters these words.

Within Europe the Directive provides for a Groupwide resolution plans, and in particular provides for national resolution authorities to co-operate in implementing these plans. It is important to note here that although all bank resolution authorities will require a bank which is the parent of a multinational group to prepare a group resolution plan, there may well be a significant difference between a group plan which is designed to assess the issue from the point of view of the regulated bank, and a group plan which is designed to ensure that the group as a whole is resolved in a co-ordinated and fair fashion. Thus, even though the notion of the group resolution plan is not new, the approach which is required under the directive may well be very different from the approach used in current group plans.

One of the primary difficulties the draftsmen of the directive faced is that the Directive would apply to a world in which national resolution authorities remain in sole charge of their regimes. Since the formation of a single European resolution authority is (necessarily) outside the scope of the directive, provisions are made for national authorities to discuss matters with each other, with the European Banking Authority empowered to intermediate in disputes between them. Although this approach may appear inefficient, it is probably the only practical mechanism which can be applied. It is also the approach which would have to be applied outside the EU – in the absence of a plenipotent authority, any progress will in practice require compromise between nationally potent authorities.

Finally a mention should be made of the mechanisms provided in the draft directive for dealing with resolution authorities outside the EU. The directive accepts in broad terms that where an entity based outside the EU has branches in the EU, the relevant EU resolution authorities should co-operate with the resolution authority of the home member state, subject to a right vested in the EBA to refuse such co-operation. This provides a useful base for dealing with cross-border branches. However it is unfortunate that these provisions are focused only on the activities of cross-border branches. Provisions of this kind would have been of little use in a case such as Lehman, where the important issues arose not out of the existence of cross-border branches, but from the effecting of cross-border business, and in particular the necessity for resolution authorities of different legal entities in different jurisdictions to co-operate with each other. This is probably the most substantial lacuna in the draft directive.

Finally we should note a curious set of measures deal with "groupwide financial support". One way of dealing with group resolution is to require full cross-guarantees between all group members – this has the effect of making the failure of any group member a matter for all group members, and to a large extent renders illusory the separation into separate legal entities which is at the base of any group structure. The measures in the directive permit (but do not mandate) entry into such mutual guarantee arrangements between members of the same group, but provide for no consequence if such an arrangement is in fact entered into. Resolution authorities are given the right to "veto" groupwide support arrangements, but not – it appears – to veto individual intra-group guarantees.

Charles Randell*

Group Resolution under the EU Resolution Directive

I. Introduction

Large financial institutions operating across borders are organised as groups of legal entities. Since the onset of the global financial crisis, three things have become clear: first, that the uncoordinated resolution of failing large financial groups is highly value-destructive and may present significant threats to financial stability; secondly, that where the coordinated resolution of a major financial group cannot be achieved, fear of financial instability may lead the authorities to opt for taxpayer bailout; and thirdly, that achieving coordination between multiple authorities across borders, at a moment of severe stress in the financial markets, is very challenging and requires extensive preparation, agreement and trust between the authorities.

The Recovery and Resolution Directive proposed by the European Commission in early June 2012[1] (the "Resolution Directive") contains provisions aimed at ensuring that financial groups can be resolved in a coordinated way across borders. These provisions cover group recovery and resolution planning, assessment and restructuring of groups to ensure resolvability, the giving of intragroup financial support, group resolution colleges and resolution schemes, and negotiation of agreements with authorities outside Europe. Since the publication of the Resolution Directive, further initiatives to address the problem of groups have been brought forward: first, the Commission's "banking union" proposals; and secondly, the proposals of the Liikanen Group established by the Commission.[2]

---

* Partner, Slaughter and May; Director, Prudential Regulation Authority; Visiting Fellow, Queen Mary University of London. The views expressed in this paper are personal and do not represent the views of Slaughter and May or the Prudential Regulation Authority.

1 European Commission, "Proposal for a Directive of the European Parliament and the Council establishing a framework for the recovery and resolution of credit institutions and investment firms and amending Council Directives 77/91/EC and 82/891/EC, Directives 2011/24/EC, 2002/47/EC, 2004/25/EC, 2005/56/EC, 2007/36/EC and 2011/35/EC and Regulation (EU) no 1093/2010", available at: http://ec.europa.eu/internal_market/bank/docs/crisis-management/2012_eu_framework/COM_2012_280_en.pdf.

2 High-level Expert Group on Reforming the Structure of the EU Banking Sector chaired by *Erkki Liikanen*, Final Report (2 October 2012), available at: http://ec.europa.eu/internal_market/bank/docs/high-level_expert_group/report_en.pdf.

Part II of this paper summarises why the failure of financial groups represents a particular problem for both counterparties and resolution authorities. Part III summarises the key provisions of the Resolution Directive that address the resolution of groups. Part IV discusses the strengths and weaknesses of the Resolution Directive's approach to group resolution, including in the key areas of financing and burden-sharing and cooperation with authorities outside Europe. It also touches on the implications of the proposals of the Liikanen Group regarding the structure of banks. Part V discusses how the Resolution Directive may be affected by the Commission's proposals for a banking union. Part VI concludes.

II. The Problem of Groups

During the global financial crisis, it has become apparent that the group structures of financial institutions operating across borders, and in particular of global systemically important financial institutions ("G-SIFIs"), are a major component of the challenge presented by their failure.

At the heart of the group problem lies the fact that group structures lead to a territorial approach to supervision, intervention and distribution of assets to creditors in insolvency. As a result, the failure of a large cross-border financial group may lead to a "sudden stop" in which the going concern value of the group is lost and assets are trapped in limbo while complex cross-border legal disputes are resolved, spreading contagion to counterparties. The impact of the group's failure on counterparties and taxpayers in the various jurisdictions where group entities are incorporated or operate may differ significantly. Group structures also contribute to complexity and lack of transparency for supervisors, investors and counterparties; to limitations on the authorities' powers of supervision and intervention; to difficulties in coordinating the actions of multiple regulators across borders; and, in particular, to difficulties of reaching agreement in financing and burden-sharing in resolution.

A. Why groups lead to territoriality

Prior to the global financial crisis, academic writing about cross-border bank insolvency tended to focus on the topic of universality and territoriality in national insolvency regimes. In its most extreme form, a universality regime asserts jurisdiction over all of the worldwide assets and liabilities of a failing entity, and treats creditors equally regardless of their nationality or the location of their claim; whereas a territoriality regime ring-fences the assets of the failing entity that are within its jurisdiction and affords priority to the claims of local creditors in distributing those assets.

Academics and policymakers have long debated the strengths and weaknesses of the two approaches and the problems that arise when the differing approaches of two or more jurisdictions collide.[3] However, the global financial crisis has highlighted the fact that large financial institutions, including G-SIFIs, are generally structured as groups, made up of many legal entities – sometimes several thousand of them in one group – located in many jurisdictions. These may include jurisdictions (such as tax havens) where the group may have little in the way of "real activity" and where regulation may be light or non-existent. These group structures lead to the result that, regardless of whether the approach taken by the insolvency regime of an individual territory towards a particular entity is universal or territorial, the failure of the group will in practice unfold on territorial lines: each individual group entity will be subject to insolvency proceedings in its home jurisdiction, in which its (often predominantly local) assets will be realised and distributed for the benefit of its (often predominantly local) creditors, without regard to the interests of the group or those of the creditors of other group members.

As the Governor of the Bank of England has famously remarked, global banks are "global in life, but national in death". While the financial group appears to be healthy, it is run as a single unit and liquidity may be pooled at group level, justifying some regulators' treatment of the parent company as a "source of strength" to other group members, and a consolidated approach to prudential supervision. However, once financial stress arises, the concerns of regulators, counterparties and directors of individual legal entities may lead to the increased ring-fencing of assets and liquidity within particular group entities. The existence of the other legal entities, previously a source of strength, becomes a source of weakness. The parent company is no longer able to freely direct the transfer of the group's assets and its creditors are structurally subordinated to those of operating entities.

The increasing trend towards collateralisation of the wholesale funding of financial institutions, through instruments such as repo or covered bonds, means that at times of stress such intragroup funding and asset transfers as are possible give rise to a game of musical chairs, with the creditors of any group entity who have failed to collateralise their claims likely to be caught out at the point of failure.

---

3 See, e.g., *Lynn M. LoPucki* "The Case for Cooperative Territoriality in International Bankruptcy", (2000) 98 Mich. L. Rev. 2216; *Andrew T. Guzman* "International Bankruptcy: In Defense of Universalism", (2000) 98 Mich. L. Rev. 2177.

Once insolvency proceedings are in train, the ring-fencing becomes complete. The assets of particular legal entities are disposed of by the relevant national insolvency official, and any value realised is used to repay the entity's creditors. Legal regimes do not generally enable the assets and claims of one group entity to be consolidated with those of another.

The territorial insolvency of a financial group can be hugely wasteful. The franchise value of the group may be lost (as was the case with Lehman) and significant deadweight costs may be incurred in dealing with the assets of each legal entity separately.

B. Complexity and lack of transparency

The group structures of large financial institutions also bring complexity and lack of transparency for regulators, investors and counterparties.

Regulators of a large financial institution have to try to understand the implications of the many intragroup transactions and relationships that are characteristic of such groups and may, in addition, find that they are unable to gain ready access to all the information they need to regulate the group and make decisions about its resolution. In some cases, simply identifying to which of the entities in a financial group counterparties have exposure is a significant challenge, as underlined by the "legal entity identifier project" being currently undertaken by the Financial Stability Board.[4] Once the entity is identified, evaluating the risks from and dependencies on other parts of the group is a further challenge: issues such as reliance on intragroup services, pooling of liquidity and assets, cross-default risks and intragroup guarantees may not be readily apparent from financial statements and regulatory capital returns. Consolidated supervision is only a partial answer, because the incentives of consolidated supervisors and host supervisors are not always fully aligned and they may decline to share information, particularly in times of crisis.[5] There may also be legal limitations on the ability of super-

4 Financial Stability Board, "A Global Legal Entity Identifier for Financial Markets" (8 June 2012), available at: http://www.financialstabilityboard.org/publications/r_120608.pdf.

5 *Katia D'Hulster* "Cross Border Banking Supervision: Incentive Conflicts in Supervisory Information Sharing between Home and Host Supervisors" (1 November 2011) World Bank Policy Research Working Paper 587, available at: http://www-wds.worldbank.org/servlet/WDSContentServer/WDSP/IB/2011/11/03/000158349_20111103150252/Rendered/PDF/WPS5871.pdf; *Richard Herring* "Conflicts between Home and Host Country Prudential Supervisors" (no date), available at: http://fic.wharton.upenn.edu/fic/papers/07/0733.pdf.

visors to obtain information about unregulated or off-balance-sheet entities, and to pass information to supervisors in other jurisdictions.

Investors and counterparties face a similar problem of complexity and lack of transparency. They may find it difficult to gain access to reliable and up-to-date information to assess the financial condition of the particular group entity with which they are dealing. The group's consolidated financial statements are of little use in evaluating the consequences of its failure, when the group effectively becomes deconsolidated into its constituent parts. Counterparties may therefore insist on guarantees and cross-default clauses, which make it more difficult for regulators to close one group entity without closing them all. The difficulty that investors and counterparties encounter in obtaining access to relevant entity-level information may also lead to them placing undue reliance on regulatory supervision or on the assessments of rating agencies.

C. Limitations on the scope of regulators' powers of supervision and intervention

Regulators' powers of supervision and (where they exist) intervention have focused on legal entities carrying on "regulated activities", such as accepting deposits or securities dealing. Other significant group entities, such as parent companies or affiliates providing essential services to the group, have often not been adequately covered. The gaps in regulatory coverage have been exacerbated by the growth in unregulated financial activities, or "shadow banking", which has been incentivised by the imposition of capital and other regulatory requirements on only the regulated activities. It is likely that the majority of the legal entities in a large financial group will be unregulated entities which lie outside the scope of any pre-existing intervention powers.

D. Regulatory coordination issues

Where a financial group operates through many regulated entities in many different countries, the efficient resolution of the group may require rapid and effective coordination between the group's many regulators. Failure to coordinate is likely to lead to ring-fencing, as discussed in Part II.A above. Ring-fencing is not, however, the only problem caused by the failure of authorities to coordinate their actions: other problems may include the withholding of information and the precipitate closure of a firm by one authority without consulting others, or the threat of such closure.

Coordination failures of this kind are partly a result of the conflicting mandates and incentives of regulatory authorities, who may seek to maximise the recoveries of depositors and other counterparties in their own jurisdiction and to minimise the cost of the failure to the financial services industry or taxpayers in that jurisdiction. In the absence of a framework for authorities in different jurisdictions to make credible *ex ante* commitments to each other about the strategies that will be followed if a resolution becomes necessary, the authorities find themselves in a "prisoner's dilemma". Cooperative action would be more beneficial for all concerned, but cannot be guaranteed, so authorities may seek to take pre-emptive and non-cooperative action. Coordination failures may also simply result from the "fog of war" surrounding the failure of a large cross-border financial institution, where strategies have to be rapidly improvised on the basis of imperfect information.

The most difficult aspect of a cross-border resolution strategy for a large financial group is likely to be the financing, and sharing of the costs, of the resolution. Improvising an agreement between the authorities of several jurisdictions on financing and burden-sharing *ex post*, i.e. once the group is failing or has failed, is likely to be difficult, if not impossible.[6] However, reaching agreement on an *ex ante* financing and burden-sharing arrangement is also challenging. To be worthwhile, any *ex ante* financing or burden-sharing commitment by the authorities of different jurisdictions has to be capable of specific application to a range of different failure scenarios: woolly statements may simply exacerbate the areas of dispute, and without mechanisms for resolving disputes and sanctions for breach, effective commitments may not be possible.

III. The Resolution Directive's approach to the problem of groups

A. Background

European financial services policy before the global financial crisis

Until the onset of the global financial crisis, issues relating to the resolution of financial groups were not at the forefront of European policymakers' minds. The

6 *Charles Goodhart and Dirk Schoenmaker* "Fiscal Burden-Sharing in Cross-Border Banking Crises" (2009) 5 International Journal of Central Banking 141–165.

main focus of European financial services policy was the pursuit of the single market, which led to the grant of "passporting" rights to credit institutions and investment firms. Under these passporting rights, credit institutions and investment firms authorised in their home European jurisdiction may establish branches and offer financial services in other member states. The sole European instrument addressing the cross-border failure of credit institutions was the Winding-up of Credit Institutions Directive.[7] This Directive, which does not cover investment firms, provides that insolvency proceedings or reorganisation measures relating to a European credit institution in its home jurisdiction must be recognised in all other member states (universality). The Directive does not address the problem of resolving groups and, as was demonstrated when the Icelandic banks collapsed leaving depositors with their UK and Dutch branches exposed to an unfunded Icelandic deposit guarantee scheme, the Directive does not necessarily guarantee the timely or fair resolution of individual credit institutions across Europe.

Experience from the global financial crisis

The first phase of the global financial crisis, starting in the autumn of 2007, demonstrated the importance of national resolution tools. Without these tools, even relatively small financial institutions, such as Northern Rock, proved to be too big to fail.

The second phase of the crisis, in the second half of 2008, demonstrated the importance of separability of essential activities of financial groups and cross-border coordination. During this phase, major financial institutions, such as Citigroup, RBS and ING, had to be bailed out by their governments, because the necessary plans and structures were not in place to resolve their complex and global activities. The only significant cross-border institution that was allowed to fail, Lehman, caused major spillover effects in Europe and coordination between US and European governments and other authorities was found wanting. The coordination problems encountered by the authorities also affected insolvency officials, as can be seen from the disputes between the officials administering the estates of the main Lehman group companies on each side of the Atlantic.

In Europe, the crisis then entered a third phase as the serious flaws in the eurozone project became apparent – a phase which continues today. Weaker sovereign debtors within the single currency area have been shown to be inextricably

7 Directive 2001/24/EC of the European Parliament and the Council of 4 April 2001 on the reorganisation and winding-up of credit institutions.

interconnected not only with their own banking systems but also with other eurozone member states and their banking systems. As a result, the stronger members of the eurozone have had to commit funds not only to support sovereign borrowers in weaker countries but also to bail out their banking systems, through mechanisms such as the European Financial Stability Facility and the European Stability Mechanism. This phase has also been characterised by the "Balkanisation" of the single market in financial services: cross-border financial activity in Europe has shrunk dramatically, as financial institutions, under pressure from their home governments and regulators to preserve capital, have retreated to their home jurisdictions.

The international policy response to the crisis

Many of the problems of groups identified in Part II above have been recognised in the work of the Cross-Border Bank Resolution Group of the Basel Committee on Banking Supervision and the Financial Stability Board (the "FSB"). The "Key Attributes of Effective Resolution Regimes for Financial Institutions"[8] ("Key Attributes"), published by the FSB in October 2011 and endorsed by G20 leaders at the Cannes Summit in November 2011, address the issue of scope described in Part II.B by requiring that resolution regimes should extend beyond those group entities carrying on regulated activities to their holding companies and to non-regulated affiliates that are significant to the business of the group, as well as branches of foreign firms. They also recognise the problems of territoriality and regulatory coordination by requiring that a national resolution authority should have a statutory duty to "duly consider the potential impact of its resolution actions on financial stability in other jurisdictions" and a mandate that empowers and strongly encourages the authority wherever possible to act to achieve a cooperative solution with foreign resolution authorities; that national laws should not discriminate against creditors on the basis of their nationality, the location of their claim or the jurisdiction where it is payable; and that jurisdictions should provide for transparent and expedited processes to give effect to foreign resolution measures. Home and key host authorities of all G-SIFIs should maintain crisis management groups ("CMGs") with the objective of enhancing preparedness for, and facilitating the management and resolution of, a cross-border financial crisis affecting the firm.

8 Financial Stability Board, "Key Attributes of Effective Resolution Regimes for Financial Institutions" (October 2011), available at: www.financialstabilityboard.org/publications/r_111104cc.pdf.

Cooperation should be underpinned by an institution-specific cooperation agreement for each G-SIFI. While the possibility of these agreements being binding is left open, there is no requirement that they should be so. These agreements will set out, among other things, the parties' commitments, in accordance with the Key Attributes, to share information on a timely basis and keep each other informed; to review the overall resolution strategy for the relevant financial institution at the level of top officials; and to engage in periodic simulation exercises to ensure that the institution's resolution plan is viable. The authorities should have power to request, when necessary, the adoption of appropriate measures, such as changes to a firm's business practices, structure or organisation, to reduce the complexity and costliness of resolution. To enable the continued operation of systemically important functions, authorities should evaluate whether to require that these functions be segregated in legally or operationally independent entities that are shielded from group problems.

Recovery and resolution plans (RRPs) should be put in place for all G-SIFIs and for any other firm that its home authority assesses could have an impact on financial stability in the event of its failure, and should be informed by resolvability assessments. For G-SIFIs, the home resolution authority should lead the development of the group resolution plans in coordination with all members of the firm's CMG.

The European policy response

Since the onset of the global financial crisis, some EU member states have introduced domestic legislation addressing the resolution of failing banks. The United Kingdom was the first to do so, with the Banking (Special Provisions) Act 2008. The UK legislation was originally limited in scope to deposit-taking entities, but the Banking Act 2009 broadened the resolution powers to holding companies and made provision for improving the insolvency regimes applicable to banks and investment firms. The United Kingdom legislation was followed by legislation in a number of other European jurisdictions, including Denmark, Germany, the Netherlands and Belgium. In some cases, such as Greece, Ireland, Portugal and Spain, the introduction of bank resolution legislation has taken place in the context of a rescue package from the IMF and/or European countries or institutions.

Legislative action at a European level has been much less swift. The Larosière Report of February 2009 highlighted the importance of crisis prevention, crisis management and crisis resolution tools, and concluded that "the lack of consistent crisis management and resolution tools across the Single Market places Europe at a disadvantage vis-à-vis the US and those issues should be addressed by the adoption at EU level of adequate measures".[9] The European Commission subsequently adopted three Communications: in October 2009,[10] proposing, in outline, changes on crisis management and resolution; in May 2010,[11] on the financing of resolution; and in October 2010,[12] setting out in more detail the proposed framework for crisis management in the financial sector. This last Communication was supplemented by a DG Markt Working Document, published in early 2011.[13]

However, the publication of a proposed Directive was repeatedly delayed by the policy paralysis that has affected the eurozone crisis more generally. In particular, fear about the effect that the "bail-in tool" required by the FSB's Key Attributes (under which the debt of a failing bank can be converted into equity by the authorities) would have on the already dysfunctional eurozone bank funding markets triggered an extended discussion about whether bail-in should apply to existing debt at all and, if so, how long the transition period to implementation should be.

B. The Directive

In early June 2012, the European Commission finally published its proposed Resolution Directive to establish a framework for the recovery and resolution of credit institutions and investment firms. The proposed Resolution Directive seeks to address a number of the problems created by cross-border financial groups in the recovery and resolution context: by requiring the preparation of plans for the recovery and resolution of groups as a whole; requiring assessments of the resolv-

---

9 The High-Level Group on Financial Supervision in the EU chaired by *Jacques de Larosière*, Report (25 February 2009), para 131. The Report is available at: http://ec.europa.eu/economy_finance/focuson/crisis/documents/de_larosiere_report_en.pdf.

10 Commission Communication, "An EU Framework for Cross-Border Crisis Management in the Banking Sector", COM 2009 561 final (20 October 2009), available at: http://eur-lex.europa.eu/LexUriServ/LexUriServ.do?uri=COM:2009:0561:FIN:EN:PDF.

11 Commission Communication, "Bank Resolution Funds", COM (2010) 254 final (26 May 2010), available at: http://ec.europa.eu/internal_market/bank/docs/crisis-management/funds/com2010_254_en.pdf.

12 Commission Communication, "An EU Framework for Crisis Management in the Financial Sector", COM (2010) 579 final (20 October 2010), available at: http://ec.europa.eu/internal_market/bank/docs/crisis-management/framework/com2010_579_en.pdf.

13 DG Internal Market and Services Working Document, "Technical Details of a Possible EU Framework for Bank Recovery and Resolution" (4 January 2011), available at: http://ec.europa.eu/internal_market/consultations/docs/2011/crisis_management/consultation_paper_en.pdf.

ability of groups and the use of powers to address impediments to resolvability; introducing a regime for the provision of intragroup financial support by healthy group entities to group entities experiencing financial difficulty; requiring the establishment of resolution colleges for groups, with powers of decision for the European Banking Authority (the "EBA") in cases where members of the resolution college disagree with the group resolution authority's decision to implement group resolution; providing for the negotiation of agreements with jurisdictions outside Europe, and for the recognition of resolution proceedings of those jurisdictions; and providing for the mutualisation of national financing arrangements in the case of a group resolution, on the basis of a financing plan for the resolution of the group drawn up by the group level resolution authority or, in cases of dispute, determined by the EBA.

1. Group recovery and resolution planning (Articles 7, 8, 11 and 12)

The Resolution Directive proposes that parent undertakings or institutions that are subject to consolidated supervision in Europe draw up and submit to the consolidating supervisor a group recovery plan, including a recovery plan for the whole group and recovery plans for each institution within the group. The aim of the group recovery plan is stabilisation of the group as a whole or any institution in the group in a coordinated way. The plan is required to include a range of recovery options, and to address coordination and consistency of measures. It is also required to include, where applicable, any intragroup financial support arrangements (see Part III.B.3).

The consolidating supervisor is to transmit the group recovery plan to the relevant European host authorities, and to review the plan in consultation with them. All of these authorities are to endeavour to reach a joint decision on the plan, within a period of four months, failing which the consolidating supervisor will make its own decision. Any competent authority that disagrees with that decision may refer the matter to the EBA, which will determine the matter within one month.

Similar requirements and processes are proposed for group resolution plans, which are to be drawn up by the group level resolution authority, acting jointly with the other relevant resolution authorities. Group resolution plans are required to include a plan for resolution at the level of the parent undertaking or institution subject to consolidated supervision and resolution plans for individual subsidiary institutions and branches in member states. The group resolution plans should identify how the group resolution actions could be financed and, where appropriate, set out principles for sharing responsibility for that financing between sources of funding in different member states, but should not assume extraordinary public financial support other than use of the resolution financing arrangements to be established pursuant to the Resolution Directive. The principles for sharing responsibility for financing "shall be set out on the basis of equitable and balanced criteria and shall take into account, in particular, the economic impact of the resolution in the member states affected and the distribution of the supervisory powers between the different competent authorities".[14] Disagreements between the group resolution authority and any individual resolution authority about the group resolution plan are to be subject to the same process of referral to the EBA as group recovery plans.

2. Resolvability of groups (Article 13, 14 and 15)

The Resolution Directive proposes that resolution authorities will assess the resolvability of groups (i.e. whether it is feasible and credible to liquidate the group under normal insolvency proceedings or to resolve it by applying resolution tools and powers, without giving rise to significant adverse consequences for the financial system and ensuring the continuity of critical functions). The EBA is to develop, and submit to the Commission, draft regulatory technical standards for the assessment of resolvability.

The Resolution Directive envisages that impediments to resolvability, at both the individual institution and group levels, will be addressed by the resolution authorities, who will have wide ranging powers, including requiring restrictions on or changes to businesses or group structures. At the group level, the group level resolution authority takes the lead in submitting a report on impediments to resolution and measures to remove them. Again, disagreements between the group level resolution authority and the resolution authorities of subsidiaries are to be determined by the EBA.

3. Intragroup financial support (Title III, Chapter III)

The Resolution Directive proposes that the parent of a European financial group and its subsidiaries should be able to enter into an agreement with each other, under which financial support may be provided to any party to the agreement

14 Article 11(3)(e) of the proposed Resolution Directive.

that experiences financial difficulties. The financial support may take the form of loans, guarantees or assets for use as collateral in dealings with third parties.

At the point when it is made, all parties to a financial support agreement must be in compliance with regulatory capital and liquidity requirements, and not at risk of insolvency. The proposed agreement is to be assessed by the consolidating supervisor and transmitted to other competent authorities. If they are unable to reach a joint decision, the EBA will determine the matter. Member states may require that the agreement must also be approved by the shareholders of each party to it. The provision of financial support under the agreement is subject to a number of conditions, including the condition that providing the support does not jeopardise the entity providing it and that it is "reasonably certain" that it will be paid back. The competent authority that is responsible for the entity providing the support may prohibit the provision of support if it considers that the conditions are not met. The consolidating supervisor or competent authority responsible for the entity that was to receive the support may refer the matter to the EBA for determination.

4. Group resolution, including resolution colleges (Title V)

Group resolution authorities are to be required to establish resolution colleges, with responsibilities that include the development of group resolution plans, group resolvability assessments, deciding whether to implement group resolution and coordinating the use of resolution financing arrangements. The group level resolution authority, the resolution authorities of each member state where there is a subsidiary covered by consolidated supervision and the EBA will be members of the resolution college. The group level resolution authority will decide which members of the resolution college participate in particular meetings or activities of the college "on the basis of the specific needs", and may also decide to invite the resolution authorities of countries outside Europe where the group has subsidiary institutions to participate, as observers.

Resolution actions by one authority relating to a member of the group are to be coordinated with the group level resolution authority and other resolution authorities. If the group resolution authority, after consultation with other resolution authorities, assesses that the failure of a group member or the resolution action proposed by its resolution authority would have a detrimental impact on the group or affiliated institutions in other member states, the group level authority is to propose a "group resolution scheme" and to submit it to the resolution college.

This group resolution scheme is required to outline the resolution actions to be taken in relation to the parent undertaking or particular group entities with the objective of preserving the value of the group as a whole, minimising the impact on financial stability in the member states in which the group operates and minimising the use of extraordinary public financial support; to specify how those resolution actions should be coordinated; and to establish a financing plan, as discussed in Part III.B.6 below.

5. Relations with third countries (Title VI)

Title VI of the proposed Resolution Directive provides that the Commission may submit proposals to the Council for the negotiation of agreements with "third countries" (i.e. non-European countries) regarding the means of cooperation in the planning and process of resolution. Until such agreements are concluded, the EBA will conclude non-binding framework cooperation agreements with the authorities in these countries, to which the appropriate competent authorities and resolution authorities will also accede.

The EBA is required to grant recognition to resolution proceedings relating to a non-European institution in its jurisdiction of incorporation unless to do so would have an adverse effect on financial stability in a member state, independent resolution of a branch of the institution in Europe is necessary to give effect to the resolution objectives set out in the proposed Resolution Directive[15] or creditors, including depositors, in Europe would not receive equal treatment with the foreign creditors in the proceedings.

6. Financing of group resolution (Article 98)

Title VII of the proposed Resolution Directive addresses financing of resolution, and proposes the establishment of a "European System of Financing Arrangements". This system is to consist of three parts: national resolution financing arrangements, to be funded by both *ex ante* and *ex post* contributions from institutions authorised in the relevant country; a requirement that the national financing arrangements of each member state be obliged to lend to the financing arrangement of another member state if it is not able to access sufficient funding; and a requirement for the "mutualisation" of national financing arrangements in

15 Set out in Article 26 of the proposed Resolution Directive.

the case of group resolution. In the event of group resolution, the group resolution authority will establish a financing plan specifying the extent of the contributions of each national financing arrangement to the funding of the group resolution, applying the principles referred to in Part III.B.1 above. In cases of dispute, this financing plan will be subject to determination by the EBA.

IV. Assessment of the Resolution Directive's Group Provisions

The Resolution Directive's provisions about groups have the potential to address some, but not all, of the four problems that cross-border financial groups present for resolution, as outlined above in Part II above. Whether the Resolution Directive will be part of the solution to the eurozone crisis that is currently afflicting many financial institutions in Europe is unclear, given the timetable for its adoption and implementation, which stretches out to 2018. It appears unlikely that member states will fully support the proposed "European System of Financing Arrangements". Even if the Resolution Directive is implemented in the form proposed by the Commission, it will of course only take effect in Europe: and many G-SIFIs headquartered in Europe have important operations outside Europe, just as many G-SIFIs headquartered outside Europe have important operations in Europe. Further progress in addressing the resolution of these groups will depend on the success of negotiations by the Commission and the EBA with authorities in the countries concerned.

A. Territoriality

Group recovery planning

The proposed Resolution Directive endeavours to address the problem of ring-fencing of assets in the run-up to the failure of a financial group, through its proposal to require the preparation of a group recovery plan and to ensure that intragroup financial support arrangements can be permitted. However, the effectiveness of these measures remains to be seen. Although the group recovery plan is subject to determination by the EBA in the event of disagreement between the competent authorities of a group, the EBA's determination relates to the plan, rather than to its implementation in a particular case. The decision whether to implement recovery plans for individual entities in the group or to implement a group recovery plan lies, in the first instance, with the management of the group.

Their ability to opt for the group recovery plan is likely to be dependent on the continued availability of funding for the group as a whole, which may in turn depend on decisions taken by the management of individual entities and by the competent authorities responsible for those entities. The intragroup financial support regime's requirement that repayment of the support is "reasonably certain" is unlikely to be clearly met in many cases: by definition, the group entity requiring the support is likely to be in difficulty and to be unable to obtain the support from other sources. Both in its ordinary role as supervisor and by virtue of the special powers of objection to be conferred on it in relation to intragroup financial support arrangements by the Resolution Directive, the national supervisor of a group entity will, therefore, continue to have significant discretion in deciding whether and when to allow forbearance in the application of prudential rules, and whether and when to impede the transfer of funds or assets. Whether or not supervisors decide to prohibit intragroup financial support, creditors dealing with individual group entities may separately impose restrictions on their ability to grant such support.

Group resolution

If recovery is not possible, resolution will ensue. The proposed Resolution Directive does not, and realistically cannot, change corporate insolvency law, which generally requires that insolvency proceedings of group entities do not consolidate their estates, and leads to territoriality in the recovery and distribution of assets to creditors.

However, by promoting the possibility of group resolution, the proposed Resolution Directive aims to ensure that groups remain intact wherever possible, avoiding the disruption and destruction of value so graphically illustrated by the Lehman case. The Directive does not provide a definition of "group resolution"; group resolution is in effect defined by reference to its objectives rather than its form in any particular case. Those objectives are: to avert the detrimental impact on the group of its failure or of national resolution or insolvency measures; to preserve the value of the group as a whole; to minimise the impact on financial stability in the relevant member states; and to minimise the use of extraordinary public financial support.

The emerging conclusion of the resolution planning processes under way for G-SIFIs in the United States and Europe is that for many of the largest, most complex and interconnected financial groups, the application of the "bail-in" tool to debt of the parent company is likely to provide the most efficient resolution option.[16] Bail-in at the level of the parent entity of the group would convert the claims of creditors of that entity to equity, strengthening the consolidated capital position of the group, and (it is hoped) enabling it to continue its operations without the necessity for further measures at the level of the operating entities. This approach is known as "single point of entry bail-in" or "highest point of entry bail-in". Applying bail-in to multiple group entities is highly complex and risks fragmenting the ownership of the group.[17]

While highest point of entry bail-in may be the group resolution scheme which produces the greatest welfare for the creditors of the group taken as a whole, and the greatest benefit for financial stability in all jurisdictions in which the group operates, it will not always be the most beneficial strategy for creditors of the parent company, nor will they necessarily perceive it to be fair. Their outcome, converted into equity holders in the parent company, may be worse than it would have been if the parent had allowed one or more subsidiaries to enter insolvency or resolution proceedings, but better than it would have been if the parent company itself had been wound up. In those circumstances, no compensation will be available to bailed-in creditors from the resolution financing arrangements since their position will not be worse off than it would have been in liquidation.

Because highest point of entry bail in results in the uneven distribution of losses caused by the resolution between creditors of the group, the incentives of the group level resolution authority may not always lead it to propose group resolution in this form. The Resolution Directive proposals contain a *lacuna* here, in that the ability of the EBA to intervene only arises where a group resolution scheme is proposed by the group level resolution authority;[18] it is for consideration whether the EBA should also be able to require a group resolution scheme to be followed where the group resolution authority has not proposed one, or whether such a provision would represent an unacceptable in road into national fiscal sovereignty. The position is most acute where the group either is not systemic in its home state or will not fail if certain of its foreign subsidiaries are allowed to fail, and those subsidiaries are systemic in other member states. In

16 *Gregory Baer* of JP Morgan Chase & Co, "Orderly Liquidation of a Failed SIFI" (March 2012), available at: http://www.law.harvard.edu/programs/about/pifs/symposia/europe/baer.pdf; see also the proceedings of the FDIC"s 25 January 2012 Systemic Risk Advisory Committee Meeting, available at: www.fdic.gov/about/srac/2012/2012_01_25_meeting.html.

17 *Simon Gleeson* "Legal Aspects of Bank Bail-Ins", Special Paper (January 2012), LSE Financial Markets Group Paper Series, available at: www2.lse.ac.uk/fmg/workingPapers/specialPapers/PDF/SP205.pdf.

18 Article 83(6) of the proposed Resolution Directive.

those circumstances, the group level resolution authority may not been keen to implement group resolution.

These differing incentives of the group level and subsidiary resolution authorities may also result in a range of additional coordination problems, discussed further in Part IV.D below.

B. Complexity and lack of transparency

Complexity

The provisions in the proposed Resolution Directive relating to recovery and resolution planning, the conduct of resolvability assessments and the removal of impediments to resolution have the potential to make a significant impact in dealing with the problem of complexity highlighted in Part II.B above. The questions that remain relate to the will of member states and their authorities to enforce the simplification and rationalisation of group structures, and the speed with which any simplification and rationalisation will be achieved.

At the heart of the issue lies the question whether essential and non-essential financial services should be permitted to co-exist within a single legal entity and, if not, the degree of separation of those activities that should be required. There is no doubt that the resolution of deposit-taking and other essential activities con be made significantly more difficult if they have to be separated from other non-essential activities at the point of resolution. For this reason, the UK's Independent Commission on Banking[19] concluded that the European deposit-taking activities of UK financial groups should not be allowed to co-exist within the same legal entities as investment banking, and the UK Government has committed to require that these activities be insulated from each other through the use of separate subsidiaries.[20] The Liikanen Group appointed by the European Commission has recently proposed that a version of this rule should be introduced at the European level for larger banks, with proprietary trading and other significant trading activities of the bank to be assigned to a separate legal entity within the group if those activities amount to a significant share of the bank's business or can be con-

---

19 Independent Commission on Banking, "Final Report and Recommendations" (September 2011), available at: www.hm-treasury.gov.uk/d/ICB-Final-Report.pdf.

20 HM Treasury, "The Government Response to the Independent Commission on Banking" (December 2011), available at: http://cdn.hm-treasury.gov.uk/govt_response_to_icb_191211.pdf.

sidered significant from the viewpoint of financial stability.[21] Unless separation is mandated at a European level, the judgment when to enforce separation may rest with the group level resolution authorities in the relevant member states, who may pursue the issue with varying degrees of enthusiasm. For a number of European G-SIFIs who engage in "universal banking" through a single legal entity, enforcement of separation would of course be highly unwelcome.

If separation is required, further thought will have to be given to both the intragroup financial support provisions and the group resolution provisions in the proposed Resolution Directive. The grant of intragroup financial support by the "essential" part of the group to its "non-essential" part (such as the grant of support by a deposit-taking entity to an entity engaged in proprietary trading) should be restricted – an issue which the Resolution Directive does not currently recognise. For this reason, the intragroup financial support provisions of the proposed Resolution Directive may not be acceptable in their current form. The group resolution provisions will need to accomodate two levels of group resolution: resolution of the entire group, including the part that includes the investment banking and trading activities; and resolution of the sub-group that contains the deposit-taking activities. Efficient resolution of the deposit-taking sub-group may require that sufficient "bail-inable" senior debt is available at the level of the relevant intermediate holding company.

Transparency

Understandably, the focus of the Resolution Directive is almost exclusively on actions by financial institutions and the authorities regulating them. There is little in the Resolution Directive to promote transparency in the interests of investors and counterparties. In fact, resolution efforts may widen the transparency gap between the position of the authorities and the position of investors and counterparties. The Resolution Directive envisages that the authorities will receive a significant volume of additional information, including recovery plans, and will make resolution plans; understandably no provision is made for coun-

---

21 The Liikanen Group suggests a two-stage process for deciding whether separation will be required for a particular bank. First, it will be determined whether the bank's assets held for trading and available for sale exceed either (a) 15–25% of the bank's total assets or (b) €100 billion. If so, the bank will move to the second stage, and supervisors will determine whether separation is needed, based on whether the relevant assets held for trading or available for sale exceed a given percentage of the bank's total assets. The Commission will determine this given percentage for banks generally. The smallest banks will in any event be excluded from the separation requirement. Report, note 3, supra, page v.

terparties and investors to have access to this information. Whilst it can be argued that the existing European Directives on Transparency and Market Abuse provide some safeguards to investors and may lead to the publication of additional information relating to the risks of resolution, it is unclear to what extent financial institutions will publish information about resolution. The fact that the resolution plans "belong" to the authorities rather than to the institution provides a basis for arguing that the institution has no information to disclose.

The non-disclosure of resolution plans to investors and counterparties increases the reliance that they place on the authorities or on rating agencies, which is of course undesirable. In addition, the uncertainties with which investors and counterparties are presented in the absence of such disclosure, and the very broad discretions conferred on the authorities, raise issues of the Rule of Law. One way to address this is to develop and publicise a "presumptive path" for the resolution of each financial institution, but such a step may limit the flexibility of the authorities to respond to uncertain and circumstances. Finding the right balance in this area remains a challenge.

C. Limitations on the scope of regulators' powers of supervision and intervention

The Resolution Directive will substantially address the existing gaps in resolution powers within Europe. Many European jurisdictions do not yet have basic resolution powers for deposit-taking institutions, let alone investment firms, holding companies or group entities providing essential services.

Outside the group resolution context, however, the Resolution Directive does not address all the gaps in regulatory coverage that have been identified since the onset of the global financial crisis. For example, the resolution of financial market infrastructure, such as central counterparties, is still a work in progress, as is the supervision of a variety of shadow banking activities.

The most significant unresolved obstacle to group resolution is, however, the cross-border effectiveness of resolution actions. While the Resolution Directive provides the framework to develop and implement a group resolution scheme at the European level, for many G-SIFIs the implementation of such a scheme without (as a minimum) recognition of the resolution measures in jurisdictions outside Europe could be disastrous. Put simply, the Resolution Directive cannot by itself solve the Lehman problem. The problem of cooperation both within and outside Europe is discussed further in Part IV.D below.

D. Regulatory coordination issues

To achieve its objective of efficient resolution of groups, the Resolution Directive will need to produce coordination and cooperation between European authorities in the resolution actions that they take and in the financing of those actions, as well as coordination and cooperation with authorities outside Europe.

Resolution colleges

The resolution colleges proposed by the Resolution Directive will play the central part in securing the necessary coordination between the various authorities. However, they raise issues of size, membership and conflict with other supervisory groups.

On the issue of size and membership, the Resolution Directive proposes that the group level resolution authority, the resolution authorities of each jurisdiction where a financial group has a subsidiary covered by consolidated supervision and the EBA should be members of the resolution college. In addition, the competent ministries of the member states concerned may also attend. The resolution authorities of non-European jurisdictions where the group has a subsidiary institution may also be invited to attend. These rules would result in very large resolution colleges and it is questionable how well they would function. The provision in the Resolution Directive that "the group level resolution authority shall decide which authorities and ministries should participate in particular meetings or activities of the college, on the basis of the specific needs"[22] is unlikely to be seen as a sufficiently transparent basis to address the problem of outsize resolution colleges.

On the other hand, no provision is made for any authority from a member state where the group has a branch to attend, which could mean that the resolution authority of a member state where the group has a relatively minor subsidiary will be present, but not the authority from the member state where it has its most systemically significant operations. In this respect, the Resolution Directive needs to be corrected.

On the issue of conflict and coordination, supervisory colleges of prudential regulators for large financial groups already exist. In addition, the FSB's Key Attributes propose that there should be Crisis Management Groups, whose membership would not of course be restricted to European authorities. There is, therefore, the potential for a European G-SIFI to have at least three overlapping groups

22 Article 80(3) of the proposed Resolution Directive.

of regulators. The division of responsibility between these various groups and their efficient interaction needs further work, and it is for consideration whether the architecture of the groups should be simplified.

Role of the EBA

Disputes between members of the resolution college will need to be resolved very swiftly, and here the EBA is to play a key role. The resolution of complex disputes between the authorities of European member states about the structure of their banking groups and their resolution is a complex and politically sensitive task. The EBA would, therefore, need adequate resources to perform this task, which would have to be very considerable and which it does not currently have. In addition, the EBA would need to be seen to have the necessary independence and legitimacy to support its decisions. In order to defuse the political sensitivity of its decisions, the EBA will need to ensure that its determinations are, so far as possible, evidence-based and accompanied by rigorous cost-benefit analysis.

As discussed in Part V below, the proposed banking union may further complicate the issue of the EBA's independence and legitimacy.

Financing

Both the question of the financing plan for a group resolution scheme and the proposed European System of Financing Arrangements are likely to be highly controversial, since they may be seen as a threat to the fiscal sovereignty of member states. To the extent that financing arrangements are unfunded, the state is in practice the lender of last resort; and to the extent that it is required to be funded, the levy on the industry may be seen as a tax which member states consider lies within their sphere of decision-making, rather than that of Europe.

Experience has shown that it is difficult, if not impossible, to develop concrete rules for the sharing of the burden of the resolution of a cross-border financial group. The best known example of an agreement addressing burden-sharing in the resolution of banks is the cooperation agreement reached between the authorities in the Nordic and Baltic regions,[23] and the Resolution Directive appears to have been influenced by this agreement, since the factors that are proposed to influence cost-sharing (impact of the resolution in the member states

---

23 "Cooperation Agreement on Cross-Border Financial Stability, Crisis Management and Resolution between relevant Ministries, Central Banks and Financial Supervisory Authorities of Denmark, Estonia, Finland, Iceland, Latvia, Lithuania, Norway and Sweden" (17 August 2010).

affected, and distribution of the supervisory powers between the different competent authorities) are very similar. However, general factors such as these do not lead to a certain cost allocation in any particular case. It is likely that the financing aspect of the group resolution plan will be too generic to enable any very specific agreement on financing to be reached. The complex question of financing and burden-sharing will, therefore, be left until the group resolution scheme is presented at the point of failure, when the host authorities have a very limited period to challenge the proposals of the group level resolution authority: if such a challenge is made, the EBA has to decide the matter within 24 hours, and there is unlikely to be time for any appeal. It is difficult to believe that member states will be comfortable to submit these key financial questions to such a process.

Similarly, given the requirement in practice that member states act as lender of last resort to their resolution financing arrangements, member states may consider that the requirement to permit the financing arrangements of other member states to borrow from their own is incompatible with their stewardship of taxpayers' interests.

Non-European entities

G-SIFIs headquartered in Europe generally have significant operations outside Europe, and many financial institutions operating in Europe are part of a G-SIFI that is headquartered outside Europe. It is therefore critical that, in addition to achieving European coordination, resolution efforts are coordinated across all jurisdictions where a threat to financial stability may arise.

There may in practice be no politically acceptable alternative to the Resolution Directive's approach of conferring the role of developing agreements and cooperation arrangements on the Commission and the EBA respectively, but it does mean that the negotiations have the potential to become a many-sided game in which extraneous issues may be brought into play. At present, the authorities in a member state which is host to a significant subsidiary of (say) a US financial group may negotiate a bilateral arrangement with the US authorities. Where the US financial group's failure would present a systemic risk in that member state but not in others, a bilateral negotiation is likely to be the most efficient way forward. The mechanisms in the Resolution Directive appear to confer negotiating powers in these circumstances on the Commission (subject to the Council of Ministers) and the EBA, which may result in negotiations being delayed as a multiplicity of parties have the potential to raise other issues which are of interest to them.

This loss of negotiating autonomy would be particularly difficult for the United Kingdom, given the number of non-European financial institutions that operate in the City of London. From the viewpoint of the UK authorities, the negotiation of bilateral agreements with non-European jurisdictions of particular significance to the UK, such as the United States and Switzerland, is likely to be more expeditious and controllable than the process proposed in the Resolution Directive.

V. Impact of the proposed Banking Union

Following the publication of the Resolution Directive, proposals for a "banking union" were published by the President of the European Council on 26 June 2012[24] and endorsed by the eurozone member states at a summit on 29 June 2012.[25] This proposed banking union had four elements:

- the assumption of responsibility for prudential supervision of credit institutions in the eurozone by the European Central Bank (the "ECB"), resulting in a "single supervisory mechanism" for banking supervision;
- a single prudential rulebook applicable across the EU, in line with the proposed revisions to the Capital Requirements Directives (CRD IV/CRR);
- a harmonised recovery and resolution framework on the basis of the proposed Resolution Directive; and
- a common deposit guarantee scheme for the EU.

It is too early to judge whether and in what form banking union may proceed. Detailed legislative proposals to give effect to the single supervisory mechanism were published by the Commission on 12 September 2012.[26] It is a measure of the

---

24 President of the European Council, "Towards a Genuine Economic and Monetary Union" (26 June 2012), available at: http://ec.europa.eu/economy_finance/focuson/crisis/documents/131201_en.pdf.

25 Conclusions of the European Council on 28/29 June 2012, EUCO 76/12 (29 June 2012), available at: http://www.consilium.europa.eu/uedocs/cms_Data/docs/pressdata/en/ec/131388.pdf.

26 Commission Communication, "A Roadmap towards a Banking Union", COM (2012) 510 final (12 September 2012), available at: http://ec.europa.eu/internal_market/finances/docs/committees/reform/20120912-com-2012-510_en.pdf; Commission Proposal for a Council Regulation conferring specific tasks on the European Central Bank concerning policies relating to the prudential supervision of credit institutions, COM (2012) 511 final (12 September 2012), availableat:http://ec.europa.eu/internal_market/finances/docs/committees/reform/20120912-com-2012-511_en.pdf; and Commission Proposal for a Regulation of the European Parliament and of the Council amending Regulation (EU) no.1093/2010 establishing a European Supervisory Authority (European Banking Authority), available at: http://ec.europa.eu/internal_market/finances/docs/committees/reform/20120912-com-2012-512_en.pdf.

depth of the Commission's concerns about the eurozone crisis that it proposed the extraordinarily ambitious deadline of 1 January 2013 for the establishment of the single supervisory mechanism. It is now clear that any legislation will be implemented over a significantly longer timetable. In addition, it now appears that the common deposit guarantee scheme has, for the time being, foundered on the objections of Germany to the mutualisation of financing that it would involve.[27] The European System of Financing Arrangements in the proposed Resolution Directive is surely likely to be scaled back. So the banking union will be a very imperfect one, for some time to come.

It is notable that the Commission's proposals do not seek to confer functions on the ECB relating to resolution. In any event, such a step would have required a change to the provision of the Treaty on the Functioning of the European Union ("TFEU") on which the Commission relies in seeking to establish the single supervisory mechanism. Article 127(6) TFEU provides that the Council may confer on the European Central Bank "specific tasks ... concerning policies relating to the prudential supervision of credit institutions and other financial institutions with the exception of insurance undertakings": the ECB's rôle in banking union is already at, and some might argue beyond, the limit of this provision. Instead, the Commission's Communication, "A Roadmap towards a Banking Union", states that the Commission envisages making a future proposal for a "single resolution mechanism" which "would be more efficient than a network of national resolution authorities, in particular in the case of cross-border failures, given the need for speed and credibility in addressing banking crises. It would also entail significant economies of scale, and avoid the negative externalities that may derive from purely national decisions."[28] No further details are given of this possible future single resolution mechanism. In this context, it is interesting to reflect on the resources that a competent Europe-wide resolution authority would need to have: the US Federal Deposit Insurance Corporation, which has jurisdiction over a similar number of banks as those in the eurozone, but operates in a simpler environment as regards both language and law, has some 8,000 full time equivalent employees.[29]

---

27 The Commission's Communication, "A Roadmap towards a Banking Union", merely notes that implementation of high standards of supervision and resolution "will help build the necessary trust between Member States, which is a pre-condition for the introduction of any common financial arrangements to protect depositors and support orderly resolution of failing banks" (p4).

28 Note 25, supra, p9 of the Communication.

29 FDIC 2011 Annual Report, Appendix 6. Available at: http://www.fdic.gov/about/strategic/report/2011annualreport/contents.html.

Although the ECB will not be responsible for implementing resolution, it will, as supervisor, have the ability to pull the trigger for resolution by concluding that a bank does not meet the conditions for continued authorisation, although it is required to exercise its power "in cooperation with the relevant resolution authorities".[30] It will also be responsible for the early intervention phase of a bank's demise, with powers to approve actions which may have an impact on resolution options, such as the implementation of a recovery plan or the giving of intragroup financial support. Close liaison with any single resolution authority would therefore be required.

The proposed commencement of the single supervisory mechanism, before the proposed deadline for implementation of the Resolution Directive, the shelving of the proposed common EU deposit guarantee scheme, the probable collapse of the European System of Financing Arrangements and and the deferral of a single resolution mechanism raise the question of what consequences would flow from a finding by the ECB as supervisor that a eurozone bank ceased to meet the conditions for continued authorisation. If the bank concerned was not systemic, or the country concerned had already put bank resolution legislation in place, it might be possible to proceed to an orderly resolution of the bank. In all other cases, however, bail-out (perhaps using the European Stability Mechanism[31]) might be the most attractive option. There has been much talk of the European Stability Mechanism directly recapitalising banks (although it currently appears that northern eurozone members oppose this in the case of "legacy problems") but no discussion of using the same funds to make direct loans to resolution funds.

Of course, if the bank in question could not fulfil the requirements of the state aid rules, including adequate remuneration of the aid received and a return to viability, any bail-out would not be consistent with EU state aid rules.

Perhaps the unkind conclusion that could be drawn from this conundrum is that the ECB will, for the foreseeable future, have to be careful to avoid concluding that any systemically important eurozone bank group with cross-border activities has to be resolved, since the instruments to handle the resolution, and the facility for funding the costs of the resolution, are not in place. It therefore seems that the forbearance that has been practised by both national supervisors and the EBA in the last few years may be continued for some years to come in the

30 Article 4(1)(k) of the proposed Resolution Directive.
31 *Jean Pisani-Ferry and Guntram B. Wolff* "The Fiscal Implications of a Banking Union" (September 2012) Bruegel Policy Brief, available at: http://aei.pitt.edu/36833/1/The_fiscal_implications_of_a_banking_union_%28English%29.pdf.

case of systemically important banks. Neither the proposed Resolution Directive nor any of the banking union proposals contain a framework to ensure "prompt corrective action".[32]

Since it is clear that the ECB is not currently resourced or configured in way that would enable it to take on the resource-intensive role of supervising a large number of banks, in practice any banking union will involve, at least in the short term, the delegation of functions by the ECB to existing national supervisors. The coordination problems outlined in Part IV.D above in relation to supervisory colleges (of which the ECB will be a member in parallel with national supervisors) and resolution colleges (to which the ECB may not necessarily belong) may become even more acute. The question of allocation of the costs of a financing plan for a group resolution will also become more difficult: the proposal in the Resolution Directive to allocate the burden of financing a group resolution between sources of funding in different member states according to "the distribution of supervisory powers between the different competent authorities"[33] does not really work where the ECB is the competent authority in all the member states concerned.

The issue of the legitimacy of the decisions of the EBA has also been brought to the fore by the proposed single supervisory mechanism, since in practice the ECB will have very significant influence in the EBA and the balance of power may be seen to move away from non-eurozone countries, notwithstanding the safeguards proposed by the Commission. The Commission's proposals envisage that "to reflect the ECB's supervisory responsibilities, representatives from competent authorities from participating Member States shall coordinate and express, for matters falling in the competences of the ECB, a common position" in the decision-making of the EBA. In practice, this will give the ECB a veto right over many EBA decisions.[34]

---

32 *Jacopo Carmassi, Carmine Di Noia and Stefano Micossi* address the question of forbearance and propose that prompt corrective action should be a feature of banking union: "Banking Union: A federal model for the European Union with prompt corrective action', CEPS Policy Brief (18 September 2012).

33 Article 11(3)(e) of the proposed Resolution Directive.

34 In the area of the EBA's determinations of disputes under the Resolution Directive, the Commission envisages that decisions will be taken by a panel consisting of the chairperson and two members appointed by the Board of Supervisors from among its voting members, one of whom shall be from a non-eurozone member state. These decisions can then be rejected by a simple majority of the Board of Supervisors which must include at least three votes from members of eurozone member states and three votes from member states which are not part of the single supervisory mechanism. Proposed amending Regulation, note 25, supra.

In the longer term, the establishment of a single resolution authority within the area covered by banking union would address many of the considerable coordination issues relating to the resolution of European financing groups, but will require concerns about unified resolution funding arrangements and loss of fiscal sovereignty to be overcome. In this regard, it is perhaps notable that "strengthening democratic legitimacy and accountability" was the shortest and least detailed section in the document issued by the President of the European Council proposing banking union.

V. Conclusion

The Resolution Directive will, if adopted in its current form, represent the first part of a coherent Europe-wide framework for the resolution of financial groups. If it is implemented with the necessary rigour, both as regards resolution planning and as regards the removal of impediments to resolution, the number of groups that are too big to fail will be reduced. However, the eurozone crisis, to which the proposed Resolution Directive is in part a response, is moving with much greater speed and determination than either the Commission or member states. The proposed Resolution Directive would be required to be partially implemented by member states by the beginning of 2015, with the "bail-in" provisions to be implemented by the beginning of 2018. Yet it is quite foreseeable that the eurozone crisis may require the decisive resolution of one or more financial groups before then.

Following implementation of the proposed Resolution Directive, financing and burden-sharing in resolution are likely to remain significant unresolved obstacles to the delivery of cooperation and coordination between the authorities of different jurisdictions. Both the question of the financing plan for a group resolution scheme addressed in the proposed Resolution Directive and the Directive's proposed European System of Financing Arrangements are likely to be highly controversial, since they may be seen as a threat to the fiscal sovereignty of member states. Eurozone funding of resolution costs, including loans to resolution funds from the European Stability Mechanism, will be needed.

The losses incurred in the resolution of a large and interconnected cross-border financial group are likely to be minimised by group resolution, which is likely in most cases to take the form of "highest point of entry bail-in" – the conversion of debt of the parent company to equity. However, this resolution strategy does not necessarily remove the burden-sharing issue.

For these and other reasons, coordination will remain a major challenge. The resolution colleges proposed by the Resolution Directive will play the central part in securing the necessary coordination between the various authorities. However, they raise issues of size, membership and conflict with other supervisory groups. Where resolution colleges cannot agree in a timely fashion, a considerable burden will fall on the EBA in its arbitral role – one for which the EBA is not currently equipped. It is also unclear whether supervisors and the EBA will show the necessary resolve to insist on the simplification of group structures to make resolution of complex groups a practical possibility.

It also remains to be seen whether the Resolution Directive will be successful in promoting coordination of resolution actions with authorities outside Europe, without which it will not be possible to resolve the largest European financial groups, including G-SIFIs. This will require the conclusion of difficult negotiations with other jurisdictions, and it is important that the Commission pursues these swiftly without allowing extraneous issues to delay the conclusion of agreements.

Banking union, as currently proposed by the Commission, will not provide a complete answer to the coordination and burden-sharing issues. The establishment of a single resolution authority within the area covered by banking union, and the establishment of a common European deposit guarantee fund, would address many of the considerable coordination issues relating to the resolution of European financing groups, but the Commission has stopped short of proposing these in view of concerns of member states about unified funding arrangements and loss of fiscal sovereignty. As a result, the ECB will have the power to withdraw a bank's authorisation but may not have confidence that such a step will be followed by the necessary coordinated resolution actions, supported by resolution funding. In the case of systemically important banks at least, there is a risk that this incomplete banking union will lead to further forbearance, and the survival of "zombie banks" which are unable to perform the role of lending to the real economy that is so vital to address the recessions and depressions that are taking hold in Europe.

Living Wills – The Centerpiece of Resolution

Eva Hüpkes*

"Living Wills" – An International Perspective

Introduction

Facing the complexities of the Lehman bankruptcy, the court-appointed liquidator Tony Lomas noted that "... if we had walked in here on that Sunday, and there had been a manual there that said, 'Contingency plan: if this company ever needs to seek protection in court, this is what will happen' wouldn't that have been easier?"[1] In his Mansion House speech of 17 June 2009, the Governor of the Bank of England *Mervyn King* suggested that it would be wise "to require any regulated bank itself to produce a plan for an orderly wind down of its activities. That would provide the information to the authorities the absence of which made past decisions about the future of institutions difficult." He also noted that "it would be sensible for the various authorities to work across national boundaries to identify detailed plans for how each large cross-border financial institution could be wound down."[2] "Making a will should be as much a part of good housekeeping for banks as it is for the rest of us," he observed.

Living wills are plans that outline options to restore financial strength and viability when the firm comes under severe stress and that set out steps the authorities would take if a firm is placed into resolution. They are intended to facilitate the effective use of resolution powers to protect systemically important functions, with the aim of making the resolution of any firm feasible without disruption to the financial system and without exposing taxpayers to loss.

This paper discusses the design and implementation of ex ante plans for resolution in the light of the new Financial Stability Board (FSB) standard for resolution regimes, the 'FSB Key Attributes of Effective Resolution Regimes' (FSB Key Attributes).[3]

The first section of this paper briefly recalls the shortcomings in the pre-crisis world that led to the development of the living will concept. The second section

* The views expressed are those of the author and do not necessarily reflect the views of the FSB or its members.

1 Quoted by *Jennigher Hughes* "Winding up Lehman Brothers", in Financial Times, 7 November 2008.

2 Speech by *Mervyn King* Governor of the Bank of England at the Lord Mayor's Banquet for Bankers and Merchants at the City of London at the Mansion House on 17 June 2009.

3 Key Attributes of Effective Resolution Regimes for Financial Institutions, October 2011, available at http://www.financialstabilityboard.org/publications/r_111104cc.pdf.

discusses the FSB standard for recovery and resolution as set out in the FSB Key Attributes. The third section considers the challenges that need to be addressed when developing living wills in a world in which finance is global, but resolution continues to rely on the exercise of public power in a national (or regional) context.

The pre-crisis world

In the pre-crisis world many jurisdictions lacked suitable tools to resolve failing financial institutions. A substantial number relied on general insolvency regimes that were administered by the courts and were applied too late and were too slow to resolve financial institutions without causing massive losses and a very significant erosion of confidence. Supervisory and crisis resolution frameworks were misaligned. Supervisors practiced global consolidated supervision and looked at financial groups as a single economic entity cutting across legal entities and jurisdictions. By contrast, corporate insolvency proceedings tended to be territorial and entity-centric so that the individual legal entities making up the group would be resolved in the event it failed. The authorities in key jurisdictions did not engage in advance planning. They had not contemplated the cross-border failure of a financial group nor had they established processes that would ensure the effective coordination of the resolution or insolvency proceedings among the relevant authorities in the jurisdictions where the failing firm had operations. They were confronted with the unpleasant choice of either permitting a highly unpredictable corporate bankruptcy process or bailing out the failing institution.

Failure resolution was further complicated by the fact that resolution policy and procedures differed greatly across major financial centers. The US had a well-developed resolution regime for deposit taking institutions, but other important jurisdictions such as the UK and Germany did not – they only introduced them after the crisis.[4] The high-level supervisory MoUs and best efforts declarations to cooperate, where they existed,[5] were of little help when the crisis broke.

4 See Basel Committee, Resolution policies and frameworks – progress so far, July 2011.

5 In the EU, there were regional and national MoUs, such as those among the central banks of the Nordic region and between the Dutch and Belgian authorities, motivated by the presence of large cross border financial groups in these regions (the Nordea group in the Nordic countries and the Fortis group in the Benelux). An MoU on high-level principles of co-operation between the banking supervisors and central banks on crisis management was adopted in March 2003. In January 2001 EU banking supervisors and central banks in their capacity as payment systems

The Lehman case revealed a number of cross-border complexities such as conflicting judgments on financial contracts[6] and differences in valuation, automatic stays and intra-group claims.

At the Pittsburgh Summit in September 2009, the G20 called for "internationally-consistent firm-specific contingency and resolution plans" for all systemically important financial firms. At Seoul in November 2010, the G20 further stipulated "Globally systemically important financial institutions should be subject to "a sustained process of mandatory international recovery and resolution planning."

At the Cannes Summit in November 2011, the G20 endorsed the FSB Key Attributes, which set out the essential features that should be part of resolution regimes in all jurisdictions. They include a requirement for "an ongoing process for recovery and resolution planning, covering at a minimum domestically incorporated firms that could be systemically significant or critical if they fail."[7]

The twelve Key Attributes

A necessary prerequisite for effective recovery and resolution planning is the existence of a legal and institutional framework that provides for a resolution regime with the needed authorities and powers to execute a resolution plan. The Key Attributes set out the features that such a regime should have. They apply to resolution regimes for all financial institutions that could be systemically significant or critical if they fail. Financial institutions include banks, insurance companies, investment and securities firms and financial market infrastructure (FMIs). The KAs also cover the resolution of financial groups and conglomerates and therefore extend to holding companies as well as non-regulated operational entities within a financial group or conglomerate. KAs 8 to 10 set out special

overseers signed an MoU which contains provisions dealing with the exchange of information in the event of liquidity or solvency problems. In May 2005 an MoU on co-operation between the banking supervisors, the central banks and the finance ministries in financial crises was signed, including arrangements for the development of contingency plans for crises, along with stress testing and simulation exercises.

6 The "Lehman flip clause case" revealed a major discrepancy. Whereas UK courts upheld the flip clause provisions, US courts declared them unenforceable. See Christopher Whittall, DERIVATIVES: US lawsuit re-opens "flip clause" debate, International Financing Review, 13 February 2012 available at http://www.ifre.com/derivatives-us-lawsuit-re-opens-flip-clause-debate/20048554.article.

7 FSB Key Attribute 11.1.

requirements, including a resolution planning requirement, for financial institutions that are designated as global systemically important financial institutions (G-SIFIs) by the FSB.[8]

In November 2011, the FSB released a list of 29 institutions which have been identified as globally systemically important institutions (G-SIFIs) based on a methodology developed by the Basel Committee.[9] The FSB announced that this list will be reviewed and updated on an annual basis. These firms are subject to specific resolution planning requirements which include mandatory recovery and resolution plans, regular resolvability assessments and institution-specific cross-border cooperation agreements. National authorities may decide to extend these recovery and resolution planning requirements to other institutions in their jurisdictions.

Their Preamble describes the public policy objective and key functions of effective resolution regimes as making feasible the "resolution of failing or problem financial institutions without severe systemic disruption and without exposing taxpayers to loss while preserving the vital economic functions."

- Key Attribute 1 sets out the scope of the new standard: any financial institution that could be systemically significant or critical if it fails should be subject to a resolution regime that has the attributes set out by the FSB. Thus, the scope includes not only banks, but also other non-bank financial institutions such as insurers, investment firm and financial market infrastructures ('FMIs'), including central counterparties. To facilitate comprehensive group-wide solutions, the resolution authority should extend to holding companies of failing financial firms as well as non-regulated operational entities within a financial group that are significant to the regulated business of the financial group.
- Key Attribute 2 provides that the resolution regime should be administered by a designated administrative authority or authorities with the expertise, resources and the operational capacity and independence to effectively apply the resolution measures. The resolution authority (or authorities in jurisdictions where more than one authority is charged with the exercise of resolution powers) should have unimpeded access to firms as necessary for the

8 The first list of global systemically important banks (G-SIBs) was published by the FSB in November 2011: http://www.financialstabilityboard.org/publications/r_111104bb.pdf. The list will be updated annually, and in the future will include financial institutions other than banks, such as insurers that are assessed as global systemically important insurers (G-SIIs).

9 Financial Stability Board, Policy Measures to Address Systemically Important Financial Institutions, 4 November 2011, at http://www.financialstabilityboard.org/publications/r_111104bb.pdf.

purposes of resolution planning, and the preparation and implementation of resolution measures. The resolution authority and its staff should be protected against liability for actions taken and omissions made while discharging their duties in the exercise of resolution powers in good faith, including when taking actions in support of foreign resolution proceedings. Where different resolution authorities are in charge of resolving entities of the same group within a single jurisdiction, the resolution regime of that jurisdiction should identify a lead authority ('group resolution authority') that coordinates the resolution of the legal entities within that jurisdiction. Consistent with the overall objectives of resolution as set out in the Preamble of the Key Attributes, the resolution authority should in the exercise of its resolution powers and as part of its statutory mandate promote financial stability and the continued performance of critical functions and duly consider the potential impact of its resolution actions on financial stability in other jurisdictions. Such a statutory mandate sets the resolution authorities apart from bankruptcy authorities under general corporate insolvency law whose primary mandate is to protect the interests of individual creditors. Judicial authorities administering a corporate insolvency regime do not generally have a mandate to consider the financial stability implications of bankruptcy measures.

- Key Attribute 3 sets out the range of powers that resolution authorities should have at their disposal. These include powers to achieve a sale or transfer of the shares in the failing firm or of all or parts of the firm's assets and liabilities to a third party, either directly or through a bridge institution, without such transaction requiring the consent from shareholders or counterparties. Key Attribute 3 also stipulates that authorities should have the requisite powers to achieve the orderly closure and wind-down of all or parts of the firm's business with timely payout or the transfer of insured deposits. Key Attribute 3 also recommends that authorities be given the statutory power to convert debt instruments into equity in order to achieve a creditor-financed recapitalisation ('bail-in') in either of two ways: (i) by way of recapitalising the entity that is no longer viable, or (ii) alternatively, by capitalising a newly established entity or bridge institution to which the distressed firm's critical functions have been transferred following closure of the non-viable firm (the residual business of which would then be wound up and the firm liquidated). Under the first option the bail-in tool would be used to convert debt into equity of the non-viable entity to absorb losses and recapitalise this entity so as to return it to viability. Under the second option, the critical and core business operations of a failed firm would be transferred to a newly established (bridge) institution. Bailed-in creditors of the failed entity would then receive equity stakes in the newly established institution. The concept of bail-in is important as it seeks to minimize the frictions and non-linearities associated with closure and liquidation. It offers the possibility for bailed-in creditors whose investments might otherwise be lost in liquidation to recover value. It also presents an alternative to temporary government ownership and to solutions, such as a sale or merger with an existing institution, which can increase concentration and thereby exacerbate the 'too big to fail' problem. The Key Attributes stipulate that bail-in powers should be exercised in a manner that respects the hierarchy of claims in liquidation. The extent to which banks maintain a sufficient level of bail-in debt so that bail-in may be a suitable resolution option may be reviewed as part of resolvability assessments (see Key Attribute 10 below). "Bail-in within resolution" needs to be distinguished from the conversion or write-down of equity and subordinated creditors based on contractual provisions. The latter would normally be triggered before any bail-in within resolution is carried out. A further distinction needs to be made between traditionally subordinated claims and "co-co" obligations with early triggers, which will be subject to conversion or write-down well before the resolution stage is reached. The Key Attributes also recognize the need for special tools to resolve insurance companies. These include powers to undertake a portfolio transfer of all or part of the insurance business to another insurer without the consent of each and every policyholder and powers to discontinue the writing of new business by an insurance firm in resolution while continuing to administer existing contractual policy obligations. In applying resolution powers to individual components of a financial group located in its jurisdiction, the resolution authority should be required to take into account the impact on the group as a whole and on financial stability in other affected jurisdictions, and undertake best efforts to avoid taking actions that could reasonably be expected to trigger instability elsewhere in the group or in the financial system. Resolution by means of application of one or a combination of resolution tools should be initiated when a firm is no longer viable or likely to be no longer viable, and has no reasonable prospect of becoming so. This means that resolution should be possible before the total equity value of a firm has been extinguished.

- Key Attribute 4 recognizes the importance of legal certainty and enforceability of financial contracts, including netting and collateralisation agreements. Entry into resolution and the exercise of any resolution powers should not, however, constitute an event that entitles any counterparty of the firm in resolution to exercise acceleration or early termination rights under such agreements if the substantive obligations under the contract continue to be performed, such as would be the case if the contracts were transferred to a sound financial firm or bridge institutions.[10] Should acceleration or termination rights nevertheless be exercisable, resolution authorities should have the power to stay such rights temporarily. The objective is to avoid the unnecessary termination of large volumes of financial contracts and resulting fire sales where the contracts can be continued, for instance by way of transfer to a sound financial market participant or bridge bank, in a manner that does not interfere with payment or delivery obligations under the contract.

- Key Attribute 5 stresses the need for legal certainty and predictability with regard to the exercise of resolution powers and stipulates that resolution powers should be exercised in a way that respects the hierarchy of claims. Authorities should have some flexibility to depart from the general principle of equal (*pari passu*) treatment of creditors of the same class if necessary to contain the potential systemic impact of a firm's failure or to maximise the value for the benefit of all creditors as a whole, provided that all creditors receive at a minimum what they would have received in a liquidation of the firm ('no creditor worse off than in liquidation' safeguard). Judicial review mechanisms should not constrain the implementation of, or result in a reversal of, measures taken by resolution authorities acting within their legal powers and in good faith. Instead, they should provide for redress by awarding compensation, if justified.
- Key Attribute 6 requires jurisdictions to put in place privately-financed funding mechanisms that can provide temporary financing to facilitate the resolution of the firm. Such funding mechanism may consist of resolution funds financed by levies on the industry or mechanisms that rely on ex post recovery from the financial firms or industry as a whole. They also include deposit insurance funds, which can be used to facilitate the resolution of a firm's deposit-taking activities, e.g. by funding the transfer of insured deposits to a sound institution or bridge bank. The resolution authority or authority extending the temporary funding should make a provision to recover any losses incurred from shareholders and unsecured creditors or, if necessary, from the financial system more widely.
- Key Attribute 7 sets out legal framework conditions that should facilitate the resolution of cross-border institutions. Recognizing that cross-border firms remain governed by national laws administered by national authorities, it provides that the statutory mandate of a resolution authority should empower and strongly encourage the authority wherever possible to act to achieve a cooperative solution with foreign resolution authorities. Legislation

---

10 See Key Attribute 4 and Annex IV.

and regulations in jurisdictions should not contain provisions that trigger automatic action in that jurisdiction as a result of official intervention or the initiation of resolution or insolvency proceedings in another jurisdiction. Jurisdictions should provide for transparent and expedited processes to give effect to foreign resolution measures. Depending on the nature of the resolution measure this may be achieved either by way of a recognition process or by taking measures under the domestic resolution regime that support implementation and are consistent with the resolution measures taken by the foreign home resolution authority. Such recognition or support measures should enable a foreign home resolution authority to gain rapid control over the firm (branch or shares in a subsidiary) or its assets that are located in the host jurisdiction, as appropriate, in cases where the firm is being resolved under the law of the foreign home jurisdiction.

- Key Attribute 8 requires home and key host authorities of all G-SIFIs to maintain CMGs with the objective of enhancing preparedness for, and facilitating the management and resolution of a failing cross-border firm. CMGs should include as necessary the supervisory authorities, central banks, resolution authorities, finance ministries and the public authorities responsible for guarantee schemes of jurisdictions that are home or host to entities of the group and material to its resolution, and should cooperate closely with authorities in other jurisdictions not represented on the CMGs where firms have a systemic presence.
- Key Attribute 9 calls for institution-specific cooperation agreements to be in place between the home and relevant host authorities that need to be involved in the preparation and management of a crisis affecting a firm that has been designated as globally systemically significant. Effective resolution in a cross-border context requires an understanding among the relevant home and host authorities on how they will cooperate over the resolution of individual firms, both in the planning phase and during a crisis. Annex I to the Key Attributes "*Essential elements of institution-specific cooperation agreements*" sets out the necessary core elements of such agreements. These agreements should, inter alia, establish the objectives and processes for cooperation through CMGs; define the roles and responsibilities of the authorities pre-crisis (that is, in the recovery and resolution planning phase) and during a crisis; set out the processes for information sharing, including sharing with any host authorities that are not represented in the CMG, and for coordination in the development of the RRPs. They should also provide for meetings to be held at least annually, involving top officials of the home and relevant host authorities, to review the robustness of the overall resolution strategy for G-SIFIs; and provide for regular (at least annual) reviews by

appropriate senior officials of the operational plans implementing the resolution strategies.

- FSB Key Attribute 10 calls for regular resolvability assessments of at least those firms that have been designated as globally systemically significant.[11] Resolvability assessments should constitute a continuous and iterative process aimed at identifying and addressing material obstacles to resolvability until an adequate level of resolvability is reached. They should be led by the home authority and coordinated with key host authorities. Annex II to the Key Attributes document elaborates on the elements of such assessments and the process for carrying them out. Resolution authorities should, in coordination with other relevant authorities, assess in particular: the extent to which critical financial services, and payment, clearing and settlement functions can continue to be performed; the nature and extent of intra-group exposures and their impact on resolution if they need to be unwound; the extent to which the institution holds sufficient 'bail-inable' debt to allow for a creditor-financed recapitalization of the firm in distress or of a newly established firm by way of conversion of the debt into equity; the capacity of the firm to deliver sufficiently detailed accurate and timely information to support resolution; and the robustness of cross-border cooperation and information sharing arrangements. Resolvability assessments should extend to the group as a whole and be conducted by the home authority of the G-SIFI and coordinated within the firm's CMG taking into account national assessments by host authorities. Host resolution authorities that conduct resolvability assessments of subsidiaries located in their jurisdiction should coordinate as far as possible with the home authority that conducts resolvability assessment for the group as a whole. The Key Attributes do not express any preference for a particular group structure or business model. However, given that structural factors may limit authorities' choices of resolution options, authorities should have the requisite powers to address such factors where financial, legal operational structures render a firm unresolvable by requiring changes to the manner in which the firms operate or to their legal structures.
- Key Attribute 11 sets out a requirement for an adequate and credible recovery and resolution plan (RRP) for all G-SIFIs and any firm the failure of which is assessed by its home authority to have a potential impact on financial stability. It should be informed by resolvability assessments and take account

11 See Key Attribute 10.1.

of the specific circumstances of the firm and reflect its nature, complexity, interconnectedness, level of substitutability and size.

- Key Attribute 12 requires jurisdictions to remove legal, regulatory or policy impediments that hinder the appropriate exchange of information, including firm-specific information, between supervisory authorities, central banks, resolution authorities, finance ministries and the public authorities responsible for guarantee schemes. The sharing of all information relevant for recovery and resolution should be possible in normal times and during a crisis at a domestic and a cross-border level. Firms should be required, to be able to demonstrate, as part of the recovery and resolution planning process, that they are able to produce the essential information needed to implement RRPs within a short period of time.

Key elements of Recovery and Resolution Plans ("living wills")

The Key Attributes require that adequate and credible Recovery and Resolution Plans (RRPs) are in place for those firms whose failure is deemed by their home authorities to have a potential impact on financial stability. This requirement should apply, at a minimum, to all G-SIFIs (see Key Attribute 11.2).[12]

Objectives

The objective of the resolution planning requirement is to establish an integrated process of supervision and resolution that will enable authorities to prepare for and to carry out an orderly resolution. One of the purposes of the planning process is to introduce new discipline into the financial system. It requires authorities to understand what critical functions are performed by the firm, and it requires authorities to identify the most suitable options for preserving these functions. The very act of considering potential failure compels firms to better understand their commercial drivers and operational dependencies. If bail-outs are no longer

---

12 Annex III of the Key Attributes provides more specific guidance as regards the process of resolution planning.

inevitable and if resolution is a credible option, managers and investors will have an incentive to act early to address problems.

The RRPs should take account of the specific circumstances of the firm and reflect the nature, complexity, interconnectedness, level of substitutability and size of the firm. Most importantly, RRPs should not assume that taxpayers' funds can be used to resolve the firm.

RRPs should provide guidance to firms and authorities in a recovery or resolution scenario. The RRPs are not binding on the authorities and do not prevent authorities from implementing a different strategy in the event that the firm needs to be resolved. They nevertheless increase predictability by permitting managers and investors to develop expectations as to how authorities would act in a crisis. RRPs have two parts:

(i) a recovery plan that outlines the steps the firm itself could take to restore financial strength and viability when the firm comes under severe stress; and
(ii) a resolution plan that outlines resolution actions that authorities can take to protect systemically important functions and resolved firm feasible without severe disruption and without exposing taxpayers to loss.

Recovery plan

Authorities should regularly review recovery plans as part of the supervisory process, assessing whether they are credible and can be effectively implemented. The authorities should have the power to require the implementation of recovery measures. Firms should be obliged to update their recovery plans at regular intervals and when events occur that materially change the firm's structure or operations, its strategy or its aggregated risk exposure. They should use an appropriate number of market-wide (systemic) stress scenarios and firm-specific (idiosyncratic) stress scenarios to test the robustness of their recovery plans.

Recovery plans should include a range of measures that will be effective in a variety of circumstances, including recapitalisation after extraordinary losses, capital conservation measures such as suspension of dividends and payment of variable remuneration as well as sales of subsidiaries and spin-offs of business units. One of the essential elements of recovery plans is that they should set out clear backstops and escalation procedures, identifying the criteria (both quantitative and qualitative) that would trigger implementation of the plan (or individual measures in the plan) by the firm. Such triggers should be designed to prevent undue delays in the implementation of recovery measures.

Resolution plan

The resolution plan should facilitate the effective use of the resolution authority's powers. It should help the authorities achieve an orderly resolution in the event that recovery measures are not feasible or have proved to be ineffective. The authorities are responsible for developing and maintaining, and where necessary, executing the resolution strategies set out in resolution plan.

At the national level, all relevant authorities involved in supervision, implementation of corrective actions and resolution should participate in the RRP process. Firms should be required to provide on a timely basis data and information, including strategic and scenario analysis, required by the authorities for resolution planning.

Cross-border resolution planning

In the case of G-SIFIs, the home resolution authority should lead the development of a group resolution plan in coordination with all members of the firm's CMG. Host resolution authorities may maintain their own resolution plans for the firm's operations in their jurisdictions, cooperating as far as possible with the home authority to ensure that the plan is as consistent as possible with the group plan.

Home authorities of G-SIFIs should have in place a process for ascertaining which jurisdictions that are not included in the CMG consider the local operations of the firm to be systemically important for the local financial system, and the reasons for that judgment. The home authorities should maintain contact with such non-CMG jurisdictions and ensure that appropriate modalities for cooperation and information sharing are in place. Resolution plans should include a high-level substantive summary of the key resolution strategies and operational plans for their implementation. They should include the identification of the firm's essential and systemically important functions, a description of the main measures that will be used to implement the resolution strategies and an assessment of potential impediments to their successful implementation. The Key Attributes call for regular meetings of top officials of the home and key host authorities of G-SIFIs, where appropriate with the CEO of the firm, to review at least annually the overall resolution strategy (see Key Attribute 11.6). Appropriate senior officials of the home and host authorities should, at least annually, review the resolution plans for each G-SIFI and engage in periodic simulation or scenario exercises to test the viability of the plans.

The FSB has given priority to the development by home authorities of high-level resolution strategies that may consist of either 'single point of entry' or 'top down' approaches and 'multiple-entry' resolution approaches along national, regional or functional lines. These resolution strategies should provide the necessary direction for more detailed work in CMGs on how to make them operational, and inform the development of cooperation agreements, RRPs and resolvability assessments.[13]

- A "single point of entry" approach involves entry by a single national resolution authority at the top holding or parent company level of the group[14] – most probably in the jurisdiction responsible for the comprehensive consolidated supervision of the group. Resolution powers are applied at parent level and in a manner that avoids the need to apply resolution at a lower level within the group, including at the level of foreign subsidiaries. This approach may consist in a bail-in of debt at holding company level and the transfer of assets or a controlled wind-down of operations, with or without the use of a bridge entity.
- A "multiple point of entry" approach involves the simultaneous or consecutive entry into resolution of multiple parts of the group and application of resolution tools by two or more resolution authorities. It would likely result in a break-up of the group along national, regional or functional lines.

Status of implementation of the resolution planning requirements

Jurisdictions have taken important steps towards the implementation of the resolution planning requirement.

In the United States, the Dodd-Frank Wall Street Reform and Consumer Protection Act (Title I) requires companies covered by the act to prepare resolution plans on the premise that they will be resolved under the US Bankruptcy Code (Title I plans). The prevailing view is that in practice G-SIFIs would not be resolved under the Bankruptcy Code. Instead, the resolution powers conferred on

13 See Financial Stability Board, Implementing the FSB Key Attributes of Effective Resolution Regimes – how far have we come?, 15 April 2013.

14 In this note, references to a holding company include a parent operating company, recognizing that an SPE resolution of the latter entails additional challenges, which should be considered in the resolution plan.

the FDIC by Title II of the Act would be used. Nonetheless, the FDIC would use the Title I plans as a source of information and potential strategies.

In the United Kingdom, firms are required to produce a "resolution pack" containing the necessary information to enable the authorities to plan for resolution.

The European Commission's provisional draft directive for a crisis management framework includes a requirement that banks and investment firms develop and maintain both recovery and resolution plans. Firms should be required to draw up recovery plans setting out arrangements and measures to enable it to take early action to restore its long-term viability in the event of a material deterioration of its financial situation. Group resolution plans should include a plan for the group as well as plans for each institution within the group. Supervisors will assess and approve recovery plans. Resolution plans should be prepared by the relevant resolution authorities in cooperation with supervisors.

Conclusion

The Key Attributes provide a comprehensive framework for the resolution of large and complex financial institutions active in multiple jurisdictions.

To implement the Key Attributes in their national legal and regulatory frameworks and to remove the remaining obstacles to cross-border cooperation, authorities and firms still have considerable work ahead of them. Challenges arise from the remaining differences among national resolution regimes. For instance, differences in the treatment or ranking of creditor claims may make authorities reluctant to agree to cooperative solutions if as a result of deference to a foreign authority, local creditors are treated less favourably than under the national regime. Impediments to information sharing between members of a CMG can create obstacles to joint resolution planning and hamper effective cooperation in a crisis. Different funding arrangements across jurisdictions can complicate cross-border coordination, for instance, if a resolution fund can be used in some jurisdictions only after an institution has been closed and placed in receivership whereas in others resolution funding may be made available prior to closure in the context of a 'going concern' bank restructuring. Finally, the scope of resolution regimes matters. Institutions that engage in shadow banking[15] activities not

---

15 The FSB describes the 'shadow banking system' as 'credit intermediation involving entities and activities outside the regular banking system'. See Shadow Banking: Strengthening Over-only operate outside of the safety net and regulatory perimeter, they also tend not to be covered special resolution regime. Resolution planning will need to be stepped up significantly to address these and other issues so that cross-border cooperation will take place seamlessly in times of crisis.

sight and Regulation, Recommendations of the Financial Stability Board, 27 October 2011 at http://www.financialstabilityboard.org/publications/r_111027a.pdf.

Mathias Otto*
Living Wills – The In-House Perspective

Table of Contents

I. Introduction

It was an as bold as morbid message that kicked off the political discussion on living wills in early autumn of 2009. Regulators announced their intention to force the large banks to draw up "living wills" so that they have to consider and reduce their complexity[1]. Such living wills should serve as "prestructured euthanasia" for ailing banks and "[e]very large institution will have to have an in-house 'undertaker' responsible for mapping out how it would be wound down if it was going to the wall"[2]. And the G20 Leaders stated in the communiqué of their

* The opinions expressed here are those of the author. This paper was finalized on 2 November 2012 and does not reflect legal or policy developments since then.
1 Financial Times, 3 September 2009: "FSA's Turner backs living wills for banks"; Financial Times, 14 September 2009: "Living Wills 'to be forced on UK banks'".
2 Speech of UK Financial Services Minister *Paul Myners* at the Financial Times Global Finance Forum on 18 September 2009, HM Treasury press release 82/09 (http://webarchive.nationalarchives.gov.uk/20100407010852/http://www.hm-treasury.gov.uk/press_82_09.htm).

summit in Pittsburgh of 24–25 September 2009: "Systemically important financial firms should develop internationally-consistent firm-specific contingency and resolution plans."[3]

It can therefore hardly surprise that the industry signaled not only its willingness to engage in a constructive dialogue but that its reaction was otherwise frosty and ranged from qualifying the proposed requirement on banks "to draw up some form of step-by-step instruction manual for their own dismantling" as "both misjudged in conception [...] and wasteful of valuable resources"[4], to the concern that regulators "may find themselves 'shadow managing' a business in the desire to eliminate negative outcomes"[5] and to the conclusion that "living wills will be very theoretical and lead to inefficient structures"[6].

Whilst all these points remain valid concerns, a number of banks has in the meantime set up huge projects to prepare their living wills or, as they are called now, recovery and resolution plans, and is in a regular dialogue with the relevant regulatory authorities on the progress made. With the dust of the political discussion having settled to a large extent, the time is right for a more in-depth view on this phenomenon.

At a number of occasions the financial crisis exposed the problem that a financial institution in difficulties can hijack regulators, governments and parliaments because of its size, its complexity, its services provided or simply because of the perception that its collapse could ignite a wider crisis of confidence into the financial system. The phenomenon is widely known as the "too-big-to-fail" dilemma. Indeed, since 2007 numerous financial institutions in Europe and the United States had to be rescued with almost unimaginable amounts of taxpayers' money. And the collapse of Lehman Brothers in September 2008 showed how big and far reaching the shockwaves of a disorderly market exit of a large financial firm are. It has therefore only been fair that regulators and politicians are looking for mechanisms through which an ailing firm can leave the market place without disrupting it.

---

3 Point 13, fourth indent (pg. 9), published at http://www.g20-g8.com/g8-g20/root/bank_objects/EN_declaration_finale_pittsburgh2009.pdf.

4 Institute of International Finance (IIF): "A Global Approach to Resolving Financial Firms: An Industry Perspective" (May 2010), pg. 20 at paragraph 41 (http://www.iif.com/regulatory/resolution/).

5 British Bankers Association (BBA): "Next steps for banking" – a BBA series, Chapter 3 (November 2009), pg. 3 (http://www.bba.org.uk/download/694).

6 *Josef Ackermann* according to The Telegraph, 2 November 2009: "FSA's Lord Turner: splitting banks will make sector more risky".

The fact that the business of financial institutions is intermediation and that therefore financial institutions are by definition highly interconnected with both one another and the real economy should not discourage us from this task. It shows, however, how complicated it is.

II. The framework for living wills

The requirement to prepare living wills is already reality – at least for the large financial institutions perceived to be of global systemic relevance and known as "Global Systemically Important Financial Institutions" or "G-SIFIs". They will submit their first recovery and resolution plans by the end of 2012. And in the U.S., the Dodd-Frank Act[7] requires large bank holding companies – measured by their consolidated assets – to prepare resolution plans already by mid 2012.

Three aspects of the current framework for living wills warrant discussion in more detail: the legal basis, the threshold above which a living will is required, and the interrelationship of living wills with other concepts that respond to the "to-big-to-fail" problem like capital surcharges.

1. Legal basis for requiring living wills

In sharp contrast to the current dynamics in supervisory practice, only two countries with major financial centers have enacted living will legislation with a clear statutory basis to require banks and their holding companies to prepare living will: the United States and Switzerland. In the U.S., Section 165 (d) of the Dodd-Frank Act[8] requires that bank holding companies with assets of $ 50bn. or more prepare a plan "for rapid and orderly resolution in the event of material financial distress or failure". Switzerland amended its Banking Act effective 1 March 2012 by a "too-big-to-fail law"[9] and now requires that each of its systemically relevant

7 Dodd-Frank Wall Street Reform and Consumer Protection Act (Pub.L. No. 111-203, 124 Stat. 1376 (2010)).

8 Codified at 12 U.S.C. 5365 (d).

9 Amendment "Stärkung der Stabilität im Finanzsektor; too big to fail" (Strengthening the stability of the financial sector; too big to fail) of 30 September 2011, promulgated 21 February 2012 (AS 2012, pg. 811).

banks develops contingency plans which ensure the continuation of systemically relevant functions of that bank in case of its imminent insolvency[10].

Otherwise, the legal terrain is uncertain. The G20 summit in Cannes on 4 November 2011 endorsed a policy framework developed by the Financial Stability Board (FSB) which comprises also an international standard for resolution regimes[11]. On the same day, the FSB published two documents: the "Policy Measures to Address Systemically Important Financial Institutions"[12] which state that the "G-SIFIs will need to meet the resolution planning requirements by end-2012"[13] and the "Key Attributes of Effective Resolution Regimes for Financial Institutions"[14] which set forth the key elements of a recovery and resolution plan.

It is worth bearing in mind that the G20 Leaders are the finance ministers and central bank governors of the G20 countries and that the FSB comprises representatives from the finance ministries, central banks and bank supervisory authorities. All of them are bound to operate within the framework of the existing laws in their country. Therefore, everything agreed and committed on this level which needs to be implemented and is imposed on individual financial institutions needs to secure a proper legal basis in the respective national laws or EU regulations[15].

When the FSB framework was endorsed by the G20, Europe was still in a sort of consultation mode. Following its Communication on a framework for crisis management in the financial sector of 2010[16], the European Commission had launched a consultation on technical details of such a framework at the begin-

10 Articles 9 (2)(d) and 10 (2) of the Swiss Banking Act.

11 Published at http://www.g20-g8.com/g8-g20/g20/english/for-the-press/news-releases/cannes-summit-final-declaration.1557.html, paragraph 28.

12 FSB: "Policy Measures to Address Systemically Important Financial Institutions", Annex "G-SIFIs", published at http://www.financialstabilityboard.org/publications/r_111104bb.pdf.

13 *Ibid.* at paragraph 6.

14 Published at http://www.financialstabilityboard.org/publications/r_111104cc.pdf.

15 In his discussion paper for the German Lawyers' Conference 2010, *Höfling* therefore questions the current legal basis of these international regulatory standard setters and urges that the mission, organization and procedures for national authorities to participate in these bodies should be codified by an act of law of the respective national parliaments (*Wolfram Höfling*, "Finanzmarktregulierung – Welche Regelungen empfehlen sich für den deutschen und den europäischen Finanzsektor?", Gutachten F zum 68. Deutschen Juristentag (2010), pg. 33 *et seqq.* (on pg. 39)).

16 Communication from the Commission to the European Parliament, the Council, the European Economic and Social Committee, the Committee of the Regions and the European Central Bank of 20 October 2010: "An EU Framework for Crisis Management in the Financial Sector" (COM(2010) 579 final).

ning of 2011[17] and had announced its intention to adopt a legislative proposal on bank recovery and resolution in June 2011. Eventually, this proposal came a year later. Only on 6 June 2012, the European Commission published the draft of a directive for a framework for the recovery and resolution of banks[18]. Already three weeks before this proposal, the European Banking Authority (EBA) published a discussion paper on a draft template for recovery plans[19]. This proposal is based on Article 25 (1) of the EBA Regulation[20] which mandates the EBA to "contribute to and participate actively in the development and coordination of effective and consistent recovery and resolution plans". The basis for such development is, however, not specified and in its proposal the EBA acknowledges that it "may identify best practices" but that only "the forthcoming European Commission proposal for EU legislation [...] is expected to detail the nature and content of R[ecovery and] R[esolution] P[lan]s, clarify the scope of their application, and further define the role and powers of the EBA and national competent authorities"[21]. The EBA's proposal had a comment period of one month until 15 June 2012. This left the industry and other interested parties just nine calendar days to reflect in their comments also the draft regulation on recovery and resolution of banks proposed by the European Commission. And the legislative process for the directive has not even started.

In the UK, the Financial Services Act 2010[22] mandates the Financial Services Authority (FSA) to "exercise its power to make general rules" that require banks

---

17 DG Internal Market and Services Working Document "Technical details of a possible EU framework for bank recovery and resolution" published on 6 January 2011 (press release IP 11/10). (http://ec.europa.eu/internal_market/consultations/docs/2011/crisis_management/consultation_paper_en.pdf).

18 European Commission: "Proposal for a directive of the European Parliament and of the Council establishing a framework for the recovery and resolution of credit institutions and investment firms and amending Council Directives 77/91/EEC and 82/891/EC, Directives 2001/24/EC, 2002/47/EC, 2004/25/EC, 2005/56/EC, 2007/36/EC and 2011/35/EC and Regulation (EU) No. 1093/2010 (COM(2012) 280)" published 6 June 2012 (http://ec.europa.eu/internal_market/bank/docs/crisis-management/2012_eu_framework/COM_2012_280_en.pdf).

19 EBA: "Discussion Paper on a template for recovery plans (EBA/DP/2012/2)" published 15 May 2012 (http://www.eba.europa.eu/cebs/media/Publications/Discussion%20Papers/DP%202012%2002/Discussion-Paper-on-Template-for-Recovery-Plans.pdf).

20 Regulation (EU) No. 1093/2010 of the European Parliament and of the Council of 24 November 2010 establishing a European Supervisory authority (European Banking authority), amending Decision No. 716/2009/EC and repealing Commission Decision 2009/78/EC (OJ L331, 15 December 2010, pg. 12).

21 *Ibid.* on pg. 4.

22 Financial Services Act 2010 ch. 28 (http://www.legislation.gov.uk/ukpga/2010/28/introduction).

to prepare, and keep up-to-date, a recovery plan and a resolution plan[23]. On this basis, the FSA published a consultation paper on recovery and resolution plans in August 2011[24] with a comment period until 9 November 2011. Oddly enough, the agreements at the G20 summit in Cannes were reached with the participation of the UK already five days *before* expiry of the comment period for the FSA's consultation.

In Germany, the Restructuring Act of 2010[25] grants the Federal Financial Supervisory Authority (BaFin) wide restructuring and reorganization powers but it does not impose any planning requirements for living wills on banks. The BaFin's current requirement that certain banks prepare a recovery and resolution plan will therefore have to be based on the general norm that each bank must maintain a proper risk management that addresses the nature, scope, complexity and risks of its business (Section 25a of the German Banking Act (KWG)). On 1 November 2012, the BaFin eventually launched a public consultation on a draft circular dealing with minimum requirements for recovery plans[26] which is also meant to implement the FSB's Key Attributes into the German regulatory practice.

All this is not meant to challenge the legality of the current living wills exercise[27]. The list of countries with recovery and resolution legislation published by the FSB[28] is impressive but one should note that in most countries this process started after the FSB's Key Attributes had been published and before banks were pushed to write up such plans. This questions the haste with which regulatory reform including living wills is pushed forward and the lack of both vertical coor-

23 Section 7 which inserts new Sections 139B–139F into the Financial Services and Markets Act 2000; see Sections 139B (1) and 139 (1).

24 FSA: Consultation Paper CP 11/16 of 9 August 2011 "Recovery and Resolution Plans".

25 Restrukturierungsgesetz of 9 December 2010 (BGBl. I pg. 1900), introducing restructuring powers for the Federal Financial Supervisory Authority (BaFin) in Sections 48a *et seqq.* of the Banking Act (KWG) and introducing the Act on the Reorganization of Credit Institutions (Kreditinstitute-Reorganisationsgesetz – KredReorgG).

26 Consultation 12/2012 ("Entwurf Mindestanforderungen an die Ausgestaltung von Sanierungsplänen"), published at http://www.bafin.de/SharedDocs/Veroeffentlichungen/DE/Konsultation/2012/kon_1212_masan_ba.html.

27 The G20 summit in Los Cabos from 18–19 June 2012 reiterated the commitment to the FSB Key Attributes and the support of "the ongoing elaboration of recovery and resolution plans and institution-specific cross-border cooperation agreements for all G-SIFIs" (paragraph 41 of the G20 summit communiqué – http://www.telegraph.co.uk/finance/g20-summit/9343250/G20-Summit-communique-full-text.html).

28 FSB: "Resolution of Systemically Important Financial Institutions – Progress Report" (November 2012), pg. 5 *et seqq.* (http://www.financialstabilityboard.org/publications/r_121031aa.pdf).

dination within the hierarchy of rule makers and proper involvement of parliaments in the development of far reaching rules.

2. Applicability to large and systemically relevant banks

Further inconsistency comes from different thresholds above which a firm is required to develop a recovery and resolution plan.

a) Limitation to systemic relevance?

The Dodd-Frank Act simply refers to a firm's total assets and requires that bank holding companies with assets of $ 50bn. or more prepare a living will[29]. Total assets also determine the deadline by which a firm has to submit its initial resolution plan: the plans of large firms with consolidated assets of $ 250bn. or more are due by 1 July 2012, firms with consolidated assets of $ 100bn. or more are given until 1 July 2013 and the remaining firms have to file their initial plan by the end of 2013[30]. It is estimated that more than 120 financial institutions will fall under this regime[31]. Also the UK FSA's consultation paper proposes a total assets oriented threshold[32].

Obviously, total assets as the dividing line makes it easy to determine which firms fall into the resolution planning requirement and which ones are exempt. Otherwise, the threshold is quite crude. It perceives systemic relevance as a mere function of size. It ignores off-balance sheet positions as well as the nature of the services provided and the firm's interconnectedness with other market participants as criteria. And it thus risks missing firms that should also have a resolution plan and burdening other firms disproportionately.

---

29 See *supra* note 8.

30 Regulation QQ (12 C.F.R. § 243.3 (a)).

31 *Joseph Karl Grant:* "Planning for the Death of a Systemically Important Financial Institution Under Title I § 165 (d) of the Dodd-Frank Act: The Practical Implications of resolution Plans or Living Wills in Planning a Bank's Funeral", 6 Virginia Law & Business Rev. 469, 476 (2012); *Marcia L. Goldstein, Heath P. Tarbert* and *Kathlene M. Burke:* "Navigating Dodd-Frank's Resolution Plan Requirement", New York Law Journal, 5 December 2011 (http://www.newyorklawjournal.com/PubArticleNY.jsp?id=1202534237120&slreturn=1#).

32 *Supra* note 24, point 1.18: Investment firms with assets exceeding £ 15bn. in addition to all UK incorporated deposit-takers (point 1.15).

A more refined methodology was applied by the Basle Committee in determining the group of G-SIFIs for the Financial Stability Board (FSB)[33]. It considered not only the size of firms but also their complexity, substitutability and the level of their cross-border activities and eventually came up with a list of 29 banks which have to prepare living wills[34].

Also the amended Swiss Banking Act limits resolution planning to systemically relevant banks (Article 9 (2)(d)). Systemic relevance is determined by the Swiss National Bank on the basis of the market share of a bank in functions that are indispensable for the Swiss economy and not substitutable, the ratio of the bank's total assets to the Swiss gross domestic product, the volume of its deposits and its risk profile (Article 8).

The crisis has shown, however, that the systemic relevance of a firm has also a huge subjective element. If the potential collapse of a small bank is perceived as the signal on the wall that a bigger problem might be looming, this firm becomes systemically relevant and its rescue becomes a "must" in order to calm down concerns on the stability of financial system even before they arise and to avoid that the perception becomes a self fulfilling prophecy.

It is therefore important to caution against measuring systemic relevance only against numbers and to remind that also the public perception of the concrete situation at hand needs to be factored into the analysis. On this basis, one should anticipate that in a second and third wave ultimately every financial firm will have to prepare a living will.

The draft of the EU directive on recovery and resolution planning[35] points in this direction. It requires that each credit institution and financial firm in the European Union draws up and maintains a recovery plan (Article 5) and furnishes information to the relevant resolution authority for it to prepare and implement a resolution plan (Articles 9 and 10). Depending on the anticipated impact of the failure of an institution "due to the nature of its business, its size or its interconnectedness to other institutions or to the financial system in general, on financial markets, on other institutions, on funding conditions", national authorities may apply the rules on the content and details of recovery plans and information to be

33 Basel Committee on Banking Supervision: "Global systemically important banks: assessment methodology and the additional loss absorbency requirement – Rules text" (November 2011).

34 See *supra* note 12. The list was updated on 1 November 2012 and shrunk to 28 banks (FSB: "Update of group of global systemically important banks (G-SIBs)" Annex I, published at http://www.financialstabilityboard.org/publications/r_121031ac.pdf).

35 See *supra* note 18.

provided for resolution planning in a simplified manner (Article 4). But they will not be able to completely ignore non-SIFIs in that regard.

Also international bodies have started looking beyond firms of global relevance. In April 2012, the FSB proposed to generally apply the G-SIFI framework also to banks of domestic systemic relevance and to defer the designation as "D-SIB" (domestic systemically relevant bank) to the local regulator[36]. A half year later, the Basel Committee published its framework for dealing with D-SIBs.[37] And the BaFin's consultation paper on minimum requirements for recovery plans foresees already that these requirements shall also apply to banks with only domestic systemic relevance[38]. Whilst this development is heading into the right direction, it leaves the regulators with the tough *ex ante* determination of a firm's systemic relevance and risks to miss unforeseen situations in which a firm may be perceived as too important to fail because it is perceived (rightly or not) to represent a wider issue in the system. Real life is more colorful than any imagination driving the preselection.

b) Limitation to banks?

Finally, the current focus of the "too-big-to-fail" discussion only on the banking sector ignores the fact that there are also non-bank financial firms of a size, complexity and interconnectedness with other financial firms and the real economy that easily compares to systemically important banks. The question, how a large insurance company or clearing system in trouble would be able to exit the market in an orderly fashion at no cost for the taxpayer without having a recovery and resolution plan in place and without having assessed the resolution powers of the competent authorities is raised surprisingly rarely[39].

---

36 FSB: "Extending the G-SIFI Framework to domestic systemically important banks" (Progress Report to G-20 Ministers and Governors, 16 April 2012), published at http://www.financialstabilityboard.org/publications/r_120420b.pdf.

37 Basel Committee on Banking Supervision: "A framework for dealing with domestic systemically important banks" (October 2012).

38 *Supra* note 26, point C.1.

39 Deutsche Bank Research: "Identifying systemically important financial institutions (SIFIs)" (11 August 2011), pg. 14 *et sq.* (http://www.dbresearch.de/PROD/DBR_INTERNET_EN-PROD/PROD0000000000276722/Identifying+systemically+important+financial+institutions+%28SIFIs%29.pdf).

It is worth noting in this context that the Dutch Intervention Act of 2012[40] which grants resolution powers on ailing financial firms to the Dutch Central Bank and the Ministry of Finance expressly applies to both banks and insurance companies[41]. Moreover, two recent developments are reassuring in this context: the European Commission's consultation on a possible living will framework for non-bank financial institutions, in particular insurance and reinsurance companies[42] and the consultative report of the Basel Committee and the International Organization of Securities Commissions (IOSCO) on how financial market infrastructures could be resolved and which planning is necessary in this regard[43]. All this shows that recovery and resolution planning is a key topic throughout the financial sector and it may easily lead to a best practice that will inspire also firms outside the financial sector.

3. Relationship between living wills and capital surcharges

Finally, when discussing living wills, one should remember that the Financial Stability Board offers two concepts to deal with the "too-big-to-fail" problem of G-SIFIs: first, ask them to demonstrate their resolvability by way of a living will agreed with the supervisory authority and, in addition, ask them to hold a special capital surcharge to address their potential non-resolvability because of their size, complexity and interconnectedness[44]. But if a G-SIFI has a living will agreed with its regulator and has thus demonstrated its resolvability, there is no logical basis to also impose a special capital surcharge for potential non-resolvability just because of the systemic relevance of the institution.

---

40 Wet van 24 mei 2012: Wet bijzondere maatregelen financiële ondernemingen (Law of 24 May 2012 on Special Measures on Financial Firms), Staatsblad 2012, 241, commonly referred to as the "Intervention Act".

41 Article 1 C of this law introduces a new chapter 3.5.4A into the Dutch Financial Supervision Act (Wet op het financieel toezicht – Wft); see in particular the definition of "problem institution" (probleeminstelling) in Article 3:159a (h) Wft.

42 European Commission (DG Internal Market and Services): "Consultation on a possible recovery and resolution framework for financial institutions other than banks" published on 5 October 2012 at http://ec.europa.eu/internal_market/consultations/2012/nonbanks/consultation-document_en.pdf.

43 Recovery and resolution of financial market infrastructures – Consultative Report (July 2012) (http://www.iosco.org/library/pubdocs/pdf/IOSCOPD388.pdf).

44 FSB, Policy Measures (*supra* note 12), paragraph 4 (ii) and (iii).

Both tools are communicating tubes which reinforce one another[45] but which the FSB has failed to calibrate to one another. Where a capital surcharge applies because the firm appears to be not resolvable if it falls into difficulties, this surcharge will have to be removed (or at least be reduced) where a recovery and resolution plan shows that the firm is indeed or has become resolvable. This would also create an incentive not only for recovery and resolution planning, but also for structural measures that enhance such plans. And conversely, the threat of capital surcharges leaves a strong incentive to keep the firm's structure resolvable and the living will up to date.

In this regard, the Swiss approach is the most advanced one. The "too-big-to-fail law"[46] introduced not only the requirement to prepare recovery and resolution plans but also higher capital requirements for systemically relevant banks. Their regulatory capital shall, among other things, "provide incentives to limit the degree of their systemic relevance and to improve their resolvability"[47]. According to the legislative materials, the firm-specific capital requirement is expressly meant to be a reflection of the resolvability analysis and to follow the quality of the recovery and resolution plan[48]. It will be interesting to see which experience the Swiss banks are going to make with this concept over a series of planning cycles.

III. Key elements of a living will

As the official name given by the FSB suggests, living wills comprise two parts: recovery planning and resolution planning. This marks two different phases of a crisis and two lines of defense for the taxpayer. The first part describes how the firm would recover and return to a normal business mode at times of stress. The second part deals with a situation where these efforts failed and the systemically relevant functions of the firm need to be isolated in such a manner that the distressed firm can exit the market without severe disruption. The first part accommodates action by management whilst the second part accommodates action by the competent resolution authority. Therefore, the recovery part is effectively

---

45 *Emilios Avgouleas, Charles Goodhart* and *Dirk Schoenmaker:* "Living Wills as a Catalyst for Action", Duisenberg School of Finance (DSF) Policy Paper No. 4 (May 2010), pg. 2.

46 See *supra* note 9.

47 Article 9 (2)(a) no. 3 of the Swiss Banking Act.

48 Botschaft zur Änderung des Bankengesetzes (Stärkung der Stabilität im Finanzsektor; too big to fail), BBl. 2011, pg. 4717.

a contingency plan for situations of severe stress and the resolution part of the plan is a tool that ensures that the firm can provide the resolution authority with meaningful information in a timely manner in a situation where the firm has otherwise lost its autonomy.

1. Recovery planning

a) Scenarios to be assumed

Recovery plans serve as a roadmap for a distressed firm to return to a normal business mode[49], though this may potentially end up in a different size or business model. Therefore, the firm has to define scenarios that would trigger the plan and options to cope with the situation. The FSB expects that recovery plans address stress scenarios that "should be sufficiently severe" and consider firm specific and system-wide scenarios[50]. But who defines which scenarios are sufficiently severe? Presumably it is the firm itself that prepares the plan. The immediate purpose of the plan, however, is to satisfy the supervisory authority that the firm is resolvable. So it will ultimately be the supervisor who determines the level of stress to be assumed. In its draft minimum requirements for recovery plans, the BaFin already expressly reserves the right to determine specific scenarios which a particular bank has to address[51]. Recovery planning is an iterative process in which one can always construe that an awful situation could get even worse. No doubt, to meet the purpose of a recovery plan, the stress scenarios assumed have to be ambitious but they should be still realistic and reasonable. One can hardly plan what to do if the sky falls on our head ...

b) Ways and means for recovery

The earlier a stress situation is identified, the easier it will be to address it. Risk monitoring and early warning tools are therefore essential. A firm specific parameter is the development of the demand for capital through the growth of its risk-weighted assets (or, with regard to the leverage ratio, its total assets) as well as capital consumption through write-downs, provisioning needs or simply loss

49 FSB, Key Attributes (*supra* note 14), Annex III, point 1.5.
50 FSB, Key Attributes (*supra* note 14), Annex III, point 1.3.
51 BaFin, Consultation 12/2012 (*supra* note 26), point E.3.2 (2) last paragraph.

making activities. Related to that is the supply with capital and in particular the firm's ability to form capital through profits to be retained. Also the ability to generate capital through the conversion of certain debt is an important factor whilst new issuances at times of stress or closed markets are an unrealistic option even if proper authorizations are in place. To which extent the conversion of debt will be recognized for recovery planning is an open question at this point. The discussion of which liabilities should be subject to a mandatory bail-in mechanism is still ongoing[52] and the regulatory recognition of conditional capital instruments (CoCos) is still uncertain since they were not accepted for the SIFI capital surcharge[53].

Another firm specific parameter is its liquidity profile. Liquidity is binary – the firm is either able or not able to pay when due – and therefore warrants particular attention. Apart from spotting maturity mismatches and contingent funding needs (*e.g.*, because of a ratings downgrade), the firm will also consider the diversification and depth of its funding base and the mechanisms to distribute and balance liquidity within its group. Finally, it will consider which assets are unencumbered and could be mobilized as collateral for covered bonds or for posting with the central bank.

It will also be relevant for the firm to assess its competitive position in key products and markets as well as their relevance and value contribution to the firm. This leads over to system-wide parameters like macro-economic data and general economic, social and political trends. In the light of these parameters, the recovery plan will also consider the firm's legal entity architecture and how it maps against the business activities[54]. The legal entity structure of a group

---

52 DG Internal Market and Services Working Document "Discussion paper on the debt write-down tool – bail-in" published on 30 March 2012 (http://ec.europa.eu/internal_market/bank/docs/crisis-management/discussion_paper_bail_in_en.pdf). The European Commission's proposal for a recovery and resolution directive (*supra* note 18) would create a new category of capital instruments to that effect (Article 39).

53 FSB, Policy Measures (*supra* note 12), point 4 (iii). In particular the Swiss FINMA advocated CoCos ("Addressing 'Too Big To Fail' – The Swiss SIFI Policy" published 23 June 2011, point 4.2.2 (http://www.finma.ch/e/finma/publikationen/Documents/be-swiss-SIFI-policy-june-2011-summary-20110624-e.pdf)) and also the Bundesbank and the UK FSA argued in favour of CoCos (*Andreas Dombret:* "Reform of the global financial system", lecture on 17 June 2011, end of point 3.1 (http://www.bundesbank.de/download/presse/reden/2011/20110617.dombret.en.pdf); *Thomas F. Huertas:* "Living Wills: How Can the Concept be Implemented?" speech on 12 February 2010, under "Raising additional capital" (http://www.fsa.gov.uk/pages/library/communication/speeches/2010/0212_th.shtml)).

54 *Huertas* (*supra* note 53), end of the chapter "Recovery plans"; *Avgouleas/Goodhart/Schoenmaker* (supra note 45), pg. 4.

is not only a tribute to current regulatory requirements but also a reflection of past requirements, acquisitions, tax laws, specialization within the group and so forth. A recovery plan can help to indentify not only hurdles for recovery and resolution but also inefficiencies that may have evolved over time and thus invite the firm to consider also immediate structural changes.

But even before a recovery plan comes into play, it is good business practice and prudent management to review regularly the business portfolio for its competitiveness, value creation and prospects and to initiate changes early on. If this occurs only in a stress situation when a recovery plan is activated, the firm will have to make tough choices under extreme time pressure. Should it sell the troubled activities which then will most likely have no value and stop the bleeding? Or should it sell some of its crown jewels in order to maximize the profit and boost its cash position? The first option may not find a buyer or only under conditions that effectively leave the risk with the seller. The second option may undermine the prospects of the firm and its ability to recover further. And both options are likely to lead to fire sale prices. Moreover, the experience with the sale of businesses imposed by the European Commission as a condition for its antitrust approval suggests that the sale of a business will hardly ever be a short term recovery measure[55].

c) What is new?

Some ingredients of the foregoing have been in place even before the crisis. The comparison of capital demand and capital supply in a regular and structured process is known as the Internal Capital Adequacy Assessment Process (ICAAP) mandated under the Basel 2 framework[56]. Basel 2 also requires in very general terms that "[e]ach bank must have adequate systems for measuring, monitoring and controlling liquidity risk"[57], a topic on which Basel 3 now elaborates in greater detail and by imposing specific ratios[58]. And just like an umbrella principle that overwhelms all that, the Basel Committee's "Core Principles for Effective

---

55 The proposal of *Huertas* (*supra* note 53) under "Sale or run down of business" therefore appears to underestimate these intricacies.

56 Basel Committee for Banking Supervision: "International Convergence of Capital Measurement and Capital Standards – A Revised Framework" (June 2004), Principle 1 for the supervisory review process (paragraph 725 *et seqq.*).

57 Paragraph 741.

58 Basel Committee for Banking Supervision: "Basel III: International framework for liquidity risk measurement, standards and monitoring" (December 2010).

Banking Supervision" published already back in 1997 require "that banks have in place a comprehensive risk management process"[59].

Notwithstanding all the above, when sailing into a crisis one has seen a number of banks that were far from being ready to weather even a stiff breeze. It seems that some firms had taken these requirements and the challenges they present too lightly. Resolution planning requirements therefore just echo these shortcomings. The grip by the regulators on the firms' planning for economic contingencies has become significantly tighter and the view to be adopted has become much more holistic than before the crisis.

2. Resolution planning

Resolution planning is for a time where the firm has lost its autonomy, where the resolution authority has taken over the steering wheel and is about to implement drastic measures by separating the good and relevant parts of the firm from the rest and winding the latter down. Resolution planning is therefore predominately something for the resolution authority itself. In order to be effective, however, it has to rely on a lot of information and data to be made available by the distressed firm. And the firm has to prepare for that.

For the firm, the resolution part for the plan means therefore that it creates an inventory with up-to-date and meaningful information on its structure, licenses, key counterparties and critical service providers and the key terms of the relevant contracts[60]. And one should not forget that it will be equally important to identify key functions and personnel that will be critical to maintain the necessary processes and to logistically support the restructuring proceeding. Unfortunately, this aspect is mostly neglected in the current discussion. But people are a core asset of each financial services firm. Any resolution authority would be lost if it walked in and relied just on the resolution plan and the corresponding data base.

This sounds like documentation and record keeping requirements which have been in place almost forever[61]. But their main purpose is to provide the basis for internal and external audits and not to produce information and sort data in a way that suits emergency situations. The resolution part of a living will therefore clearly enhances these requirements to enable the resolution authority to make and implement far reaching decisions on a well informed factual basis and in an

59 Principle 13, restated as Principle 7 in the revised Core Principles of October 2006.

60 *Avgouleas/Goodhart/Schoenmaker* (*supra* note 45), pg. 5 *et seq.*

61 *Cf.* for example Section 25a (1) of the German Banking Act (KWG).

extremely short period of time. This challenge is unprecedented. But it tells not only the resolution authorities but also the financial firms a lot about themselves.

IV. International cooperation

1. A practical need

Financial supervision and resolution powers flow from a country's sovereignty and hence are limited by territories and legal entities. This leads to overlaps and conflict-of-law issues where a firm is engaged in cross-border activities. Mechanisms to remove such conflicts and inefficiencies range from home-host cooperation including mutual recognition[62] to the establishment of colleges of supervisors[63] and to supranational structures like the new European supervisory architecture[64] or the concentration of the supervision of banks in the Euro zone with the European Central Bank recently proposed by the European Commission[65]. In a globalized economy, preparation for crisis management and resolu-

62 Since its inception, the Basel Committee has issued countless papers that aim to enhance the cross border-cooperation of supervisors, for example: "Report to the Governors on the supervision of banks' foreign establishments" (BS/75/44e), published on 26 September 1975 and revised by the "Principles for the supervision of banks' foreign establishments" (May 1983); "Exchanges of information between supervisors of participants in the financial markets" (April 1990); "Information flows between banking supervisory authorities" (April 1990); "Minimum standards for the supervision of international banking groups and their cross-border establishments" (July 1992); "Essential elements of a statement of cooperation between banking supervisors" (May 2001); "High-level principles for the cross-border implementation of the New Accord" (August 2003).

63 The Declaration of the G20 Summit in Washington DC of 15 November 2008 foresees as one action point the "[s]upervisors should collaborate to establish supervisory colleges for all major cross-border financial institutions" by 31 March 2009 (under "Reinforcing International Cooperation"), New York Times of 16 November 2008 (accessible through http://www.nytimes.com/2008/11/16/washington/summit-text.html?pagewanted=all). For the European Union see Article 131a of the Banking Directive (2006/48/EC) (introduced by Directive 2009/111/EC (CRD 2)).

64 Regulations (EU) No. 1093/2010, 1094/2010 and 1095/2010 of 24 November 2010 creating the European Banking Authority (EBA), the European Insurance and Occupational Pensions Authority (EIOPA) and the European Securities and Markets Authority (ESMA), respectively.

65 European Commission: "Proposal for a Council Regulation conferring specific tasks on the European Central Bank concerning policies relating to the prudential supervision of credit institutions (COM(2012) 511)" published on 12 September 2012 at http://ec.europa.eu/internal_market/finances/docs/committees/reform/20120912-com-2012-511_en.pdf.

tion planning therefore inevitably requires close cooperation of authorities in multiple countries[66]. The FSB's Key Attributes call for the creation of Crisis Management Groups (CMGs) of the home and key host authorities "with the objective of enhancing preparedness for, and facilitating the management and resolution of, a cross-border financial crisis affecting the firm"[67].

This suggests that there should be one plan per group which then sets the framework for country specific plans that cover the relevant local operations. And it suggests that the host country plan for the local operations is tied into the global plan of the parent[68]. It is unfortunate to note in this connection that about a hundred non-U.S. banks with operations in the United States have to submit resolution plans for their U.S. operations[69] in a separate process outside the CMG that has been formed for them and in some cases even before the global plan under the FSB Key Attributes is due.

2. The complexity of Crisis Management Groups

A Crisis Management Group foreseen by the FSB includes "the supervisory authorities, central banks, resolution authorities, finance ministries and the public authorities responsible for guarantee schemes"[70] of the relevant jurisdictions. For Germany this translates into the Federal Financial Supervisory Authority (BaFin), the Bundesbank and the Federal Ministry of Finance. Given the importance of London and New York as financial market places, it is fair to assume that the UK and U.S. authorities will be members of most of the Crisis Management Groups. This gives them particular influence on the future development of living wills.

The UK would also bring three authorities to the table: its FSA (to be replaced by the Prudential Regulatory Authority once the UK has finalized its regulatory reform[71]), the Bank of England and H.M. Treasury. For European banks, also the European Banking Authority (EBA) will play a role[72] and the European Central Bank may as well claim a seat.

But where the U.S. joins a Crisis Management Group, the group will grow exponentially to reflect all the fragmentation of the supervisory system in the

66 *Grant* (*supra* note 31), pg. 504; *Avgouleas/Goodhart/Schoenmaker* (*supra* note 45), pg. 9.
67 FSB, Key Attributes (*supra* note 14), Key Attribute 8.1.
68 This is expressly foreseen in the BaFin's Consultation 12/2012 (*supra* note 26), point C.3.
69 *Goldstein/Tarbert/Hearth* (*supra* note 31).
70 *Ibid.*
71 Part 4 of the Financial Services Bill (HL Bill 25 as brought from the Commons on 23 May 2012).
72 See Article 25 (1) of Regulation (EU) No. 1093/2010 (*supra* note 20).

United States. The Federal Reserve will be represented with the relevant Federal Reserve Bank as well as with the Board of Governors of the Federal Reserve System. Licenses are issued by state authorities like the New York Financial Services Department or by the Office of the Comptroller of the Currency (OCC), so that at least one of them would also become part of the group. And finally, one should not forget the Federal Deposit Insurance Corporation (FDIC) with its resolution powers, the Securities and Exchange Commission (SEC), the Commodity Futures Trading Commission (CFTC) and the Treasury Department.

Such a trilateral Crisis Management Group already adds up to fourteen to fifteen authorities. And this does not yet reflect the growing importance of Asia.

The draft to a EU directive on recovery and resolution planning foresees resolution colleges at group level which comprise the resolution authorities of the parent bank and each member state where the relevant bank operates a subsidiary and the EBA[73]. With twenty-seven EU member states and three additional members of the European Economic Area[74] a resolution college can become an equally large group. And it may even be expanded further by inviting the resolution authorities from outside the EU/EEA if the bank in question has also subsidiaries in such countries[75].

The mere internal coordination task faced by a Crisis Management Group or a resolution college can therefore hardly be overestimated. This does not mean that regulators should shy away from it. But it contrasts to another trend that is occurring in parallel to intensified international cooperation. More and more regulators seek to ringfence capital, liquidity and other resources within their respective remits. This does not appear to follow a particular master plan. It seems to flow more from a subliminal desire to achieve greater autonomy in financial supervision in their own jurisdiction, to be less dependent on the cooperation by fellow regulators and a reduced willingness to strike compromises on the priorities on the supervisory agenda. And it certainly reflects the fact that the supervisory authorities are ultimately accountable to their respective national parliaments rather than supranational bodies. But if this trend persists, international cooperation will degenerate to a lip service and Crisis Management Groups will be no more than a fig leaf, though at tremendous costs for the industry. In fact, in the

73 See *supra* note 18, Article 80 (2).
74 Under Article 36 of the Agreement on the European Economic Area signed in Oporto on 2 May 1992 (OJ L 1, 3 January 1994, pg. 3) the application of EU legislation can be extended to the EEA.
75 Article 80 (2) paragraph 4.

recent crisis banks were rescued entirely by their respective home countries and taxpayers[76] or broken up into national components[77].

3. Ambiguity with source-of-strength concepts

There is a second ambiguity in international cooperation that needs to be addressed in a Crisis Management Group. In an integrated group, the foreign operations and the subsidiaries are typically intertwined with the other parts of the group and rely ultimately on the group parent as their source of strength. When acquiring a business or setting up a new one, the ability of the ultimate parent to support it is one of the standard points of scrutiny for the regulator when reviewing the transaction[78]. In a crisis situation it is therefore fair to assume that the host authorities would probably first turn to the group parent and explore how deep its pockets are – regardless of the existence or non-existence of formal support arrangements with or support undertakings of the parent.

A discussion on capital surcharges for subsidiaries that are classified of local systemic relevance[79] therefore appears as a departure from this longstanding practice. It has also the same flaws as capital surcharges for G-SIFIs that are not calibrated against the quality of recovery and resolution plans of these institu-

76 *Avgouleas/Goodhart/Schoenmaker* (*supra* note 45), pg. 13.

77 For details of the split of Fortis and Dexia see the press releases of the Dutch government of 6 October 2008 ("Overname Fortis België en Luxemburg door BNP Paribas") (http://www.rijksoverheid.nl/documenten-en-publicaties/persberichten/2008/12/03/overname-fortis-belgie-en-luxemburg-door-bnp-paribas.html) and of Dexia of 10 October 2011 ("The Belgian, French and Luxembourg states provide strong support to Dexia in the implementation of the restructuring plan announced on 4 October") (http://www.dexia.com/EN/journalist/press_releases/Documents/111008_cp_EN.pdf), respectively.

78 For Europe see Article 19a (1)(c) of the Banking Directive (2006/48/EC) (introduced by Directive 2007/44/EC) and paragraph 61 of the "Guidelines for the prudential assessment of acquisitions and increases in holdings in the financial sector required by Directive 2007/44/EC" issued by CEBS, CEIPOS and CESR (CEBS/2008/214; CEIOPS-3L3-19/08; CESR/08-543b). In the U.S., the Federal Reserve has applied a "source of strength test" in its Regulation Y under the Bank Holding Company Act (12 C.F.R. § 225.4 (a)(1)) and the Dodd-Frank Act introduced a new Section 38A with this concept into the Federal Deposit Insurance Act (Section 616 (d), codified at 12 U.S.C. 1831o-1). Also the Basel Committee's Core Principles for Effective Banking Supervision (*supra* note 59) provide for an assessment of the shareholder as the source of strength for the subsidiary (version of 1997 on pg. 18 and – less pronounced – the principle 3, criterion 9 and principle 4, criterion 3 of the 2006 restatement).

79 Börsen-Zeitung, 13 June 2012: "Nationale Sifis bereiten Kopfzerbrechen"; Handelsblatt, 13 June 2012: "Globalen Instituten drohen strengere Auflagen für ihr Eigenkapital".

tions[80]. Therefore, potential capital surcharges for local SIFIs will have to weigh this against the local components of a living will. And recovery and resolution planning (also by the regulators) will need to factor parental or other intragroup support mechanisms and the extent to which this has been required by the host regulator into the plan. It would therefore be too narrow if such support mechanisms were only recognized for recovery and resolution planning of local branch offices of foreign banks[81].

V. Conclusions and outlook

Whether we like them or not, livings wills are about to become a reality for banks. The question marks set in this paper will not make them disappear. But summarizing the foregoing, four take-aways should be borne in mind when working on living wills these days:

First: The requirement to prepare living wills is a fall-out from the financial crisis and comes alongside with other measures like enhanced capital, liquidity and leverage requirements. The overall framework is not entirely consistent yet. This is in particular true for the treatment of G-SIFIs. Requiring them to prepare living wills that demonstrate their resolvability while subjecting them to a specific capital surcharge remains an unresolved ambiguity – with Switzerland being the only positive exemption so far.

Second: Living wills build on and enhance preexisting requirements on proper risk management. This is in particular true for the recovery part of the plan. It is a tool for management to maneuver through a crisis on the basis of good intelligence and well prepared road maps on board. This reflects good business practice and sound and forward looking management. There is therefore no good reason for limiting this requirement only to systemically important institutions, in particular since systemic relevance is to a large extent also perception and hence a function of a particular situation. As proposed by the European Commission, also smaller and less complex firms need to consider their recovery and resolution, though with smaller and less onerous plans.

Third: The resolution part of a living will forces organizations to not only look at their product silos but to focus more intensively on their legal entity architecture. They will need to have mechanisms in place to regularly review this struc-

80 See the discussion *supra* at point II.3.
81 See *e.g.*, point 1.21 of the FSA's consultation paper (*supra* note 24).

ture and adjust it as necessary. The resolution part of a living will also force firms to pay particular attention to critical interfaces and have supply and manufacturing chains properly documented. And finally, the resolution part of a living will should not only look to documentation and systems but also to key personnel on which a resolution authority will have to draw when it comes on board.

Fourth: International cooperation among the relevant authorities is a critical though hugely complex task. Regulators as well as politicians with their expectations on them should not get seduced by the idea of renationalizing banking supervision and crisis management and that financial firms can best be resolved in nationally ringfenced reservations. Crisis Management Groups are a first step towards supranational structures for the resolution of international financial firms. But they depend on harmonized national resolution regimes.

If financial firms, regulators and politicians work on living wills with this understanding in mind, living wills can help to make the troubled financial markets a better and safer place.

Randall D. Guynn*

Resolution Planning in the United States

The resolution planning process in the United States is still evolving. A resolution plan is a plan for liquidating, reorganizing, recapitalizing or otherwise resolving a systemically important financial institution ("**SIFI**") that has reached the point of insolvency, non-viability or failure. It is different from a recovery plan, which is a set of planned actions designed to prevent a financial institution from becoming insolvent or otherwise failing. Resolution planning is the last stage along the full continuum of contingency planning from risk management to recovery planning to resolution planning that is sometimes referred to as a "living will."[1]

Section 165(d) under Title I of the Dodd-Frank Wall Street Recovery and Consumer Protection Act (the "**Dodd-Frank Act**") requires all bank holding companies[2] and foreign banking organizations[3] with assets of $50 billion or more, as well as any nonbank financial institution that has been designated as systemically important,[4] to prepare and regularly update a resolution plan ("**Title**

* The author is deeply indebted to *Brandon Smith* for his excellent assistance on this paper, as well as to numerous other colleagues at Davis Polk, including *Donald Bernstein, John Douglas, Margaret Tahyar, Luigi De Ghenghi, Reena Sahni and Erika White* who shared valuable ideas and experiences with the author. Unless otherwise specified, this paper is current as of April 15, 2013.

1 The Federal Reserve and the FDIC have used the term "living will" interchangeably with the term "resolution plan," see 76 U.S. Federal Register 67323, 67323 (Nov. 1, 2011). For a description of the full continuum of contingency planning from risk management to resolution planning. See, e.g., *Davis Polk & Wardwell LLP & McKinsey & Co.*, Credible Living Wills: The First Generation (Apr. 25, 2011), available at http://www.davispolk.com/files/Publication/37a3a804-6a6c-4e10-a628-7a1dbbaece7c/Presentation/PublicationAttachment/c621815c-9413-436b-91ea-3451b2b4cf32/042611_DavisPolkMcKinsey_LivingWills_Whitepaper.pdf.

2 A "**bank holding company**" is any U.S. or non-U.S. company that controls a U.S. "bank" as defined in Section 2 of the U.S. Bank Holding Company Act of 1956.

3 A "**foreign banking organization**" is any foreign bank with a branch, agency or commercial lending subsidiary in the United States or that controls a company organized under Section 25A of the U.S. Federal Reserve Act and acquired after March 5, 1987, as well as any company that directly or indirectly controls such a foreign bank.

4 See Dodd-Frank Act, U.S. Public Law No. 111-203, § 113, 124 U.S. Statutes at Large 1375, 1398 (2010); 77 U.S. Federal Register 21637 (Apr. 11, 2012). See also *Davis Polk & Wardwell LLP*, FSOC Issues Final Rule on Designation of Systemically Important Nonbank Financial Companies (Apr. 4, 2012), available at http://www.davispolk.com/files/Publication/bd4d269c-ecc1-4757-a5ae-007f26f378e1/Presentation/PublicationAttachment/c6a028ce-271b-4aef-b140-02f4b9094236/040412_FSOC.Final.Rules.pdf.

I resolution plan").[5] According to the regulation implementing this provision, these plans must assume that the covered company is resolved under the U.S. Bankruptcy Code or other applicable insolvency law,[6] and that no "extraordinary support" from the U.S. or any other government would be available.[7] The Federal Deposit Insurance Corporation (the "**FDIC**") separately requires all U.S. insured depository institutions ("**IDIs**") with assets of $50 billion or more to submit and regularly update a resolution plan ("**IDI resolution plan**").[8] The final rules for the Title I and IDI resolution plans were designed to complement each other.[9]

Neither the Dodd-Frank Act nor any other provision of U.S. law requires a financial institution to prepare a recovery (as distinguished from a resolution) plan. Nevertheless, the Board of Governors of the Federal Reserve System (the "**Federal Reserve**"), in its capacity as a banking supervisor, has required several of the largest U.S. bank holding companies to prepare and submit recovery plans,[10] and is in the process of expanding that requirement to the largest bank and nonbank SIFIs.[11]

---

5 Dodd-Frank Act, U.S. Public Law No. 111-203, § 165(d), 124 U.S. Statutes at Large 1375, 1426 (2010).

6 See 76 U.S. Federal Register 67323, 67327 note 8 (Nov. 1, 2011). Although the regulation does not prohibit a covered company from submitting a resolution plan under Title II of the Dodd-Frank Act as a supplement to its plan under the U.S. Bankruptcy Code or other applicable insolvency law, the regulation provides that the credibility of the overall plan and whether it would facilitate an orderly resolution of the covered company will be judged assuming the covered company is resolved under the U.S. Bankruptcy Code or, if the covered company is not subject to the U.S. Bankruptcy Code, under the insolvency regime to which it is normally subject, which would not include Title II. See id.; 12 U.S. Code of Federal Regulations § 243.5(b).

7 See 12 U.S. Code of Federal Regulations § 243.4(a)(4)(ii).

8 See id. § 360.10 (the "**IDI Rule**").

9 See 76 Federal Register 67323, 67329 (Nov. 1, 2011). See also *Davis Polk & Wardwell LLP*, Credible Living Wills under the U.S. Regulatory Framework (Sep. 19, 2011), available at http://www.davispolk.com/files/Publication/d0e11d7b-2f4b-45e4-849c-2320b1e0d9c5/Presentation/PublicationAttachment/7426ca31-e687-482b-a8e0-24c3cdbc5564/091911_Credible_Living_Wills_US_Framework.pdf (discussing final rules for Title I resolution plans and interim final rules for IDI resolution plans); Davis Polk & Wardwell LLP, FDIC Releases Joint Notice of Proposed Rulemaking on Resolution Plans and Credit Exposure Reports (Apr. 5, 2011), available at http://www.davispolk.com/files/Publication/c46d3612-578c-4706-9487-01144c479a32/Presentation/PublicationAttachment/9df66ece-09fa-4dd4-b73e-031278f4e668/050411_S165d_NPR_Summary.pdf (discussing proposed rules for Title I and IDI resolution plans).

10 See *Rick Rothacker* U.S. Banks Told to Make Plans for Preventing Collapse, Reuters, Aug. 10, 2012.

11 See, e.g., Board of Governors of the Federal Reserve System, Consolidated Supervision Framework for Large Financial Institutions, SR 12–17 (Dec. 17, 2012).

Nine institutions filed initial Title I resolution plans and five filed initial IDI resolution plans on July 1, 2012 (**"Round 1 Filers"**).[12] Two additional institutions filed initial Title I and IDI resolution plans on October 1, 2012 (**"Round 1.5 Filers"**).[13] All of the Round 1 and Round 1.5 Filers have previously been designated by the Financial Stability Board (**"FSB"**) as global SIFIs (**"G-SIFIs"**).[14] The Round 1 Filers were originally required to file their first annual updates on July 1, 2013 or such other date as the regulators may specify,[15] and the Round 1.5 Filers were originally required to file their first annual updates on October 1, 2013 or such other date as the regulators may specify[16] but the regulators later specified October 1, 2013 for both groups.[17] Four additional institutions are expected to file their initial plans on July 1, 2013 (**"Round 2 Filers"**).[18] All the rest of the firms required to file plans are currently required to file their initial plans by the end

---

12 Bank of America, Barclays, Citigroup, Credit Suisse, Deutsche Bank, Goldman Sachs, JP Morgan Chase, Morgan Stanley and UBS filed Title I resolution plans. The public sections of their Title I resolution plans are available at http://www.federalreserve.gov/bankinforeg/resolution-plans.htm. Five of these institutions – Bank of America, Citigroup, Goldman Sachs, JP Morgan Chase and Morgan Stanley – were required to file IDI resolution plans because they all have IDI subsidiaries with $50 billion or more in assets. See FDIC, Bank Data and Statistics, http://www.fdic.gov/bank/statistical/ (searchable database with IDI asset size and other information). The public sections of their IDI resolution plans are available at http://www.fdic.gov/regulations/reform/resplans/index.html.

13 Bank of New York Mellon and State Street filed Title I and IDI resolution plans. The public sections of their Title I resolution plans are available at http://www.federalreserve.gov/bankinforeg/resolution-plans.htm. Both have IDI subsidiaries with $50 billion or more in total assets. See FDIC, Bank Data and Statistics, http://www.fdic.gov/bank/statistical/ (searchable database with IDI asset size and other information). The public sections of their IDI resolution plans are available at http://www.fdic.gov/regulations/reform/resplans/index.html.

14 See *Financial Stability* Board Update of group of globally systemically important banks (G-SIBs) (Nov. 1, 2012), available at http://www.financialstabilityboard.org/publications/r_121031ac.pdf (list of G-SIFIs consisting of 28 G-SIBs).

15 12 U.S. Code of Federal Regulations § 243.3(a)(3)–(4).

16 Id.

17 FDIC and Federal Reserve, *Guidance for 2013 § 165(d) Annual Resolution Plan Submissions by Domestic Covered Companies that Submitted Initial Resolution Plans in 2012* at 2 (Apr. 15, 2013), available at http://federalreserve.gov/newsevents/press/bcreg/bcreg20130415c2.pdf; FDIC and Federal Reserve, *Guidance for 2013 § 165(d) Annual Resolution Plan Submissions by Foreign-Based Covered Companies that Submitted Initial Resolution Plans in 2012* at 2 (Apr. 15, 2013), available at http://federalreserve.gov/newsevents/press/bcreg/joint_resolution_plans_foreign-based_guidance_20130415.pdf.

18 The Round 2 Filers are BNP Paribas, HSBC, Royal Bank of Scotland Group and Wells Fargo. See Statement of Federal Deposit Insurance Corporation by James R. Wigand, Director, Office of Complex Financial Institutions, and Richard J. Osterman, Jr., Acting General Counsel, Before the

of 2013 ("**Round 3 Filers**").[19] The total number of firms required to submit Title I plans was initially estimated to be 124.[20] The vast majority of this number are foreign banking organizations with worldwide assets of $50 billion or more, but with relatively small U.S. footprints.[21]

The FDIC has announced that it is preparing its own resolution plans for systemically important bank holding companies under Title II of the Dodd-Frank Act.[22] The FDIC is also probably preparing its own resolution plans for large IDIs.

The Chairman of the FDIC has said that the FDIC's preferred method for resolving the largest and most complex banking groups under Title II is called the single-point-of-entry ("**SPOE**") recapitalization model.[23] The FDIC and the Bank of England have issued a joint paper endorsing the SPOE model for resolving banking organizations with cross-border operations.[24] The FDIC has also indicated that it intends to propose a policy statement or regulation describing

Subcommittee on Oversight and Investigations, Committee of Financial Services, U.S. House of Representatives (April 16, 2013).

19 12 U.S. Code of Federal Regulations § 243.3(a)(1)(iii).

20 See 76 U.S. Federal Register 67323, 67333 (Nov. 1, 2011) (124 estimated respondents in Paperwork Reduction Act analysis consisting of 20 full resolution plan filers and 104 tailored resolution plan filers).

21 See *Victoria McGrane and Alan Zibel* FDIC Drafts Rule on 'Living Wills' for Banks, Wall St. J., Mar. 29, 2011 (quoting FDIC officials as saying that 26 of the 124 institutions required to file Title I resolution plans would be U.S. bank holding companies and the remaining 98 would be subsidiaries of foreign-owned banks); Institute of International Bankers, Comment Letter to the Federal Reserve and the FDIC on the Joint Notice of Proposed Rulemaking Implementing the Resolution Plan and Credit Exposure Requirements of Section 165(d) of the Dodd-Frank Act (June 10, 2011), available at http://www.iib.org/associations/6316/files/20110610ResPlanNPR_IIB_final.pdf (estimating that of the approximately 98 foreign banking organizations required to file U.S. resolution plans, only approximately 20 have U.S. consolidated assets of $50 billion or more).

22 Video: FDIC Systemic Resolution Advisory Committee Meeting, Panel on Title II Orderly Liquidation Authority (Dec. 10, 2012), available at http://www.vodium.com/MediapodLibrary/index.asp?library=pn100472_fdic_SRAC. Presentation slides from the meeting are available at http://www.fdic.gov/about/srac/2012/2012-12-10_title-ii_orderly-liquidation-authority.pdf.

23 *Martin J. Gruenberg*, Acting Chairman, FDIC, Remarks to the Federal Reserve Bank of Chicago Bank Structure Conference (May 10, 2012), available at http://www.fdic.gov/news/news/speeches/chairman/spmay1012.html.

24 Resolving Globally Active, Systemically Important, Financial Institutions: A joint paper by the Federal Insurance Deposit Corporation and the Bank of England (Dec. 10, 2012), available at http://www.fdic.gov/about/srac/2012/gsifi.pdf; Martin Gruenberg & Paul Tucker, Op-Ed., Global Banks Need Global Solutions When They Fail, Financial Times, Dec. 10, 2012.

in more detail how it would use its authority under Title II to resolve a covered financial company under the SPOE model.[25]

Under the SPOE model, only the parent bank holding company of a banking group would be put into a resolution proceeding. All of the parent's assets, including its ownership interests in operating subsidiaries, would be transferred to a bridge financial company. The transferred business would be recapitalized by leaving the failed company's equity capital and a sufficient amount of its unsecured long-term debt behind in a receivership. The operating subsidiaries would be recapitalized and kept out of insolvency proceedings by converting loans or other extensions of credit from the parent into new equity in the operating subsidiaries or otherwise down-streaming available parent assets to the subsidiaries. If the bridge financial holding company or any of its operating subsidiaries were unable to obtain sufficient liquidity from the market, the Federal Reserve's discount window,[26] or Section 13(3) of the Federal Reserve Act,[27] the FDIC could provide such liquidity by borrowing from the U.S. Treasury subject to certain limits contained in Title II of Dodd-Frank.[28]

The Federal Reserve Board has indicated that it is likely to propose minimum long-term unsecured debt requirements for certain U.S. bank holding companies in order to ensure that they have sufficient loss-absorbing capacity to make the SPOE recapitalization method a viable one.[29] This mandate would supplement Basel capital requirements.

Although the Title I resolution plans prepared by members of the financial industry are available to the FDIC when it prepares its Title II plans, the initial Title I plans submitted in 2012 were required to be prepared with a very different set of assumptions from the Title II plans being prepared by the FDIC. For

---

25 See, e.g., Statement of *James Wigand*, Director of the FDIC's Office of Complex Financial Institutions, in Video: Banking Law Institute 2012, Panel on Systemic Risk – the Challenge of Systemically Important Financial Institutions (SIFIs), Living Wills and Orderly Liquidation Issues (Practicing Law Institute program Dec. 19, 2012), available at http://www.pli.edu/Content/OnDemand/Banking_Law_Institute_2012/_/N-4nZ1z12whl?fromsearch=false&ID=144553.

26 See, e.g., 12 U.S. Code of Federal Regulations Part 201; The Federal Reserve Discount Window (July 21, 2010), available at http://www.frbdiscountwindow.org/discountwindowbook.cfm?hdrID=14&dtlID=43#eligibilityps.

27 12 United States Code § 343.

28 See Dodd-Frank Act, U.S. Public Law No. 111–203, § 210(n), 124 U.S. Statutes at Large 1375, 1506–09 (2010).

29 *Daniel K. Tarullo*, Governor, Board of Governors of the Federal Reserve System, Industry Structure and Systemic Risk Regulation, Speech at the Brookings Institution Conference on Structuring the Financial Industry to Enhance Economic Growth and Stability (Dec. 4, 2012), available at http://www.federalreserve.gov/newsevents/speech/tarullo20121204a.htm.

example, as noted in the FDIC's December 2012 meeting with its Systemic Resolution Advisory Committee ("**SRAC**"),[30] and in the public portions of the Title I resolution plans submitted by Round 1 Filers,[31] the FDIC and the Federal Reserve required that the initial Title I plans assume that all material entities of a particular banking group would fail,[32] whereas the SPOE plans being prepared by the FDIC under Title II do not. The FDIC has not shared its Title II resolution plans with the relevant financial institutions or tried to validate them with input from these institutions.

The FDIC and the Federal Reserve are currently exploring whether it is possible for the industry and FDIC resolution planning processes to be more complementary of each other. For example, in guidance applicable for the first annual updates of the resolution plans of Round 1 and Round 1.5 Filers, the FDIC and the Federal Reserve relaxed the unrealistic assumption that all material entities must be assumed to fail in a Title I plan, and instead will allow these filers to assume that only the top parent holding company fails.[33] The purpose of relaxing this assumption is to allow these institutions to develop SPOE resolution strategies under the U.S. Bankruptcy Code if feasible and based on a reasonable set of alternative assumptions.

This paper is organized in four parts. Part I describes the purpose of resolution planning. Part II summarizes the U.S. legal and regulatory framework for resolution planning, and compares it to the typical resolution planning process outside the United States. Part III identifies some of the "lessons learned" from the initial rounds of U.S. resolution planning. Part IV attempts to forecast how the resolution planning process and related laws and regulations may evolve in the

---

30 The Federal Deposit Insurance Corporation Holds a Meeting of the Systemic Resolution Advisory Committee, Panel on Title I Resolution Plans, SEC Wire Transcript at 12 (Dec. 10, 2012). The assumption that all material entities must fail was also noted in the presentation slides from the December 10, 2012 SRAC meeting, available at http://www.fdic.gov/about/srac/2012/2012-12-10_title-i_resolution-plans.pdf.

31 See, e.g., Citigroup Title I Resolution Plan, Public Section, at 30 (July 1, 2012), available at http://www.federalreserve.gov/bankinforeg/citigroup-20120703.pdf. See also *Davis Polk & Wardwell LLP*, Living Wills: Key Lessons from the First Wave for Second and Third Round Filers (July 11, 2012), available at http://www.davispolk.com/files/Publication/cbadd86a-3680-4305-bf10-f3ea147b57c3/Presentation/PublicationAttachment/26191e6f-06dd-4d1b-ada8-f74a977be52e/071112_Living_Wills.pdf.

32 For a material entity subject to a specialized insolvency regime other than the U.S. Bankruptcy Code, a resolution plan should discuss strategies under that applicable regime (for example, under Sections 11 and 13 of the FDI Act in the case of a material entity that is an insured depository institution). 76 U.S. Federal Register 67323, 67328–29 (Nov. 1, 2011).

33 See footnote 17 above.

United States. The paper concludes that the separate Title I and Title II resolution planning processes are likely to converge in the future.

I. Purpose of Resolution Planning

The purpose of resolution planning is to develop, in advance of any crisis, strategies for resolving SIFIs and G-SIFIs that are credible alternatives to the Hobson's choice between taxpayer-funded bailouts and "disorderly" liquidations or other strategies that risk destabilizing the financial system.[34] It is an important component of the toolkit necessary to solve the too big to fail (**"TBTF"**) problem. The TBTF problem arises when the only options available for resolving a particular SIFI are taxpayer-funded bailouts or "disorderly" liquidations or other destabilizing resolution strategies. Faced with such a choice, policymakers inevitably choose bailout as the lesser of two evils.[35]

Activating a resolution plan is a last-resort option, when various ex-ante solutions designed to reduce the likelihood of failure have been unsuccessful. Such ex-ante measures might include higher capital and liquidity requirements, better risk management and supervision, more frequent and better stress-testing, more effective early remediation, activities restrictions, size limitations, and recovery plans.[36]

II. U.S. Legal and Regulatory Framework

The U.S. legal and regulatory framework for resolution planning is comprehensive, but divergent. It currently requires certain banking organizations to prepare Title I resolution plans under one set of assumptions, while the FDIC is preparing Title II resolution plans under a different set of assumptions. This divergence is odd because one of the stated purposes for the Title I plans is to "support the

34 See *Randall D. Guynn*, Are Bailouts Inevitable?, 29 Yale Journal on Regulation 121, 123–24, (2012).

35 Id. at 127–29. See also *Hal S. Scott*, Interconnectedness and Contagion (Nov. 20, 2012), available at http://www.capmktsreg.org/pdfs/2012.11.20_Interconnectedness_and_Contagion.pdf.

36 *Randall D. Guynn*, Are Bailouts Inevitable?, 29 Yale Journal on Regulation 121, 130–35 (2012). See also Board of Governors of the Federal Reserve System, Consolidated Supervision Framework for Large Financial Institutions, SR 12–17 (Dec. 17, 2012).

[FDIC's] planning for the exercise of its resolution authority under [Title II]."[37] The FDIC and the Federal Reserve are exploring whether it is possible for these two resolution processes to be more complementary of each other. But in the meantime, the two processes are operating on separate tracks.

A. Title I Plans

Section 165(d) of the Dodd-Frank Act requires the Federal Reserve to cause certain large bank holding companies, foreign banking organizations and nonbank financial institutions to submit periodic resolution plans to the Federal Reserve, the FDIC and the Federal Systemic Oversight Council ("**FSOC**").[38] The statute requires the Federal Reserve to share the authority to review the credibility of the plans with the FDIC.[39]

If the Federal Reserve and the FDIC both determine that a particular resolution plan is either "not credible" or would not facilitate an orderly resolution under the U.S. Bankruptcy Code,[40] they are required to give the covered company a reasonable opportunity to cure the deficiency.[41] If the company fails to cure the deficiency, the agencies "may jointly impose more stringent capital, leverage, or liquidity requirements, or restrictions on growth, activities, or operations of the company, or any subsidiary thereof."[42] If the company fails to cure the deficiencies within two years after any of these sanctions are imposed on it, the agencies have the joint discretionary authority, after consultation with the FSOC, to force the company to divest certain assets or operations – that is, break it up.

It is important to note, however, that Section 165(d) does not authorize either agency to take unilateral action against a covered company based on a deficient resolution plan. Instead, it requires both agencies to agree that the plan is not credible or does not otherwise facilitate an orderly resolution, that action should be taken and on what that action should be in order for either of them to take any

37 76 U.S. Federal Register 67323, 67323 (Nov. 1, 2011).

38 Dodd-Frank Act, U.S. Public Law No. 111-203, § 165(d)(1), 124 U.S. Statutes at Large 1375, 1426 (2010).

39 Id. § 165(d)(3)–(4).

40 If the covered company is not subject to the U.S. Bankruptcy Code, then the review would be under the insolvency regime to which the covered company is ordinarily subject. See 76 U.S. Federal Register 67323, 67327 note 8 (Nov. 15, 2011).

41 Id. § 165(d)(4)–(5).

42 Id. § 165(d)(5).

action based on Section 165(d); if either agency disagrees on any of these points, the other agency has no authority to impose any sanctions under the statute.[43]

The Federal Reserve and the FDIC have also issued a regulation implementing Section 165(d). That regulation provides further details about the resolution planning requirement, including which companies are subject to it, when initial and subsequent plans must be filed, what sort of board approvals are required, what sort of information and data the resolution plans must contain, what portions of the plans will be treated as confidential, how the agencies will review the plans to determine whether they are "not credible," how the cure process will work, and whether and how any sanctions will be imposed for a plan that is found to be "not credible."

The regulators also advised the initial filers that they did not intend to conduct a credibility review of any of the initial plans, but instead would reserve their credibility reviews for future updates.[44]

1. Applicability

The regulation defines the institutions that are subject to the Title I resolution planning requirement through its definition of the term "covered company."[45] That term is defined to include any bank holding company that has total consoli-

---

43 The FDIC does, of course, have the unilateral authority to take certain actions against a covered company's IDI subsidiary for filing a deficient resolution plan under the IDI Rule if authorized to do so under the Federal Deposit Insurance Act (**"FDI Act"**). If the FDIC is not the IDI subsidiary's appropriate federal banking agency, however, its authority to take actions under the FDI Act may be severely limited. Instead, the authority to take such actions would typically lie with the IDI subsidiary's appropriate federal banking agency. 12 United States Code §1813(q). The Office of the Comptroller of the Currency (**"OCC"**) is the appropriate federal banking agency for all national banks and other federally chartered IDIs, id. § 1813(q)(1), and the Federal Reserve is the primary federal banking regulator for state-chartered banks that are members of the Federal Reserve System (**"member banks"**). Id. § 1813(q)(3). Because the IDI subsidiaries of most U.S. SIFIs are national banks or member banks, the FDIC's authority to act unilaterally against them may be quite limited.

44 76 U.S. Federal Register 67323, 67331 (Nov. 1, 2011) ("There is no expectation by the [Federal Reserve] and the [FDIC] that the initial resolution plan iterations submitted after this rule takes effect will be found to be deficient, but rather the initial resolution plans will provide the foundation for developing more robust annual resolution plans over the next few years following that initial period.").

45 12 U.S. Code of Federal Regulations § 243.2(f).

dated assets of $50 billion or more.[46] It also includes any foreign banking organization that has worldwide consolidated assets of $50 billion or more, even if its U.S. footprint is relatively small.[47] Finally, the term includes any non-bank financial company that has been designated as systemically important by the FSOC.[48] The term expressly excludes any bank holding company that is majority owned by the United States or any state and any bridge financial company organized under Title II of the Dodd-Frank Act.[49] Under both the statute and the regulation, the Federal Reserve may, pursuant to a recommendation of the FSOC, raise the $50 billion threshold applicable to any bank holding company or to any foreign banking organization.[50]

2. Timing

The regulation creates a staggered schedule for the submission of both initial plans and periodic updates. To do so, it creates three categories of filers. The first category is any covered company with $250 billion or more in nonbanking assets, or in the case of a foreign-based covered company with $250 billion or more in U.S. nonbanking assets.[51] This category of banking organization was required to file initial plans on July 1, 2012.[52] Nine banking institutions fell within the first category and filed initial plans.[53] The second category is any covered company with less than $250 billion in nonbanking assets but at least $100 billion of such assets, or in the case of a foreign-based covered company with at least $100 billion of U.S. nonbanking assets.[54] This category of filers is required to file initial

46 Id. § 243.2(f)(1)(ii).

47 Id. § 243.2(f)(1)(iii); see also 76 U.S. Federal Register 67,323, 67,326 (Nov. 1, 2011) (explaining that the assets test is based on a foreign bank's worldwide consolidated assets, but that foreign banks with relatively small nonbanking operations in the U.S. are permitted to file tailored resolution plans with reduced information requirements).

48 12 U.S. Code of Federal Regulations § 243.2(f)(1)(i).

49 Id. § 243.2(b), (f)(5).

50 Dodd-Frank Act, U.S. Public Law No. 111-203, § 165(a)(2)(b), 124 U.S. Statutes at Large 1375, 1424; 12 U.S. Code of Federal Regulations § 243.2(f)(4).

51 12 U.S. Code of Federal Regulations § 243.3(a)(1)(i).

52 Id.

53 Bank of America, Barclays, Citigroup, Credit Suisse, Deutsche Bank, Goldman Sachs, JP Morgan Chase, Morgan Stanley and UBS.

54 12 U.S. Code of Federal Regulations § 243.3(a)(1)(ii).

plans on July 1, 2013.[55] Four banking institutions fall within this category.[56] All other covered companies fall in the third category and are required to file their initial plans by the end of 2013.[57] The Federal Reserve and the FDIC also have the authority to accelerate or delay the schedule for initial resolution plans for any particular banking institution.[58]

Each covered company must submit updated resolution plans on each anniversary of its initial submission date,[59] although the agencies have the discretionary authority to accelerate or delay any deadlines, including the timing of updated annual resolution plans and they extended the due date for the first annual update for Round 1 and Round 1.5 Filers to October 1, 2013, and announced that both Round 1 and Round 1.5 Filers would in the future both file annual updates on July 1 of each year.[60]

Each covered company is also required to give the agencies notice of any event that does or could result in a material effect on the company's resolution plan, unless the event occurs within 90 days before the company's next annual submission date.[61] The agencies have the joint discretion to require a company to file an interim update of its resolution plan within a reasonable time after a material event occurs.[62] Because this authority is joint, neither agency has the unilateral authority to require a covered company to file an interim update without the consent of the other agency.

3. Board Approvals

The initial and annual resolution plans must be approved by the covered company's board of directors and noted in the board minutes.[63] In the case of a foreign-based covered company, it is sufficient to have the plans approved by a person or body that has delegated authority from the foreign company's board of directors.[64]

---

55 Id.
56 BNP Paribas, HSBC, Royal Bank of Scotland Group and Wells Fargo.
57 12 U.S. Code of Federal Regulations § 243.3(a)(1)(iii).
58 Id. § 243.3(a)(4).
59 12 U.S. Code of Federal Regulations § 243.3(a)(3).
60 Id. § 243.3(a)(4). See footnote 17 above.
61 Id. § 243.3(b)(2)–(3).
62 Id. § 243.3(b)(1).
63 Id. § 243.3(e)(1).
64 Id. § 243.3(e)(2).

4. Required Content – Generally

a. Public and Private Sections

The regulation requires each resolution plan to be divided between a public section and confidential section.[65] The public section must contain an executive summary of the resolution plan of the covered company that describes the business of the covered company and, to the extent material to understanding the covered company, includes the following information[66]:

- Names of covered company's material entities;
- A description of the group's core business lines;
- Consolidated or segment financial information about the group's assets, liabilities, capital and major funding sources;
- A description of the group's derivative and hedging activities;
- A list of the covered company's direct or indirect memberships in any material payment, clearing and settlement systems;
- A description of any foreign operations;
- The identities of material supervisory authorities;
- The identities of the principal officers of the covered company;
- A description of the corporate governance structure and processes related to resolution planning;
- A description of material management information systems; and
- A description, at a high level, of the covered company's resolution strategy, covering such items as the range of potential purchasers of the covered company, its material entities and the group's core business lines.

The confidential section of the resolution plan must include far more extensive information, including a confidential executive summary. It must also include detailed information about organizational structure, resolution strategies, corporate governance, management information systems, interconnections and interdependencies, supervisory and regulatory issues and contact information.[67] The Federal Reserve and the FDIC, however, may jointly exempt a covered company from one or more of these requirements.[68] The Federal Reserve and the FDIC also supplemented these information requirements for the initial plans of the Round 1 and Round 1.5 filers by providing them with other supervisory guidance, includ-

65 Id. § 243.8(c).
66 Id.
67 Id. § 243.4.
68 Id. § 243.4(k).

ing a requirement that all material entities must be assumed to fail and be placed into applicable resolution proceedings; but in April 2013, the regulators relaxed this mandatory assumption for the first annual update and provided updated formatting and informational requirements.[69]

b. Material Entities, Critical Operations and Core Business Lines

In the case of domestic covered companies, the information is required for their worldwide operations, including their material entities, critical operations and core business lines.[70] The regulation defines material entity, critical operations and core business lines as follows:

- **"Material entity"** means a subsidiary or foreign office of the covered company that is significant to the activities of a critical operation or core business line.[71]
- **"Critical operations"** means those operations of the covered company and its material entities, including associated services, functions, and support, the failure or discontinuation of which, in the view of the covered company or as jointly directed by the Federal Reserve and the FDIC, would pose a threat to the financial stability of the United States.[72]

---

69 See footnote 17 above. See also the Federal Deposit Insurance Corporation Holds a Meeting of the Systemic Resolution Advisory Committee, Panel on Title I Resolution Plans, SEC Wire Transcript at 12 (Dec. 10, 2012). The assumption that all material entities must fail was also noted in the presentation slides from the December 10, 2012 SRAC meeting, available at http://www.fdic.gov/about/srac/2012/2012-12-10_title-i_resolution-plans.pdf. Neither the statute nor the text of the implementing regulation requires this assumption, and the release accompanying the regulation only says that covered company "should" assume the failure of all material entities under certain circumstances. See 76 U.S. Federal Register 67323, 67328 (Nov. 1, 2011) ("When the covered company utilizes a material entity and that material entity is subject to the Bankruptcy Code, then a resolution plan should assume the failure or discontinuation of such material entity and provide both the covered company's and the material entity's strategy, and the actions that will be taken by the covered company to prevent or mitigate any adverse effects of such failure or discontinuation on the financial stability of the United States.") (emphasis added). For a material entity subject to a specialized insolvency regime other than the U.S. Bankruptcy Code, a resolution plan should discuss strategies under that applicable regime (for example, under Sections 11 and 13 of the FDI Act in the case of a material entity that is an insured depository institution). Id. at 67328–29.

70 12 U.S. Code of Federal Regulations § 243.4(a)(1).

71 Id. § 243.2(l).

72 Id. § 243.2(g).

- **"Core business lines"** means those business lines of the covered company and its material entities, including associated operations, services, functions and support, that, in the view of the covered company, upon failure would result in a material loss of revenue, profit or franchise value.[73]

In the case of foreign-based covered companies, the information is only required with respect to their operations that are domiciled or conducted in whole or in part in the United States, together with information about any interconnections or interdependencies between the U.S. and foreign operations and a description of how the U.S. resolution plan is integrated into the covered company's overall resolution or other contingency planning process.[74]

c. Tailored Plans

The regulation contains certain exemptions from its minimum content requirements for U.S. bank holding companies with relatively small nonbanking operations and for foreign-based covered companies with relatively small nonbanking operations in the United States.[75] Resolution plans that reflect these exemptions are called "tailored resolution plans."[76] To qualify for the tailored plan exemptions with respect to any particular resolution plan, a covered company must submit a request with the Federal Reserve and the FDIC to file a tailored plan at least 270 days before the relevant plan is due[77] and satisfy two additional conditions[78]:

- **Nonbanking Assets.** It must have less than $100 billion in total nonbanking assets (or, in the case of a foreign-based covered company, in total U.S. nonbanking assets); and
- **Banking Assets.** 85% or more of its total consolidated assets must be attributable to its insured depository institution subsidiaries (or, in the case of a foreign-based covered company, 85% or more of its total U.S. consolidated assets must be attributable to its U.S. insured depository institution subsidiaries, branches or agencies).

If the banking institution qualifies for the tailored plan exemptions, the required content of its plan is limited to the following[79]:

---

73 Id. § 243.2(d).
74 Id. § 243.4(a)(2).
75 Id. § 243.4(a)(3).
76 Id.
77 Id. § 243.4(a)(3)(iii).
78 Id. § 243.4(a)(3)(i).
79 Id. § 243.4(a)(3)(ii).

- **Executive Summary.** An executive summary satisfying the requirements described below;
- **Information about Nonbanking Operations.** The information specified below about organizational structure, resolution strategies, corporate governance, management information systems, supervisory and regulatory issues, but only with respect to the covered company and its nonbanking material entities and operations (*i.e.*, excluding any such information about its insured depository institution subsidiaries or, in the case of a foreign bank, its U.S. branches or agencies); and
- **Interdependencies and Interconnections, and Contact Information.** The information specified below about interdependencies and interconnections, as well as contact information, with respect to the covered company and its insured depository institution subsidiaries (or, in the case of a foreign-based covered company, its U.S. insured depository institution subsidiaries, branches or agencies) and nonbank material entities and operations, which shall be discussed in the covered company's section on resolution strategies.

d. Macroeconomic Scenarios

Each plan is required to explain how it would work under the most recent "baseline," "adverse" and "severely adverse" macroeconomic scenarios provided to the covered company by the Federal Reserve in connection with the Comprehensive Capital Analysis and Review (**"CCAR"**) stress-testing process,[80] except that the initial plan only needs to address the baseline scenario.[81] The plans are not permitted to rely on "extraordinary support" from the U.S. or foreign governments.[82] Although the regulation does not define what constitutes "extraordinary support," the release accompanying the final rule states that this assumption "is intended to prohibit the covered company from assuming in its resolution plan that the United States or any other government will provide the covered company funding or capital other than in the ordinary course of business."[83]

---

80 Id. § 243.4(a)(4)(i). See also Dodd-Frank Act, § 165(i)(1), 124 U.S. Statutes at Large 1375, 1430 (2010); *Davis Polk & Wardwell LLP*, 2013 CCAR Process Begins and U.S. Basel III Rules are Delayed (Nov. 14, 2012), available at http://www.davispolk.com/files/Publication/a531f098-49f8-4d38-a462-37ba2a1805d2/Presentation/PublicationAttachment/78874f7c-8fe8-40c2-a6fe-39335c0f6835/111412_CCAR.pdf.

81 12 U.S. Code of Federal Regulations § 243.4(a)(4)(i).

82 Id. § 243.4(a)(4)(ii).

83 76 U.S. Federal Register 67323, 67328 (Nov. 1, 2011).

5. Required Content – Specific Items

The following sections summarize the information that is required to be included in the confidential portion of each resolution plan, subject to the exemptions for tailored resolution plans discussed above.[84]

a. Confidential Executive Summary

Each plan must include a confidential executive summary describing the key elements of the plan, any material changes from the most recently filed plan, and any actions taken by the covered company to improve the effectiveness of the plan or to remediate or mitigate any material weaknesses or impediments to the effective and timely execution of the plan.[85]

b. Organizational Structure

The regulation requires the following information about a covered company's organizational structure[86]:

- **Organizational Chart.** A detailed description of the group's organizational structure, including a hierarchical list of all material entities (including intermediate holding companies) that identify the direct holder and the percentage of voting and nonvoting equity of each legal entity and foreign office listed and the location, jurisdiction of incorporation, licensing, and key management associated with each material entity and foreign office.
- **Mapping of Critical Operations and Core Business Lines to Material Entities.** A mapping of the group's critical operations and core business lines to material entities.
- **Unconsolidated and Consolidating Financial Information.** An unconsolidated balance sheet of the covered company and a consolidating schedule for all material entities.
- **Liabilities.** A description of the material components of the liabilities of the covered company, its material entities, critical operations and core business lines that, at a minimum, separately identifies short-term and long-term liabilities, secured and unsecured liabilities, and subordinated liabilities.

---

84 See 12 U.S. Code of Federal Regulations § 243.4(a)(3).
85 Id. § 243.4(b).
86 Id. § 243.4(e).

- **Collateral.** A list and description of the processes used by the group to determine the persons to which the covered company or any material entity has pledged collateral, the persons who hold the collateral and the jurisdictions in which the collateral is located, and, if different, the jurisdictions in which the collateral is enforceable against the covered company or any material entity.
- **Off-Balance Sheet Exposures.** A description of material off-balance sheet exposures (including guarantees and contractual obligations) of the covered company and its material entities, including a mapping to the group's critical operations and core business lines.
- **Booking Practices.** A description of the practices of the covered company, its material entities and the group's core business lines related to the booking of trading and derivatives activities.
- **Material Hedges.** A list and description of the material hedges of the covered company, its material entities and its core business lines related to the booking of trading and derivatives activities, including a mapping to legal entity.
- **Hedging Strategies.** A description of the hedging strategies of the group.
- **Exposure Limits.** A description of the process used by the covered company and its material entities to establish exposure limits.
- **Major Counterparties.** A list of the major counterparties of the covered company and its material entities, and a description of the interconnections, interdependencies and relationships with such major counterparties.
- **Failure of Major Counterparty.** An analysis of whether the failure of each major counterparty would likely have an adverse impact on or result in material financial distress to or failure of the covered company.
- **Financial Market Utilities.** A list of each trading, payment, clearing or settlement system of which the covered company, directly or indirectly, is a member and on which the covered company or any material entity conducts a material number or value of trades or transactions, including a mapping of membership in each such system to the covered company, its material entities, and the group's critical operations and core business lines.

c. Resolution Strategies

The regulation also requires the information set forth below about a covered company's resolution strategies.[87] The purpose of the strategies is to describe the

---

87 Id. § 243.4(c).

covered company's plan for its "rapid and orderly resolution,"[88] which is defined as "a reorganization or liquidation of the covered company (or, in the case of a covered company that is incorporated or organized in a jurisdiction other than the United States, the subsidiaries and operations of such foreign company that are domiciled in the United States) under the Bankruptcy Code[89] that can be accomplished within a reasonable period of time and in a manner that substantially mitigates the risk that the failure of the covered company would have serious adverse effects on financial stability in the United States."[90]

- **Resolution Strategies.** A description of the covered company's resolution strategy, including a detailed description of the:
  - **Key assumptions and supporting analyses**, including of economic or financial conditions.
  - **Range of specific actions** to be taken to facilitate a rapid and orderly resolution of the covered company, its material entities, and the group's critical operations and core business lines in the event of material financial distress or failure of the covered company.
  - **Funding, liquidity and capital needs** of, and resources available to, the covered company and its material entities, a mapping of such needs to the group's critical operations and core business lines in the ordinary course of business and in the event of material financial distress to or failure of the covered company.
  - **Strategy for maintaining the operations of, and funding**, for the covered company and its material entities, and a mapping of such operations and funding to the group's critical operations and core business lines.
  - **Strategy for the failure or discontinuation of any material entity, core business line or critical operation**, and the actions to be taken to prevent or mitigate any adverse effects of such failure or discontinuation on the financial stability of the United States, except that no such strategy is required for any material entity that is not subject to the U.S. Bankruptcy Code (but instead is subject to another insolvency regime

88 Id.
89 If the covered company is not subject to the U.S. Bankruptcy Code, then rapid and orderly resolution means a reorganization or liquidation of the company under the insolvency regime to which the covered company is ordinarily subject. See 76 U.S. Federal Register 67323, 67327 note 8 (Nov. 15, 2011).
90 12 U.S. Code of Federal Regulations § 243.2(o).

such as the FDI Act or the Securities Investor Protection Act), has less than $50 billion in assets and does not conduct a critical operation.[91]
  - **Strategy for insulating any insured depository institution subsidiary** from risks arising from the activities of nonbank subsidiaries (other than subsidiaries of the IDI).
- **Timing.** A description of the time period(s) expected to successfully execute each material aspect and step of the plan.
- **Material Weaknesses or Impediments.** A list of the potential material weaknesses or impediments to the effective and timely execution of the plan, and the actions or steps to be taken to remediate or otherwise mitigate the weaknesses or impediments, including a timeline for such action.
- **Processes.** A description of the processes used by the covered company to:
  - **Value and Marketability.** Determine current market values and marketability of the core business lines, critical operations and material asset holdings of the covered company.
  - **Feasibility.** Assess the feasibility of the covered company's plans for executing any sales, divestitures, restructurings, recapitalizations or other actions contemplated in the plan.
  - **Impact.** Assess the impact of any sales, divestitures, restructurings, recapitalizations or other similar actions on the value, funding and operations of the covered company, its material entities, critical operations and core business lines.

d. Corporate Governance

The regulation also requires the following information about corporate governance[92]:
- **Integration of Resolution Planning.** A detailed description of how resolution planning is integrated into the covered company's corporate governance structure and processes.
- **Resolution Leader(s).** A description of the senior management official(s) (including title) who is(are) primarily responsible for overseeing the develop-

---

91 Id. § 243.4(c)(1)(v). For a material entity subject to a specialized insolvency regime other than the U.S. Bankruptcy Code that has $50 billion or more in assets or conducts a critical operation, a resolution plan should discuss strategies under that applicable regime (for example, under Sections 11 and 13 of the FDI Act in the case of a material entity that is an insured depository institution). 76 U.S. Federal Register 67323, 67328–29 (Nov. 1, 2011).
92 Id. § 243.4(d).

ment, maintenance, implementation, and filing of the plan and the covered company's compliance with the applicable regulations.
- **Reporting.** A detailed description of the nature, extent and frequency of reporting to senior executive officers and the board of directors regarding the development, maintenance and implementation of the plan.
- **Contingency Planning.** A description of the nature, extent and results of any contingency planning or similar exercise (*e.g.*, a simulation of the failure and resolution of the covered company) conducted by the covered company since the date of its most recent resolution plan to assess the viability of or improve the plan.
- **Risk Measures.** A list and description of the relevant risk measures used to report credit risk exposures both internally to senior management and board of directors, as well as to investors or to federal regulators.

e. Management Information Systems

The regulation requires the following information about the company's management information systems[93]:
- **Key Systems and Applications.** A detailed inventory and description of the key management information systems and applications, including systems and applications for risk management, accounting and financial and regulatory reporting, used by the covered company and its material entities, including the name of the legal owner or licensor, the use and function of the system or application, service level agreements related thereto, any software or system licenses, and any intellectual property associated with it.
- **Mapping.** A mapping of the key management information systems and applications to the covered company, its material entities, and the group's critical operations and core business lines.
- **Reports.** Identification of the scope, content and frequency of the key internal reports used by senior management of the covered company, its material entities, and the group's critical operations and core business lines to monitor the financial health, risks and operations of the covered company, its material entities, and the group's critical operations and core business lines.
- **Access of Regulators.** A description of the process for the appropriate regulators to access these management information systems and applications.

---

93 Id. § 243.4(f).

- **Capabilities and Weaknesses.** A description and analysis of the capabilities of the management information systems to collect, maintain and report in a timely manner to management of the covered company and to the Federal Reserve the information and data underlying the resolution plan, and any deficiencies, gaps or weaknesses in such capabilities and the actions to be taken to promptly address any deficiencies, gaps or weaknesses and the time frames for doing so.

f. Interconnections and Dependencies

The regulation requires a list and mapping of any interconnections and interdependencies among the covered company, its material entities, and the group's critical operations and core business lines that, if disrupted, would materially affect the funding or operations of the covered company, its material entities, and the group's critical operations or core business lines.[94] The regulation identifies the following as examples of interconnections and interdependencies that should be included:

- common or shared personnel, facilities or systems (including information technology platforms, management information systems, risk management systems, and accounting and recordkeeping systems);
- capital, funding, or liquidity arrangements;
- existing or contingent credit exposures;
- cross-guarantee arrangements, cross-collateral arrangements, cross-default provisions, and cross-affiliate netting agreements;
- risk transfers; and
- service level agreements.[95]

The release accompanying the adoption of the final regulation also stated that "the continued availability of key services and supporting business operations to core business lines and critical operations in an environment of material financial distress and after insolvency should be a focus of resolution planning. Steps to ensure that service level agreements for such services, whether provided by internal or external service providers, survive insolvency should be demonstrated in the resolution plan."[96]

---

94 Id. § 243.4(g).
95 Id.
96 76 U.S. Federal Register 67323, 67329–30 (Nov. 1, 2011).

g. Supervisory and Regulatory Issues

Each resolution plan must identify the covered company's federal, state and foreign supervisors with authority over the safety and soundness of the covered company, its material entities, and the group's critical operations and core business lines, as well as any foreign supervisors responsible for resolving any foreign-based material entity, critical operation or core business line.[97] The plan must also include contact information for each supervisory or regulatory authority identified.[98]

h. Contact Information

Each resolution plan must identify a senior management official responsible for serving as the point of contact for the plan, as well as a senior management official at each material entity.[99]

i. Incorporation by Reference

Any plan other than a covered company's initial plan may incorporate by reference informational elements (but not strategic analysis or executive summary elements) from a resolution plan previously submitted to the Federal Reserve and the FDIC, provided that the plan seeking to incorporate such information by reference clearly indicates the informational element and which of the previous resolution plans contains the information, and the covered company certifies that the incorporated information is still accurate.[100]

6. Confidential Treatment

Section 112(d)(5)(A) of the Dodd-Frank Act requires the Federal Reserve and the FDIC to "maintain the confidentiality of any data, information, and reports submitted under" Title I of the Dodd-Frank Act,[101] which includes resolution plans submitted under Section 165(d) of that Act. The regulation implementing Section

---

97 12 U.S. Code of Federal Regulations § 243.4(h).
98 Id.
99 Id. § 243.4(i).
100 Id. § 243.4(j).
101 Dodd-Frank Act, U.S. Public Law No. 111-203, § 112(d)(5)(A), 124 U.S. Statutes at Large 1375, 1397–98 (2010).

165(d) further provides that confidentiality of resolution plans and related materials will be determined in accordance with applicable exemptions contained in the U.S. Freedom of Information Act ("**FOIA**").[102] As noted above, the regulation requires resolution plans to be divided between a public section and a confidential section.[103] It also provides that the confidential section will be treated as confidential to the extent permitted by law,[104] if a proper request for confidential treatment has been filed along with the resolution plan.[105] The regulation also provides that the submission of nonpublic information in a resolution plan will not constitute the waiver of, or otherwise affect, any privilege arising under Federal or state law, such as attorney-client privilege, to the extent permitted by law.[106]

The U.S. FOIA generally requires disclosure of any information filed with the U.S. government or any federal agency, including the Federal Reserve and the FDIC, unless it qualifies for one of several statutory exemptions.[107] In their release accompanying the regulation implementing Section 165(d) of the Dodd-Frank Act, the Federal Reserve and the FDIC indicated that the statutory exemptions for which information in the confidential portions of resolution plans are most likely to qualify are the exemptions for trade secrets and confidential or privileged commercial or financial information or for confidential supervisory information.[108] The Federal Reserve and the FDIC also acknowledged in the release that resolution plans would likely include "highly detailed, internal proprietary information" that "covered companies would not customarily make available to the public and that an agency typically would have access to and could review as part of the supervisory process in assessing, for example, the safety and soundness of a regulated institution."[109] They also acknowledged that "release of this information would impede the quality and extent of information provided by covered companies and could significantly impact the efforts of the

102 12 U.S. Code of Federal Regulations § 243.8(d)(1).
103 Id. § 243.8(c).
104 Id. § 243.8(d)(3).
105 Id. § 243.8(d)(2).
106 Id. § 243.8(d)(4).
107 5 United States Code § 552.
108 76 U.S. Federal Register 67323, 67332 (Nov. 1, 2011). See also 5 United States Code §§ 552(b)(4) (exemption for trade secrets and privileged or confidential commercial or financial information) and 552(b)(8) (exemption for confidential supervisory information); *Annette L. Nazareth & Margaret E. Tahyar*, Transparency and Confidentiality in the Post-Financial Crisis World—Where to Strike the Balance?, 1 Harvard Bus. L. Rev. 146 (2011).
109 76 U.S Federal Register 67323, 67332 (Nov. 1, 2011).

[Federal Reserve] and the [FDIC] to encourage effective and orderly unwinding of the covered companies in a crisis."[110]

7. Credibility Reviews

In order to facilitate review of a covered company's resolution plan, a covered company must provide the Federal Reserve and the FDIC with such information and access to personnel as the Federal Reserve and the FDIC jointly determine is necessary to assess the credibility of the resolution plan and the ability of the covered company to implement the resolution plan.[111] The Federal Reserve and the FDIC must rely to the fullest extent possible on examinations conducted by or on behalf of the appropriate Federal banking agency for the relevant company.[112]

Within 60 days of receiving an initial or annual resolution plan, the Federal Reserve and the FDIC must jointly determine whether the resolution plan satisfies the minimum informational requirements.[113] If the Federal Reserve and the FDIC jointly determine that it is incomplete or that substantial additional information is required to facilitate review, they must jointly inform the covered company in writing of the areas with respect to which additional information is required.[114] The covered company must resubmit its resolution plan or any additional information jointly requested no later than 30 days after receiving notice, unless the Federal Reserve and the FDIC jointly prescribe otherwise.[115]

If the Federal Reserve and the FDIC jointly determine that a resolution plan is not credible or would not facilitate an orderly resolution under the U.S. Bankruptcy Code (or other applicable insolvency law), they must jointly notify the covered company in writing of such determination.[116] As noted above, neither agency may unilaterally give such notice of deficiencies without the consent of the other. Before issuing any notice of deficiencies with respect to a covered company that is likely to have a significant impact on a functionally regulated subsidiary or a depository institution subsidiary of a covered company, the Federal Reserve ***must*** consult with each FSOC member that primarily supervises such subsidiary.[117] The Federal Reserve ***may*** also

110 Id.
111 12 U.S. Code of Federal Regulations § 243.3(d).
112 Id.
113 Id. § 243.5(a)(1).
114 Id. § 243.5(a)(2).
115 Id.
116 Id. § 243.5(b). See also 76 U.S. Federal Register 67323, 67327 note 8 (Nov. 1, 2011).
117 12 U.S. Code of Federal Regulations § 243.7(a).

consult with any other federal, state or foreign supervisor as it considers appropriate.[118] Before issuing any notice of deficiencies with respect to the U.S. operations of a foreign-based covered company, the Federal Reserve ***may***, but is not required to, consult with any foreign supervisor as it considers appropriate.[119]

The covered company must submit a revised resolution plan within 90 days of receiving notice of any deficiencies, or within such shorter or longer period as the Federal Reserve and the FDIC may jointly determine.[120] The revised resolution plan must address all deficiencies identified and discuss the following in detail:
- the revisions made to address the deficiencies;
- any changes to business operations and corporate structure the covered company proposes to undertake to facilitate implementation of the revised resolution plan (including a timeline for execution of such changes); and
- why the covered company believes the revised resolution plan is credible and would result in an orderly resolution under the U.S. Bankruptcy Code (or other applicable insolvency law).[121]

A covered company may request an extension of time to submit a revised resolution plan in response to a notice of deficiencies.[122] Such extension request must be supported by a written statement describing the basis and justification for the request.[123]

8. Sanctions for Failure to Cure Deficiencies

As an initial consequence of failure to cure deficiencies in a resolution plan, the Federal Reserve and the FDIC may jointly impose on a covered company, or any subsidiary of a covered company, more stringent capital, leverage or liquidity requirements or restrictions on growth, activities or operations.[124] The Federal Reserve and the FDIC may jointly impose such restrictions or requirements if either the covered company fails to submit a revised resolution plan within the required time period or the Federal Reserve and the FDIC jointly determine that the revised resolution plan does not adequately remedy the deficiencies identi-

118 Id. § 243.7(b).
119 Id.
120 Id. § 243.5(c).
121 Id. See also 76 U.S. Federal Register 67323, 67327 note 8 (Nov. 1, 2011).
122 Id. § 243.5(d).
123 Id.
124 Id. § 243.6(a).

fied.[125] Any requirements or restrictions imposed in response to a failure to cure resolution plan deficiencies would only apply until the date when the Federal Reserve and the FDIC jointly determine that the covered company has submitted a revised resolution plan that adequately remedies the deficiencies.[126] As noted above, neither agency may unilaterally take any action under Section 165(d) of the Dodd-Frank Act without the consent of the other.

A covered company on which the foregoing types of requirements or restrictions are imposed faces the further threat of mandated divestitures (*i.e.*, break-up) if it fails, within the first two years following the imposition of such requirements and restrictions, to submit a revised resolution plan that adequately remedies the deficiencies. After two years, the Federal Reserve and the FDIC may jointly require the covered company to divest assets or operations upon a joint determination that the divestiture of such assets or operations is necessary to facilitate an orderly resolution of the covered company under the U.S. Bankruptcy Code or other applicable insolvency law.[127]

Before making a joint determination to impose any requirements or restrictions or require any divestitures with respect to a covered company that are likely to have a significant impact on a functionally regulated subsidiary or a depository institution subsidiary of a covered company, the Federal Reserve ***must*** consult with each FSOC member that primarily supervises such subsidiary.[128] The Federal Reserve ***may*** also consult with any other federal, state or foreign supervisor as it considers appropriate.[129] Before determining to jointly impose any requirements or restrictions or require any divestitures with respect to the U.S. operations of a foreign-based covered company, the Federal Reserve ***may***, but is not required to, consult with any foreign supervisor as it considers appropriate.[130]

The Federal Reserve and the FDIC may jointly enforce any order imposing initial requirements or restrictions or divestitures.[131] The Federal Reserve, in consultation with the FDIC, may take any enforcement action under Section 8 of the Federal Deposit Insurance Act (the **"FDI Act"**) to address any violation.[132]

A resolution plan submitted under Section 165(d) of the Dodd-Frank Act has no binding effect on a court or trustee in a proceeding under the U.S. Bankruptcy

125 Id.

126 Id. § 243.6(b).

127 Id. § 243.6(c). See also 76 U.S. Federal Register 67323, 67327 note 8 (Nov. 1, 2011).

128 12 U.S. Code of Federal Regulations § 243.7(a).

129 Id. § 243.7(b).

130 Id.

131 Id. § 243.9.

132 Id.

Code, a receiver appointed or a bridge financial company chartered under Title II of the Dodd-Frank Act or any other authority that is authorized to resolve a covered company.[133]

B. IDI Plans

The requirements for IDI resolution plans are substantially similar to the requirements for Title I plans, but there are a few important differences. Because of the similarities, a covered company that has a covered insured depository institution (**"covered IDI"**) subsidiary can file the IDI chapter from its Title I plan as its IDI plan,[134] together with a cross-reference sheet showing where the information and data required by the IDI Rule is located. To the extent the IDI Rule requires additional information, filers would need to include the additional information in both their Title I and IDI plans.

1. Most Important Differences from Title I Plans

The most important differences between Title I and IDI plans relate to their objectives, scope, credibility review and consequences of submitting a deficient resolution plan.

a. Objectives

As noted above, the purpose of a Title I resolution plan is to show how a covered company can be resolved in a rapid and orderly manner.[135] The regulation implementing the Title I requirement defines a "rapid and orderly resolution" as "a reorganization or liquidation of the covered company (or, in the case of a covered company that is incorporated or organized in a jurisdiction other than the United States, the subsidiaries and operations of such foreign company that are domi-

133 Id. § 243.8(a).

134 See *Davis Polk & Wardwell LLP*, Credible Living Wills Under the U.S. Regulatory Framework (Sept. 19, 2011), available at http://www.davispolk.com/files/Publication/d0e11d7b-2f4b-45e4-849c-2320b1e0d9c5/Presentation/PublicationAttachment/7426ca31-e687-482b-a8e0-24c3cdbc5564/091911_Credible_Living_Wills_US_Framework.pdf (describing expectation that most financial institutions will submit one integrated U.S. resolution plan with separate chapters).

135 Id.

ciled in the United States) under the Bankruptcy Code[136] that can be accomplished within a reasonable period of time and in a manner that substantially mitigates the risk that the failure of the covered company would have serious adverse effects on financial stability in the United States."[137] The focus is directly on mitigating the risk that the failure of a covered company could destabilize the U.S. financial system as a result of interconnectedness and contagion.[138]

In contrast, the purpose of an IDI resolution plan is to show how a covered IDI can be resolved by the FDIC under the principal bank resolution provisions of the FDI Act[139] "in a manner that ensures that depositors receive access to their insured deposits within one business day of the IDI's failure (or two business days if the failure occurs on a day other than Friday), maximizes the net present value return from the sale or disposition of the IDI's assets and minimizes the amount of any loss realized by the creditors in the resolution."[140] While the direct focus of IDI plans is on access to deposits, value maximization and loss minimization, the release accompanying the IDI Rule indicated that resolving IDIs in this manner will serve the additional purpose of strengthening the stability of and public confidence in the U.S. banking system.[141]

b. Scope

Another important difference relates to scope. One aspect of this difference relates to the definitions of the terms "critical operations" and "critical services." The

---

136 If the covered company is not subject to the U.S. Bankruptcy Code, then rapid and orderly resolution means a reorganization or liquidation of the company under the insolvency regime to which the covered company is ordinarily subject. See 76 U.S. Federal Register 67323, 67327 note 8 (Nov. 15, 2011).

137 12 U.S. Code of Federal Regulations § 243.2(o).

138 See, e.g., *Hal S. Scott*, Interconnectedness and Contagion (Nov. 20, 2012), available at http://www.capmktsreg.org/pdfs/2012.11.20_Interconnectedness_and_Contagion.pdf.

139 Sections 11 and 13 of the FDI Act, 12 United States Code §§ 1821, 1823.

140 12 U.S. Code of Federal Regulations § 360.10(a). See also id. § 360.10(c)(2). In the preamble accompanying the IDI Rule, the FDIC stated that "[b]ased on its experience resolving failed insured depository institutions (and in particular, large and complex insured depository institutions), the FDIC has concluded that Resolution Plans for large and complex insured depository institutions are essential for their orderly and least-cost resolution and the development of such plans should begin promptly." 77 U.S. Federal Register 3075, 3075 (Jan. 23, 2012).

141 77 U.S. Federal Register 3075, 3075 (Jan. 13, 2012) ("In implementing the deposit insurance program and efficiently and effectively resolving failed depository institutions, the FDIC strengthens the stability of, and helps maintain public confidence in, the banking system in the United States.").

regulation implementing Title I requires covered companies to identify their "critical operations" and develop strategies for the continuation of such operations despite the failure of the covered companies. In contrast, the IDI Rule requires covered IDIs to identify their "critical services" and develop strategies to ensure the continuation of those services despite the failure of the covered IDIs. It makes no mention of critical operations and defines critical services quite differently than how critical operations is defined in the Title I regulation.[142] As noted above, the Title I regulation defines "critical operations" as follows:

- "**Critical operations**" means those operations of the covered company and its material entities, including associated services, functions, and support, the failure or discontinuation of which, in the view of the covered company or as jointly directed by the Federal Reserve and the FDIC, would pose a threat to the financial stability of the United States.[143]

In contrast, the IDI Rule defines "critical services" as follows:

- "**Critical services**" means services and operations of the covered IDI, such as servicing, information technology support and operations, human resources and personnel that are necessary to continue the day-to-day operations of the covered IDI.[144]

As so defined, the term critical services has a very different meaning than critical operations because, in essence, critical services are internal to the covered IDI and include all services (including shared services) and operations that are "necessary" to continue the day-to-day operations of the covered IDI. In sharp contrast, critical operations relate to the covered company's external relationships with the U.S. financial sector which, if discontinued, would pose a threat to financial stability in the United States. The two terms are about very different concepts, and they should not be confused even though they share the word "critical."

Another aspect of the difference in scope between Title I and IDI plans relates to the least-cost test. Under the FDI Act, the FDIC is required to resolve insured depository institutions in a manner that results in the least cost to the U.S. Deposit Insurance Fund of all of the alternatives,[145] unless the FDIC invokes

---

142 In its preamble accompanying the IDI Rule, the FDIC observed that the definition of "the term 'critical services' differs substantially from the term 'critical operations' as used in the Section 165(d) rule." Id. at 3079.

143 12 U.S. Code of Federal Regulations § 243.2(g).

144 Id. § 360.10(a)(5).

145 12 United States Code § 1823(c)(4).

the "systemic risk" exception to the least-cost test.[146] As a result, the IDI Rule requires each covered IDI to explain how its resolution strategies would satisfy the least-cost test.[147] In its release accompanying the IDI Rule, the FDIC acknowledged that more than one strategy might satisfy the least-cost test depending on the circumstances, and it encouraged covered IDIs to include as many alternative strategies as they wished as long as all proposed strategies are "reasonable" and at least "one is least costly relative to liquidation or other resolution methods."[148] Although nothing in the IDI Rule or the accompanying release specifically addresses whether a covered IDI may include a resolution strategy based on an assumption that the systemic risk exception has been invoked, such a strategy should be permissible as long as it is "reasonable" and the plan includes at least one alternative strategy that satisfies the least-cost test.

In contrast, Title I plans are not required to explain how their strategies would satisfy the least-cost test or any similar cost-minimization test. Instead, they are only required to explain how their strategies would result in a "reorganization or liquidation of the covered company (or, in the case of a covered company that is incorporated or organized in a jurisdiction other than the United States, the subsidiaries and operations of such foreign company that are domiciled in the United States) under the Bankruptcy Code [or other applicable insolvency law][149] that can be accomplished in a reasonable period of time and in a manner that substantially mitigates the risk that the failure of the company would have serious adverse effects on financial stability in the United States."[150] It is possible that this objective may be feasible only if the strategy minimizes creditor losses, or at least short-term creditor losses, but this cost-minimization goal is apparently only a second-order concern compared to the primary concern of mitigating destabilizing risks.

146 Id. § 1823(c)(4)(G).

147 12 U.S. Code of Federal Regulations § 360.10(c)(2)(vii).

148 77 U.S. Federal Register 3075, 3081 (Jan. 23, 2012). The FDIC identified a number of strategies as potentially satisfying the least-cost test depending on the circumstances, including purchase and assumption transactions in which the entire business of a covered IDI is sold to a third party or broken up and sold in pieces to one or more third parties, the use of a bridge bank to buy extra time for such a sale or series of sales, or the recapitalization of a failed covered IDI's business by transferring all of the failed SIFI's assets to a bridge bank and distributing the shares of the bridge bank to the d claimants left behind in the failed covered IDI's receivership in satisfaction of their claims. Id.

149 If the covered company is not subject to the U.S. Bankruptcy Code, then rapid and orderly resolution means a reorganization or liquidation of the company under the insolvency regime to which the covered company is ordinarily subject. See 76 U.S. Federal Register 67323, 67327 note 8 (Nov. 15, 2011).

150 12 U.S. Code of Federal Regulations § 243.2(o).

c. Credibility Review

Unlike the Title I regulation which does not expressly require Title I plans to be credible, the IDI Rule requires that all IDI plans be credible.[151] In addition, unlike the Title I regulation, the IDI Rule defines the credibility standard. An IDI plan "is credible if its strategies for resolving the [covered IDI], and the detailed information required by [the IDI Rule], are well-founded and based on information and data related to the [covered IDI] that are observable and otherwise verifiable and employ reasonable projections from current and historical conditions within the broader financial markets."[152] The process for reviewing the credibility of an IDI plan is similar to the process for reviewing the credibility of Title I plans, except that the FDIC alone (rather than the FDIC and the Federal Reserve acting jointly) determines whether an IDI plan is credible or not.

d. Consequences

In contrast to Title I, which expressly authorizes the FDIC and the Federal Reserve to jointly impose various sanctions on a covered company for failing to file a Title I plan that survives a credibility review, the IDI Rule does not specify any consequences for failure to submit a credible IDI plan. The FDIC may view itself as having general supervisory authority to impose sanctions on a covered IDI for which it is the appropriate federal banking agency if it determines that failure to file a credible IDI plan constitutes an unsafe or unsound operational or managerial practice.[153] But the FDIC is only the appropriate federal banking agency for state-chartered banks and thrifts that are not members of the Federal Reserve System.[154] The Office of the Comptroller of the Currency is the appropriate federal banking agency for federally chartered banks and thrifts,[155] and the Federal Reserve is the appropriate federal banking agency for state-chartered banks that are members of the Federal Reserve System.[156] As a result, the FDIC would appear to have no direct authority to take any action against these institutions for failure to file a credible IDI plan. Instead, it would appear that the FDIC would have to persuade the OCC or the Federal Reserve to take such action. This is an important limitation on the FDIC's power to impose sanctions on a covered IDI for failing

151 Id. § 360.10(c)(4)(i).
152 Id.
153 See, e.g., 12 United States Code § 1818.
154 12 United States Code § 1813(q)(2).
155 Id. § 1813(q)(1).
156 Id. § 1813(q)(3).

to submit a credible IDI plan since most systemically-important U.S. banks are either national banks or state-chartered banks that are members of the Federal Reserve System.

2. Other Differences

The IDI Rule[157] is a separate regulation from the Title I regulation. The IDI Rule was issued by the FDIC acting alone pursuant to its authority under the FDI Act. Under the FDI Act, the FDIC is charged with responsibility for insuring the deposits of U.S. insured depository institutions and with serving as the receiver of such institutions if they should fail. One of the key purposes of the IDI Rule is to ensure that the FDIC has access to all of the material information it needs to efficiently resolve a covered IDI in the event of its failure.[158]

The FDIC had begun to focus on resolution planning and its responsibilities as the receiver for failed insured depository institutions even before the enactment of the Dodd-Frank Act. Indeed, the FDIC proposed an earlier version of the IDI Rule in May 2010, two months before the Dodd-Frank Act was enacted.[159] The FDIC delayed finalizing the IDI Rule to allow for harmonization with the Title I regulation. The FDIC has stated that the final IDI Rule "is intended to complement the resolution plan requirements of the Dodd-Frank Act."[160]

a. Applicability

The IDI Rule applies to all insured depository institutions with $50 billion or more in total assets, and it refers to such institutions as covered IDIs.[161] At the time the rule was finalized, the FDIC calculated that there would be 37 covered IDIs, of which 34 have holding companies that are also subject to the Dodd-Frank Act's resolution planning requirements under Section 165(d).[162]

157 12 U.S. Code of Federal Regulations § 360.10.
158 12 U.S. Federal Register 3075, 3075 (Jan. 23, 2012).
159 75 U.S. Federal Register 27,464 (May 17, 2010).
160 77 U.S. Federal Register 3075, 3076 (Jan. 23, 2012).
161 12 U.S. Code of Federal Regulations § 360.10(a), (b)(4).
162 77 U.S. Federal Register 3075, 3076, 3084 (Jan. 23, 2012).

b. Timing

The timing for the submission of initial and annual resolution plans under the IDI Rule is aligned to the three filing categories created under the Title I regulation. Five of the nine banking organizations that filed resolution plans on July 1, 2012 were subject to the IDI Rule requirements,[163] as were the two additional Round 1.5 Filers.[164] All other covered IDIs are required to file their initial IDI plans by the middle or end of 2013.[165]

Each covered IDI must submit updated resolution plans on each anniversary of its initial submission date or such other date as the FDIC may specify.[166] Each is also required to give the FDIC notice of any event that results or could result in a material effect on the covered IDI's resolution plan, unless the event occurs within 90 days before the covered IDI's next annual submission date or such other date as the FDIC may specify.[167] However, unlike the Dodd-Frank Act's resolution planning regulation, the IDI Rule does not provide for interim updates of a resolution plan following a material event. A covered IDI would be required to address any material event, occurrence or change with respect to which it provides notice in its next annual resolution plan submission.[168]

c. Board Approvals

A covered IDI's initial and annual resolution plans must be approved by the covered IDI's board of directors (not its holding company's board) and noted in the board minutes.[169]

d. Additional Information about Resolution Strategies

The IDI Rule requires the following information about a covered IDI's resolution strategy, in addition to what is required in a Title I plan:

– **Critical Services.** Identification of critical services and providers of critical services, and a mapping of critical services to the covered IDI's material entities and core business lines. The IDI resolution plan must describe the covered IDI's strategy for continuing critical services in the event of the

163 Bank of America, Citigroup, Goldman Sachs, JP Morgan Chase and Morgan Stanley.
164 Bank of New York Mellon and State Street.
165 12 U.S. Code of Federal Regulations § 360.10(c)(1)(i)(C).
166 Id. § 360.10(c)(1)(iii)–(iv).
167 Id. § 360.10(c)(1)(v).
168 Id.
169 Id. § 360.10(c)(3).

covered IDI's failure. When critical services are provided by the covered IDI's parent company or a parent company affiliate, the resolution plan must describe the covered IDI's strategy for continuing critical services in the event of the parent company's or affiliate's failure, and the plan must assess the ability of any parent company affiliate to continue providing critical services on a standalone basis in the event of the parent company's failure.[170]

- **Interconnectedness to Parent Company's Organization.** Identification of aspects of the organizational structure, interconnectedness of its legal entities, the structure of legal or contractual arrangements of the covered IDI's parent company, or its overall business operations that would, in the event the covered IDI were placed in receivership, diminish the covered IDI's franchise value, obstruct its continued business operations or increase the operational complexity to the FDIC as receiver.[171]
- **Strategy to Separate from Parent Company's Organization.** A strategy to unwind or separate the covered IDI and its subsidiaries from the organizational structure of its parent company in a cost-effective and timely fashion, including possible remediation or mitigation steps that could be taken to eliminate or mitigate obstacles to separation.[172]
- **Strategy for the Sale or Disposition of Deposit Franchise, Business Lines and Assets.** A strategy for the sale or disposition of the deposit franchise, including branches, core business lines, and major assets of the covered IDI in a manner that ensures that depositors receive access to their insured deposits within one business day of failure (or two business days if the failure occurs on a day other than Friday), maximizes the net present value return from the sale or disposition of such assets, and minimizes the amount of any loss realized in the resolution of cases.[173]
- **Least Costly Resolution Method.** Description of how the strategies for separation of the covered IDI and its subsidiaries from the parent company's organization and the sale or disposition of the deposit franchise, core business lines, and major assets can be demonstrated to be the least costly to the FDIC's Deposit Insurance Fund of all possible methods for resolving the covered IDI.[174]

---

170 Id. § 360.10(c)(2)(iii).
171 Id. § 360.10(c)(2)(iv).
172 Id. § 360.10(c)(2)(v).
173 Id. § 360.10(c)(2)(vi).
174 Id. § 360.10(c)(2)(vii).

e. Other Additional Information

The IDI Rule also requires the following information, in addition to what is required in a Title I plan:

- **Overview of Deposit Activities and Branch Structure.** Description of the covered IDI's overall deposit activities, including unique aspects of the deposit base or underlying systems that may create operational complexity for the FDIC or result in extraordinary resolution expenses in the event of failure, and description of the covered IDI's U.S. and foreign branch organization, including identification of key personnel tasked with managing core business lines and deposit activities and the covered IDI's branch organization.[175]
- **Systemically Important Functions.** Description of systemically important functions that the covered IDI, its subsidiaries, and its affiliates provide, including the nature and extent of the IDI's involvement in payment systems, custodial or clearing operations, large sweep programs, and capital markets operations in which the IDI plays a dominant role. The IDI resolution plan must discuss critical vulnerabilities, estimated exposure and potential losses, and why certain aspects of the covered IDI's businesses could pose a systemic risk to the broader economy.
- **Cross-Border Elements.** Description of material components of the covered IDI's structure that are based or located outside the United States, including foreign branches, subsidiaries, and offices. The IDI resolution plan must provide detail on the location and amount of foreign deposits and assets, discuss the nature and extent of the covered IDI's cross-border assets, operations, interrelationships, and exposures, and map to legal entities and core business lines.

f. Confidential Treatment

Similar to the Title I regulation, the IDI Rule provides that an IDI resolution plan must be divided into public and confidential sections.[176] The public section consists of an executive summary of the IDI resolution plan that describes the business of the covered IDI and includes certain specified information. To the extent material to an understanding of the covered IDI, the public section must include[177]:

175 Id. § 360.10(c)(2)(ii).
176 See id. § 360.10(f)(1).
177 Id.

- The names of a covered IDI's material entities;
- A description of the covered IDI's core business lines;
- Consolidated financial information regarding assets, liabilities, capital, and major funding sources;
- A description of derivative activities and hedging activities;
- A list of memberships in material payment, clearing and settlement systems;
- A description of foreign operations;
- The identities of material supervisory authorities;
- The identities of the covered IDI's principal officers;
- A description of the corporate governance structure and processes related to resolution planning;
- A description of material management information systems; and
- A description, at a high level, of the covered IDI's resolution strategy, covering such items as the range of potential purchasers of the covered IDI, its material entities and core business lines.

The public sections of the IDI resolution plans of the Round 1 and Round 1.5 filers are available on the FDIC's website.[178] Some filers submitted standalone public sections for their covered IDIs, while others submitted a single public section in satisfaction of both the IDI Rule and Title I resolution planning requirements.

C. Title II Plans

As noted above, the FDIC has announced that it is preparing its own resolution plans for systemically important bank holding companies under Title II of the Dodd-Frank Act.[179] Other than very broad announcements, however, the FDIC has disclosed very little about the details of its plans for specific institutions or groups of institutions. FDIC Chairman Martin Gruenberg has announced that the FDIC's preferred strategy for resolving the largest and most complex banking groups under Title II is the single-point-of-entry (**"SPOE"**) recapitalization strat-

178 FDIC, Title I and IDI Resolution Plans, http://www.fdic.gov/regulations/reform/resplans/index.html.

179 Video: FDIC Systemic Resolution Advisory Committee Meeting, Panel on Title II Orderly Liquidation Authority (Dec. 10, 2010), available at http://www.vodium.com/MediapodLibrary/index.asp?library=pn100472_fdic_SRAC. Presentation slides from the meeting are available at http://www.fdic.gov/about/srac/2012/2012-12-10_title-ii_orderly-liquidation-authority.pdf.

egy.[180] The FDIC has also issued a joint paper with the Bank of England endorsing the SPOE strategy for resolving G-SIFIs,[181] and Chairman Gruenberg and Paul Tucker, the Deputy Governor, Financial Stability, at the Bank of England, published an editorial in the *Financial Times* lauding the virtues of the SPOE recapitalization model for resolving G-SIFIs without a taxpayer-funded bailout.[182] The FDIC has also indicated that it intends to propose a policy statement or regulation later this year describing in more detail how it would use its authority under Title II to resolve a covered financial company under the SPOE model.[183]

Under the SPOE model, only the parent bank holding company of a banking group would be put into a resolution proceeding. All of the parent's assets, including its ownership interests in operating subsidiaries, would be transferred to a bridge financial company. The transferred business would be recapitalized by leaving the failed company's equity capital and a sufficient amount of its unsecured long-term debt behind in a receivership. The operating subsidiaries would be recapitalized and kept out of insolvency proceedings by converting loans or other extensions of credit from the parent into new equity in the operating subsidiaries or otherwise down-streaming available parent assets to the subsidiaries. If the bridge financial holding company or any of its operating subsidiaries were unable to obtain sufficient liquidity from the market, the Federal Reserve's discount window,[184]

---

180 *Martin J. Gruenberg*, Acting Chairman, FDIC, Remarks to the Federal Reserve Bank of Chicago Bank Structure Conference (May 10, 2012), available at http://www.fdic.gov/news/news/speeches/chairman/spmay1012.html.

181 Resolving Globally Active, Systemically Important, Financial Institutions: A joint paper by the Federal Insurance Deposit Corporation and the Bank of England (Dec. 10, 2012), available at http://www.fdic.gov/about/srac/2012/gsifi.pdf.

182 *Martin Gruenberg & Paul Tucker*, Op-Ed., Global Banks Need Global Solutions When They Fail, Financial Times, Dec. 10, 2012.

183 For example, *James Wigand*, Director of the FDIC's Office of Complex Financial Institutions, mentioned the possibility of such a policy statement as part of a panel discussion in December 2012. Video: Banking Law Institute 2012, Panel on Systemic Risk - the Challenge of Systemically Important Financial Institutions (SIFIs), Living Wills and Orderly Liquidation Issues (Practicing Law Institute program Dec. 19, 2012), available at http://www.pli.edu/Content/OnDemand/Banking_Law_Institute_2012/_/N-4nZ1z12whl?fromsearch=false&ID=144553 ("[E]ngaging in small discussions is helpful, but we need obviously broader outreach. And one way to do that is to either issue a policy statement or perhaps a rule, and we're considering doing that. It's something that we haven't made an explicit decision on, but we do think that some mechanism such as that – a policy statement, for example, that would be issued for comment – would be helpful because it would engage a broader market in understanding what that presumptive path would be in looking at the application of the Title II authority.").

184 U.S. depository institutions have the right to borrow from the Federal Reserve's discount window as long as they are in generally sound financial condition and pledge collateral that is

or Section 13(3) of the Federal Reserve Act,[185] the FDIC could provide such liquidity by borrowing from the U.S. Treasury subject to certain limits contained in Title II of Dodd-Frank.[186]

The SPOE model provides a structural solution to at least three of the most important impediments that would otherwise apply to the successful resolution of a U.S. G-SIFI. First, by forcing a group's losses up to a parent holding company's creditors and equity holders, the SPOE model is able to keep the group's bank and other operating company subsidiaries out of resolution proceedings. This avoids the need to obtain foreign counterparty or judicial consents for transfers of assets made over resolution weekend, which might otherwise be impossible to obtain

satisfactory to the Federal Reserve and subject to the relevant haircuts established by the Federal Reserve. The main statutory provisions authorizing and governing discount window borrowing by depository institutions are in Sections 10B, 13 and 19(7) of the Federal Reserve Act, 12 United States Code §§ 347b (Section 10B); 342–347 and 372 (Section 13); 461(b) (Section 19(7)). The implementing regulations are contained in 12 U.S. Code of Federal Regulations Part 201, especially §§ 201.3(a) (general authority); 201.4(a) (primary credit); 201.4(b) (secondary credit); 201.4(c) (seasonal credit). See also Federal Reserve Banks Operating Circular 10 – Lending (Effective October 15, 2006); Federal Reserve Banks Operating Circular 8 – Collateral (Effective December 12, 2011); The Federal Reserve Discount Window (July 21, 2010), available at http://www.frbdiscountwindow.org/discountwindowbook.cfm?hdrID=14&dtlID=43#eligibilityps; James A. Clouse, Recent Developments in Discount Window Policy, 80 Federal Reserve Bulletin 965 (Nov. 1994), available at http://www.federalreserve.gov/monetarypolicy/1194lead.pdf; Brian F. Madigan & William R. Nelson, Proposed Revisions to the Federal Reserve's Discount Window Lending Programs, 88 Federal Reserve Bulletin 313 (July 2002), available at http://www.federalreserve.gov/pubs/bulletin/2002/0702lead.pdf.

185 Section 13(3) of the Federal Reserve Act, 12 United States Code § 343, provides the Federal Reserve with authority to extend secured lender-of-last-resort liquidity to non-depository institutions, including bank holding companies, broker-dealers and insurance companies, if the Federal Reserve determines that "unusual and exigent" circumstances exist. Section 1101 of the Dodd-Frank Act amended Section 13(3) to limit this authority to liquidity provided as part of a "program or facility with broad-based eligibility." Dodd-Frank Act, U.S. Public Law No. 111-203, § 1101(a), 124 U.S. Statutes at Large 1375, 2113–15 (2010). See also 12 U.S. Code of Federal Regulations § 201.4(d).

186 Dodd-Frank Act, U.S. Public Law No. 111-203, § 210(n), 124 U.S. Statutes at Large 1375, 1506–09 (2010) (orderly liquidation fund, which refers to borrowing by the FDIC from the U.S. Treasury for purposes of Title II). Section 210(n)(6) of the Dodd-Frank Act limits the exposure that the FDIC may incur on loans or guarantees made to a covered company in receivership under Title II to 10% of the book value of the covered company's total consolidated assets for up to 30 days after being put in receivership and to 90% of the fair value of the company's total assets "available for repayment" after that 30-day period (or earlier if the assets have been revalued by the FDIC in less than 30 days). See also 77 U.S. Federal Register 37554 (June 22, 2012) (final FDIC rule on calculation of its maximum obligation amount under Title II).

without multinational law reform, which could take decades to achieve if it were achievable at all. The cross-border operations of a U.S. G-SIFI are invariably at the subsidiary bank level, where foreign branches exist, and not at the holding company level. If a systemically important bank with foreign branches (**"G-SIB"**) were put into an FDIC receivership, and the FDIC attempted to resolve the G-SIB through a traditional purchase and assumption transaction or a recapitalization within resolution transaction involving the transfer of all or some of the bank's assets to a third party or a bridge bank, it would trigger these foreign counterparty and judicial consent requirements. No such consent requirements would arise, in contrast, when the assets of a bank holding company are transferred to a bridge holding company under Title II because bank holding companies do not have foreign branches. Such transfers would still require foreign regulatory approvals for any change in control of material foreign branches and subsidiaries, but such regulatory approvals would be far easier to obtain over a resolution weekend than counterparty or judicial consents for the transfer of assets.

Second, by putting only the parent bank holding company into receivership, and keeping the bank and other operating subsidiaries out of resolution or insolvency proceedings, the SPOE approach avoids triggering the right to terminate or close-out any derivative or other financial contracts as a result of the resolution or failure of the contracting party. Financial contracts entered into by U.S. G-SIFIs are virtually always entered into at the subsidiary bank or other operating subsidiary level, and not at the level of the parent bank holding company. In addition, to the extent such contracts are guaranteed by the parent holding company or contain cross-defaults to the receivership or failure of the parent holding company, Title II of the Dodd-Frank Act purports to override such rights that arise as a result of the parent holding company being put into a Title II receivership.[187] Of course, a combination of the SPOE model and Title II is not a complete solution to the cross-default problem because Title II does not apply extraterritorially. As a result, it cannot stop foreign counterparties from exercising their termination rights under contracts with respect to property outside the United States, at least if the contracts are governed by non-U.S. law. A proposed solution to the remaining cross-default problem is discussed in Section IV below.

Third, by structurally subordinating unsecured debt at the bank holding company level to unsecured debt at the bank and other operating subsidiary level and providing a mechanism for holding company-level assets to be down-streamed to recapitalize the bank and other operating subsidiaries, the SPOE model reduces

187 Dodd-Frank Act, U.S. Public Law No. 111-203, § 210(c)(16), 124 U.S. Statutes at Large 1375, 1493–94 (2010); see also 12 U.S. Code of Federal Regulations § 380.12.

or eliminates the incentive of short-term creditors at the operating company level to run when a banking group fails. It also reduces or eliminates the risk of contagion throughout the financial system. The reason is that most of the unsecured long-term debt issued by U.S. SIFIs is held at the parent bank holding company level, and most of their unsecured short-term debt is held at the bank or other operating subsidiary level.[188] Indeed, many U.S. G-SIFIs have already reduced the amount of short-term debt that they have outstanding at the holding company level to improve their liquidity ratios, and the SPOE model creates a further incentive to move all short-term debt to the operating subsidiary level.[189] In addition, most U.S. G-SIFIs already have enough long-term unsecured debt so that they could be fully recapitalized at Basel III levels after suffering losses that wipe out all of their tangible common equity at levels equal to the fully effective Basel III requirements, including applicable buffers.[190] This structural subordination effectively turns long-term unsecured debt at the holding company level into a loss-absorbing shield for short-term and other unsecured debt at the operating subsidiary level, greatly reducing or eliminating the incentive of short-term creditors to run during a financial crisis. It also does so without creating moral hazard by providing a clear structural priority rule in advance. With such clarity, the market will price each class of debt efficiently, forcing the short-term creditors to internalize the costs of their structural priority in the form of lower interest rates.

The Federal Reserve Board has indicated that it is likely to propose minimum long-term unsecured debt requirements for certain U.S. bank holding companies in order to ensure that they have sufficient loss-absorbing capacity to make the SPOE recapitalization method a viable one.[191] The proposal may also include minimum unconsolidated asset requirements at the holding company level, including intercompany loans, that could be contributed to operating subsidiar-

188 See, e.g., The Clearing House Association, Report on the Orderly Liquidation Authority Resolution Symposium and Simulation, p. 10 (Jan. 2013), available at http://www.theclearinghouse.org/index.html?f=074709.

189 See The Clearing House Association, Banking Brief White Paper Series, Ending "Too Big to Fail": Title II of the Dodd-Frank Act and the Approach of "Single-Point-of-Entry" Private Sector Recapitalization of a Failed Financial Company, pp. 6–9 (Jan. 2013), available at http://www.theclearinghouse.org/index.html?f=074717.

190 See, e.g., Goldman Sachs Investment Banking Division, FDIC Orderly Liquidation Authority and Bail-in (Nov. 2012); J.P. Morgan North America Credit Research, Tarullo Speech Increases Momentum for Debt Buffers (Dec. 6, 2012).

191 *Daniel K. Tarullo*, Governor, Board of Governors of the Federal Reserve System, Industry Structure and Systemic Risk Regulation, Speech at the Brookings Institution Conference on Structuring the Financial Industry to Enhance Economic Growth and Stability (Dec. 4, 2012), available at http://www.federalreserve.gov/newsevents/speech/tarullo20121204a.htm.

ies to recapitalize them in an SPOE receivership. Such a proposal could be issued for public notice and comment as early as the first quarter of 2013. This new mandate would supplement Basel capital requirements.

Perhaps the most detailed disclosure about the FDIC's Title II planning process was provided in a December 2012 presentation by John Simonson, Deputy Director of the FDIC's Office of Complex Financial Institutions, to the FDIC's Systemic Resolution Advisory Committee ("**SRAC**").[192] In that public presentation, Mr. Simonson disclosed that the FDIC had developed Title II resolution plans for each of the top five U.S. G-SIFIs.[193] In those plans, the FDIC applied its SPOE recapitalization strategy to each of these institutions in order to "gain comfort that [they] could in fact implement such resolution if necessary."[194] According to Simonson, the FDIC has shared summaries of those plans and apparent simulations "with some domestic and international regulators."[195] Judging by the Bank of England's willingness to issue a joint paper with the FDIC endorsing the SPOE recapitalization model and the urgency with which the Federal Reserve is considering a proposal for new long-term debt requirements to ensure the feasibility of the SPOE recapitalization strategy, the FDIC's plans and apparent simulations under Title II must have been convincing. Simonson said that the FDIC is now developing similar Title II plans for "the next group of SIFIs which includes processing and custody banks, what could be termed as large regionals, as well as foreign banking organizations."[196]

It may be possible to infer certain additional characteristics about the FDIC's Title II planning process from a simulation of the resolution of a G-SIFI under Title II that was conducted by The Clearing House Association (the "**TCH Simulation**") in early November 2012.[197] The TCH Simulation applied the FDIC's SPOE recapitalization strategy to the resolution of a hypothetical U.S. SIFI that had a large U.S. bank subsidiary with foreign branches and a large U.K. broker-dealer subsidiary. The G-SIFI was put into a Title II receivership because of a run on its

---

192 Video: FDIC Systemic Resolution Advisory Committee Meeting, Panel on Title II Orderly Liquidation Authority (Dec. 10, 2010), available at http://www.vodium.com/MediapodLibrary/index.asp?library=pn100472_fdic_SRAC. Presentation slides from the meeting are available at http://www.fdic.gov/about/srac/2012/2012-12-10_title-ii_orderly-liquidation-authority.pdf.
193 Id.
194 Id.
195 Id.
196 Id.
197 See The Clearing House Association, Report on the Orderly Liquidation Authority Resolution Symposium and Simulation (Jan. 2013), available at http://www.theclearinghouse.org/index.html?f=074709.

commercial paper and the short-term liabilities of its U.S. bank and U.K. broker-dealer subsidiaries. The run arose because of substantial losses incurred in both subsidiaries and market uncertainty about the true value of the group's assets and its liquidity position. A determination was made by the hypothetical Secretary of the Treasury to invoke Title II because the failure of the hypothetical G-SIFI would create a substantial risk of destabilizing the U.S. financial system if it were allowed to be resolved under the U.S. Bankruptcy Code and the other conditions for invoking Title II were satisfied.[198]

The report of the simulation issued by TCH concluded that the simulation was successful,[199] and TCH contemporaneously issued a white paper explaining in more detail why the SPOE model would end "too big to fail" if certain conditions are satisfied.[200] The report of the TCH Simulation includes a list of lessons learned from this simulation,[201] many of which are important. But perhaps the most important lesson was that short-term creditors are likely to immediately panic and run, and foreign regulators are likely to immediately ring-fence foreign operations, in the absence of a clearly articulated, pre-existing "presumptive path" of how the FDIC will use its authority under Title II to resolve a particular SIFI, as well as general public confidence that claims on long-term debt will be structurally or legally subordinated to claims on short-term debt. As a result, it is crucial that the FDIC and regulators around the world develop and disclose "presumptive paths" for how they will use their resolution powers, as well as methods to ensure that long-term debt is structurally or legally subordinated to short-term debt, with the line between long-term and short-term debt drawn at an original or remaining maturity of at least six months to one year.

---

198 Dodd-Frank Act, U.S. Public Law No. 111-203, § 203(b), 124 U.S. Statutes at Large at 1375, 1451 (2010).

199 The Clearing House Association, Report on the Orderly Liquidation Authority Resolution Symposium and Simulation, p. 6 (Jan. 2013), available at http://www.theclearinghouse.org/index.html?f=074709.

200 The Clearing House Association, Banking Brief White Paper Series, Ending "Too Big to Fail": Title II of the Dodd-Frank Act and the Approach of "Single-Point-of-Entry" Private Sector Recapitalization of a Failed Financial Company (Jan. 2013), available at http://www.theclearinghouse.org/index.html?f=074717.

201 See The Clearing House Association, Report on the Orderly Liquidation Authority Resolution Symposium and Simulation, pp. 7–15 (Jan. 2013), available at http://www.theclearinghouse.org/index.html?f=074709.

Indeed, the principal criticism leveled against Title II, including calls for its repeal[202] and challenges to its validity under the U.S. Constitution,[203] arise from the broad discretion it gives to the FDIC, the lack of predictability that arises from that discretion, and alleged lack of adequate due process safeguards for creditors and other stakeholders.[204] While the FDIC has the discretionary power under Title II to resolve a G-SIFI using the SPOE recapitalization model, nothing in Title II or its regulations or official policies compels it to do so or even creates a reliable presumption that it will do so. Even some of the supporters of Title II admit that these criticisms have some legitimacy, and argue that statutory amendments, regulations or policy statements are needed to constrain the FDIC's discretion, improve legal certainty and predictability,[205] and provide better due process safeguards for creditors and other stakeholders so that the FDIC's discretion under Title II cannot be abused in a manner that results in a sort of regulatory Court of Star Chamber.[206]

The critics have been particularly focused on the FDIC's broad discretion under Title II to discriminate among creditors within the same class,[207] as long as all creditors receive at least what they would have received in a liquidation of

---

202 See, e.g., *Jeb Hensarling*, Op-Ed., Dodd-Frank's Unhappy Anniversary, Wall Street Journal, July 25, 2012 (characterizing Title II as a "taxpayer-funded safety net for institutions deemed too big to fail," and calling for its repeal), available at http://online.wsj.com/article/SB10000872396390443437504577547320318621132.html.

203 See State National Bank of Big Spring v. Geithner, Case No. 1:12-cv-01032, First Amended Complaint, pp. 35–41, 48–54 (U.S. District Court for the District of Columbia, Sept. 20, 2012).

204 See, e.g., *James H. M. Sprayregon & Stephen E. Hessler*, Too Much Discretion to Succeed: Why a Modified Bankruptcy Code is Preferable to Title II of the Dodd-Frank Act (June 7, 2011), available at http://www.federalreserve.gov/SECRS/2011/June/20110607/OP-1418/OP-1418_053111_80002_310357154312_1.pdf; John B. Taylor, Preface, in Bankruptcy Not Bailout, p. x (2012); Kenneth E. Scott, A Guide to Resolution of Failed Financial Institutions: Dodd-Frank Title II and Proposed Chapter 14, in Bankruptcy Not Bailout, pp. 7–9, 11–12, 22 (2012); *David Skeel*, The New Financial Deal: Understanding the Dodd-Frank Act and Its (Unintended) Consequences, Chapters 7–8 (2011) (arguing that Title II and the bank resolution provisions on which it is modeled give the FDIC nearly unfettered discretion).

205 Global Financial Markets Association, Comment Letter to the Financial Stability Board on the Consultative Document, Recovery and Resolution Planning: Making the Key Attributes Requirements Operational (Dec. 7, 2012), available at http://www.gfma.org/correspondence/item.aspx?id=386.

206 See, e.g., *Randall D. Guynn*, Are Bailouts Inevitable?, 29 Yale Journal on Regulation 121, 152–154 (2012).

207 *Kenneth E. Scott*, A Guide to Resolution of Failed Financial Institutions: Dodd-Frank Title II and Proposed Chapter 14, in Bankruptcy Not Bailout, pp. 17–19 (2012).

the company under Chapter 7 of the U.S. Bankruptcy Code.[208] One critic argues that this type of open-ended discretion to discriminate among creditors within the same class will result in a type of bailout even if taxpayer money is not used because it will result in a subsidy or bailout of the favored class of creditors by the disfavored class, creating the same type of moral hazard as a taxpayer-funded bailout.[209] Since the main purpose of the discretion to treat similarly situated creditors differently is to permit the FDIC to discriminate in favor of short-term unsecured claims during a financial panic in order to reduce the risk of runs and contagion at other financial institutions, one way to address this criticism would be to replace the FDIC's open-ended discretion in Title II with a priority rule that clearly subordinates long-term unsecured debt to short-term unsecured debt. Another way is to make it clear that enough long-term unsecured debt is structurally subordinated to short-term unsecured debt, as is done in the SPOE recapitalization model.

The structural or legal subordination of long-term unsecured debt to short-term unsecured debt can be justified on the grounds that creditors holding these two types of claims are not similarly situated during a financial panic. Short-term creditors have negotiated and paid for the legal and practical right to run during a financial crisis by accepting a lower interest rate than would be available on long-term debt, and they can and will run unless their claims are treated as structurally or legally senior to long-term debt. In contrast, long-term creditors have not negotiated or paid for the right to run during a financial crisis and cannot do so, and they have arguably been compensated for this higher risk by receiving a higher interest rate than short-term debt. Moreover, as long as this structural or legal priority scheme is known to the market in advance, the market should price each class of debt efficiently so that short-term and long-term creditors fully internalize all of the costs and benefits of this priority scheme. This should eliminate any alleged subsidy or bailout of the short-term creditors by the long-term creditors.

208 Dodd-Frank Act, U.S. Public Law No. 111-203, § 210(b)(4), (d)(2), 124 U.S. Statutes at Large 1375, 1476–77, 1494 (2010).

209 *Kenneth E. Scott*, A Guide to Resolution of Failed Financial Institutions: Dodd-Frank Title II and Proposed Chapter 14, in Bankruptcy Not Bailout, pp. 17–19 (2012).

D. Comparison of U.S. Resolution Plans to Non-U.S. Resolution Plans

The resolution plans required under Title I of the Dodd-Frank Act and the FDIC's IDI Rule are substantially different from the resolution requirements currently imposed by non-U.S. jurisdictions. It appears that the FDIC and the Federal Reserve are the only regulators that currently require any financial institutions to submit comprehensive resolution plans that contain both resolution strategies and information and data. To the extent non-U.S. regulators require financial institutions to submit resolution plans, it appears that they only require the institutions to provide information and data on which the regulators can develop their own resolution strategies.[210] It also appears that non-U.S. regulators have not disclosed the resolution plans they have prepared for particular institutions, either to the institutions themselves or the broader market. As a result it will be difficult for foreign banking organizations to satisfy the requirement in the Title I regulation to show how the resolution strategies for their U.S. subsidiaries and operations fit into their group's overall resolution strategy, because in many instances the home-country regulators will not have required the group to prepare an overall resolution strategy or disclosed the regulator's strategy to the institution. Instead, the regulators will only have required financial institutions to collect and report to the regulators various types of information and data on which the regulators can build their own resolution plans, or to prepare recovery (as opposed to resolution) plans.

III. Lessons Learned

As noted above, the Round 1 and 1.5 filers have now filed their Title I and IDI resolution plans, and the public portions of those plans have been posted on the FDIC's and the Federal Reserve's websites. Based on advising a number of the

---

210 See, e.g., U.K. Financial Services Authority, RRP Information Pack, Supplement to FS12/1 (May 2012), available at http://www.fsa.gov.uk/pubs/discussion/fs12-01-info-pack.pdf (outlining U.K. requirements for firms to develop recovery plans and a "resolution pack" of information); see also Financial Stability Board, Key Attributes of Effective Resolution Regimes for Financial Institutions, Annex III, paragraphs 1.6, 1.9 (Oct. 2011), available at http://www.financialstability-board.org/publications/r_111104cc.pdf (stating that responsibility for developing and maintaining a recovery plan lies with a firm's senior management, while responsibility for developing and maintaining a resolution plan lies with the authorities).

Round 1 and 1.5 filers on their resolution plans, and based on the public portions of their plans, a number of lessons can be drawn from this process. At the same time, these lessons should be drawn carefully in light of the fact that the business models and legal structures of many financial institutions that have not yet filed an initial plan are somewhat to very different from those of the initial filers. Any lessons learned from the initial filers should also be tempered by the fact that the standard format for the living wills that the regulators required the initial filers to use may change for subsequent filers, as has already been the case for the first annual updates for Round 1 and Round 1.5 Filers as discussed in the April 2013 guidelines referred to in footnote 17 above. With that in mind, the following are some of the key lessons from the initial filers based on what was known immediately after their public filings.

- **The Regulators Are Still in Learning Mode and Standards Are Still Evolving.** Resolution planning is as new to the regulators as it is to the banking sector, and many staff at different levels of both the Federal Reserve and the FDIC are involved. In addition, for some banking institutions, international regulators are also part of the discussion. Subsequent filers are likely to benefit from the regulators' increased experience, including improvements in the standardized format for filing that was required of the initial filers, as well as increased consistency in the messages about expectations.
- **Resolution Planning Will Continue to Evolve After the Initial Submissions.** Resolution planning will take more than one year to fully develop. As noted in the public portions of the resolution plans filed to date, the regulators provided a number of baseline assumptions to the initial filers, including:
  - No exercise of their recovery plan;
  - An idiosyncratic scenario specific to the banking institution that does not affect the global financial markets generally;
  - The baseline stress assumptions from the Federal Reserve's CCAR stress tests;
  - All material entities have failed; and
  - No reliance on extraordinary government support.

  In future years, Title I plans will be required to address all three of the scenarios provided in the Federal Reserve's CCAR stress-testing process, namely "baseline," "adverse" and "severely adverse." In addition, the regulators have relaxed some of the mandatory assumptions for the first annual updates of the Round 1 and Round 1.5 Filers as discussed in the April 2013 guidelines referred to in footnote 17 above. This expectation of different assumptions in later years means that senior management will need to look ahead to how different resolution plan strategies might fare in a more stressed environment and possibly adjust resolution planning accordingly.

- **No Credibility Reviews of Initial Plans.** The Federal Reserve and the FDIC indicated that they did not expect to perform credibility reviews of initial resolution plans, but instead expected to reserve credibility reviews for future updates.
- **Initial Assumptions Not Realistic.** The assumptions for the initial plans, especially the assumption that all material entities fail, were not realistic, but were designed to force the initial filers to identify as many of the potential impediments to resolution as possible.
- **Resolution Planning is Driven by Legal Entity Not Business Units.** Banking institutions are business lines in life but are legal entities at death. This fundamental mismatch between the most efficient way to manage a business and create shareholder value and the most efficient way to resolve it at the point of non-viability requires a temporary paradigm shift by business leaders. It is best to develop a preliminary top-down resolution strategy first by focusing both on how systemic risk can be minimized and how the value of the business lines can be preserved in a resolution that occurs on a legal entity basis. This requires, as a first step, that core business lines, critical operations, critical services and shared services be mapped to legal entities. The second step is to map each material legal entity to its applicable insolvency regime and to evaluate the interactions of the legal regimes and other resolution processes as well as major impediments by considering the fate of the core business lines, critical operations, critical services and shared services on a legal entity basis. Firms need to prepare for some surprises in the interconnections and interdependencies among legal entities. These unexpected interconnections and interdependencies will reveal the risks of what might be cut off during a resolution proceeding.
- **Create a Preliminary Top-down Strategy First and Then Create the Focused Data Gathering Plan.** Resolution planning is data heavy, and the FDIC and Federal Reserve regulations require a rich array of data. This data will have to be gathered, be evaluated and be reliable not only every year but also after a material change in the banking institution. Most of the initial filers found that it was more efficient for a banking institution to first develop a well-defined top-down resolution strategy on a preliminary basis before beginning the data-gathering process. That strategy can later be changed if the data provides a different picture than expected. Without an initial overarching strategy, however, there is a risk of expensive back-tracking or the gathering of data that is neither relevant nor useful. The data-gathering plan

during the first year should create processes that are repeatable and that can become systems-driven in later years.

- **Internal Education and Buy-in at an Early Stage Makes for a Less Intrusive and More Efficient Process.** Key people in the business units should be educated about the objectives of resolution planning and the entity-by-entity nature of the process before being asked to provide input. This means that some initial education, including senior business manager involvement from the critical business units and demonstrated support from top corporate management, will save time and make the process for creating the resolution plan much more efficient in the long run.
- **There Are a Finite Number of Resolution Strategies.** There are only a limited number of resolution strategies. As included in the public portions and discussed publicly by the regulators, they include:
  - The sale of assets and business lines, either before a bankruptcy proceeding or under the supervision of the bankruptcy court;
  - The recapitalization of the insured depository institution outside of an FDIC receivership;
  - The purchase and assumption of some or all of the assets and liabilities by a third party buyer out of an FDIC receivership;
  - The creation of a bridge bank for the insured depository institution followed by a sale or public offering, or a recapitalization of the bridge through a conversion of debt for equity; and
  - An orderly wind-down.[211]
- **There are Many Ways to Mix and Match Resolution Strategies Among the Bank and Non-bank Affiliates.** The art, and the challenge, for a credible resolution plan is in finding the right mix and match of available resolution strategies among the bank and non-bank affiliates. To accomplish this, an understanding of both bank resolution and bankruptcy laws is essential. For example:

211 In addition, at least for Round 1 and Round 1.5 Filers a single-point-of-entry or a partial multiple-point-of-entry reorganization strategy might be possible under Chapter 11 of the U.S. Bankruptcy Code since the Federal Reserve and the FDIC have relaxed the unrealistic assumption mandated for the initial plans that all material entities must fail. See footnote 17 above. Such a strategy would involve putting the parent holding company into a Chapter 11 bankruptcy proceeding, transferring its assets and certain liabilities including interests in subsidiaries to a newly formed holding company pursuant to Section 363 of the Bankruptcy Code, and keeping the operating subsidiaries out of resolution, bankruptcy or other insolvency proceedings as in the FDIC's SPOE recapitalization model under Title II.

- At what point does the publicly-listed holding company or service company enter a Chapter 11 proceeding?
- If there is a runway period leading up to the Chapter 11 proceeding, what liquidity would be placed where among the non-bank affiliates?
- What other assumptions should be made in any runway period?
- Does it make sense to delay a proceeding for a broker-dealer under the Securities Investor Protection Act ("**SIPA**") or to start it at the same time as the Chapter 11 proceeding of its holding company parent?
- How should cross-defaults, cross-collateral and netting be treated?
- Should asset sales be made before bankruptcy or with the blessing of the bankruptcy court?
- How should international cooperation be modeled?
- Where are shared services, technology and intellectual property located and how can their continuity be assured?

The answers to these questions will vary widely among banking institutions based on differences in business models, legal entity structures and past business and legal decisions.

- **There Will Be Impediments, and the Resolution Plan Should Propose Some Solutions.** As banking institutions are developing their resolution plans and formulating their resolution strategies, it is helpful to also develop a list of potential actions that could be taken, either by the banking institution or the regulators, in the future to address impediments to resolution. Thinking about solutions signals to the regulators that the banking institution has taken the resolution planning process seriously and anticipates issues that the regulators are likely to identify, as well as provides the banking institution an opportunity to define the solution.
- **Tailored Plans for U.S. Regional Banking Institutions.** One key way in which the plans of the large U.S. regional banking institutions will differ from those of the initial filers is that many of the largest U.S. regional banking institutions will be able to use a tailored Title I plan with the result that the focus of their Title I plans will be on their nonbanking operations.[212]
- **Tailored Plans for Foreign Banking Organizations.** Foreign banking organizations with a relatively small U.S. footprint, should also be able to file tailored plans that focus mainly on their U.S. nonbanking operations.

212 For a description of the qualifications for submitting a tailored plan, see Section II.A.4.c above.

IV. The Road Ahead

The U.S. and non-U.S. G-SIFIs that filed their initial Title I and IDI plans are currently scheduled to file their first annual updated plans by the middle of 2013. The Round 2 and Round 3 filers are scheduled to file their initial plans by the middle or end of 2013. This Part IV attempts to anticipate and describe the road ahead.

A. Key Assumptions

The assumptions applicable to the ***initial*** plans will almost certainly continue to include the mandatory assumption that all material entities fail. They will also continue to include the permissible assumptions that the macroeconomic scenario is the "baseline" scenario provided by the Federal Reserve in the 2012 CCAR process and that the covered company's failure is idiosyncratic rather than part of a marketwide crisis.[213] In contrast, the regulators are likely to require the ***updated*** plans to address all three of the macroeconomic scenarios from the 2012 CCAR process – namely, the "baseline," "adverse" and "severely adverse" scenarios – and to require them to assume that the covered company's failure could occur during a marketwide crisis instead of being an idiosyncratic event.[214] As discussed in the April 2013 guidelines referred to in footnote 17 above, the regulators have now relaxed the mandatory assumption that all material entities fail for all plans other than the initial plans, in order to be more realistic and to permit covered companies to develop SPOE or partial multiple-point-of-entry recapitalization strategies under Chapter 11 of the U.S. Bankruptcy Code.

B. Evolution of Guidelines, Scrutiny and Consequences

The U.S. regulators will continue to be in learning mode, and their guidelines and expectations will probably continue to evolve over time as illustrated by the differences between their guidelines for the initial plans and their April 2013 guidelines for the first annual updated plans to be submitted by the Round 1 and Round 1.5 Filers, which are referred to in footnote 17 above. It is not clear when

---

213 See 12 C.F.R. § 243.4(a)(4)(i) (permitting initial resolution plan to assume baseline economic conditions only).

214 See id. (requiring annual resolution plan updates to take into account that failure may occur under baseline, adverse and severely adverse economic conditions).

the regulators will start subjecting the plans to credibility reviews or whether the FDIC and the Federal Reserve have agreed on when that scrutiny should begin. Perennial critics of U.S. G-SIFIs, including FDIC board member Thomas Hoenig and Federal Reserve Bank of Dallas president Richard Fisher, will continue to call for the break-up of the U.S. G-SIFIs,[215] almost certainly regardless of how resolvable their resolution plans show them to be. The increasing burden of new regulations will also continue to put downward pressure on the market value of the U.S. G-SIFIs, which could eventually result in shareholder pressure to downsize or restructure.

C. Cross-Defaults

The U.S. regulators will try to find a solution to the problem of cross-defaults, which arises when a group's financial contracts not only link termination rights to the failure of the direct counterparties, but also link them to the failure of certain affiliates. Such cross-defaults can be an impediment to a successful resolution in either a Title II or U.S. Bankruptcy Code proceeding. Title II purports to override any such rights that arise as a result of a parent holding company being put into a Title II receivership,[216] but Title II does not apply extraterritorially. As a result, it cannot stop foreign counterparties from exercising their termination rights under contracts with respect to property located outside the United States, at least under contracts governed by non-U.S. law. The regulators and the G-SIFIs are likely to focus on solving this problem through amendments to ISDA master agreements and other contracts that eliminate or limit these cross-default rights, or by requiring guarantees to be moved or cross-defaults to relate only to an intermediate holding company that is not put into receivership. Although this problem could be solved by international regulatory reform that overrides such cross-defaults, the U.S. regulators are unlikely to want to rely on such reform because it might take decades to achieve, if it is achievable at all.

215 See, e.g., *Thomas M. Hoenig*, Director, FDIC, Financial Stability Through Properly Aligned Incentives, Remarks to the Exchequer Club, Washington, D.C. (Sept. 19, 2012), available at http://www.fdic.gov/news/news/speeches/chairman/spsep1912.html; Richard W. Fisher, Introduction, in Financial Stability: Traditional Banks Pave the Way (Jan. 2013), available at http://www.dallasfed.org/microsites/fed/annual/2012/1201e.pdf. See also *Simon Johnson*, Op-Ed., Fed Should Push to Cut Biggest Banks Down to Size, Bloomberg, Oct. 14, 2012, available at http://www.bloomberg.com/news/2012-10-14/fed-should-push-to-cut-biggest-banks-down-to-size.html.
216 Dodd-Frank Act, U.S. Public Law No. 111-203, § 210(c)(16), 124 U.S. Statutes at Large 1375, 1493–94 (2010); see also 12 U.S. Code of Federal Regulations § 380.12.

D. Shared Services

The U.S. regulators are likely to encourage U.S. G-SIFIs to centralize their shared services in one or more U.S. bank subsidiaries or bankruptcy-remote companies. They will also likely encourage the SIFIs to make sure the shared service providers have the economic incentive to continue providing the services to the various members of the group, including any material entities in a resolution proceeding. This may involve amending service level agreements to make sure they work during both business-as-usual and resolution periods.

E. Private Sector Emergency Liquidity Facilities

The U.S. regulators may well try to persuade the U.S. financial industry to establish a large, private sector liquidity facility that could provide emergency secured liquidity to a well-capitalized bridge financial company (or its equivalent) in a resolution or reorganization proceeding under either Title II or the U.S. Bankruptcy Code. The FDIC could use its orderly liquidation fund authority under Title II to guarantee the obligations of the bridge financial company in a Title II proceeding.[217] The authority of any U.S. government agency to provide secured or unsecured credit or liquidity support would be much more limited in a bankruptcy proceeding.

F. Recognition of Foreign Resolution Proceedings

The U.S. and non-U.S. regulators will probably eventually decide that they need to strengthen international comity doctrines or amend the local laws that implement the United Nations Commission on International Trade Law's (UNCITRAL) Model Law on Cross-Border Insolvency, to make sure they apply to the local recognition of foreign resolution proceedings as well as foreign bankruptcy proceedings. In the U.S., that could involve amending Chapter 15 of the U.S. Bankruptcy Code[218] so that it expressly applies to resolution proceedings, including with respect to foreign banks that have branches or agencies in the United States.

217 See Dodd-Frank Act, U.S. Public Law No. 111-203, § 210(n), 124 U.S. Statutes at Large 1357, 1506–09 (2010).

218 11 United States Code § 1501 et seq. (incorporating UNCITRAL Model Law on Cross-Border Insolvency).

G. Single-Point-of-Entry under Chapter 11 of the U.S. Bankruptcy Code

The U.S. regulators are now encouraging the U.S. G-SIFIs to develop SPOE recapitalization strategies under Chapter 11 of the U.S. Bankruptcy Code and have relaxed the mandatory assumptions to facilitate such strategies as discussed in the April 2013 guidelines referred to in footnote 17. Such a strategy would involve creating a new company (**"Newco"**), and transferring all of the assets of a failed bank holding company, including its operating subsidiaries, to a Newco in a court-approved transfer under Section 363 of the U.S. Bankruptcy Code.[219] Newco would be held by an independent private trustee for the benefit of the bankruptcy estate. If appropriately structured, free assets at the banking holding company level, including intercompany loans to operating subsidiaries, could be contributed to the operating subsidiaries before the Chapter 11 filing to the extent necessary to recapitalize them. If the U.S. G-SIFIs were able to develop such SPOE strategies under the U.S. Bankruptcy Code, this would result in the Title I and Title II resolution planning process converging instead of proceeding down separate roads, which is largely the case at the present time.

H. Proposed New Chapter 14 of the U.S. Bankruptcy Code

Congress and the U.S. regulators may decide to amend the U.S. Bankruptcy Code to include a new Chapter 14 that is designed specifically for the reorganization of U.S. SIFIs, including possibly making the SPOE recapitalization model more feasible under the U.S. Bankruptcy Code if there are impediments under existing Chapter 11. This new chapter, if enacted, would likely be used as a supplement to Title II rather than as a substitute for it. If properly designed, such a new Chapter 14 could limit the need to invoke Title II to a smaller set of the most extreme cases. Professor Thomas Jackson has already proposed such a new Chapter 14.[220] It could be used as a starting point for such legislation.

219 See id. § 363 (use, sale or lease of property of a bankruptcy estate).

220 See *Thomas H. Jackson*, Bankruptcy Code Chapter 14: A Proposal, in Bankruptcy Not Bailout 25 (2012).

I. Policy Statement

The FDIC will likely issue for public notice and comment a proposed policy statement or regulation that will attempt to provide more legal certainty and predictably to the market about how it will exercise its authority under Title II. The policy statement is likely to focus on fleshing out the details of its SPOE recapitalization strategy. While the timing of any such proposal is uncertain, it is likely to be issued sometime this year.

J. Minimum Debt Requirement

The Federal Reserve is likely to issue for public notice and comment a proposed minimum long-term unsecured debt requirement applicable to the U.S. G-SIFIs and certain other large U.S. bank holding companies. The purpose of this new requirement is to make sure large U.S. bank holding companies have enough loss-absorbing capacity to make the SPOE recapitalization strategy feasible. The Federal Reserve is likely to issue such a proposal in the first half of this year.

K. Repeal, Invalidation or Amendments to Title II

Jeb Hebsarling, the Chairman of the House Financial Services Committee, is on record calling for the repeal of Title II.[221] Certain state pension funds are also seeking to have Title II, or certain portions of it, invalidated as inconsistent with the U.S. Constitution.[222] These efforts are unlikely to result in the repeal or invalidation of Title II, but they could result in amendments to Title II designed to reduce the FDIC's discretion, increase legal certainty and predictability, and strengthen due process safeguards. These amendments could be considered in the context of adding a new Chapter 14 to the U.S. Bankruptcy Code or separately as part of an overall set of technical corrections to the Dodd-Frank Act.

---

221 See, e.g., *Jeb Hensarling*, Op-Ed., Dodd-Frank's Unhappy Anniversary, Wall Street Journal, July 25, 2012 (characterizing Title II as a "taxpayer-funded safety net for institutions deemed too big to fail," and calling for its repeal), available at http://online.wsj.com/article/SB10000872396390443437504577547320318621132.html.

222 See State National Bank of Big Spring v. Geithner, Case No. 1:12-cv-01032, First Amended Complaint, pp. 35–41, 48–54 (U.S. District Court for the District of Columbia, Sept. 20, 2012).

V. Conclusion

The resolution planning process has developed rapidly in the United States, but it is still in the process of developing. It is similar to the resolution planning processes in other countries in that it requires covered companies to provide information and data to the regulators to support regulator-prepared resolution plans. But in addition to providing such information and data to the regulators, U.S. banking groups are required to develop resolution strategies under the U.S. Bankruptcy Code and other applicable insolvency laws. For the time being, the Title I and Title II resolution planning processes are running down separate paths, but the U.S. regulators are taking steps to encourage the two paths to converge and be more supportive of each other.

Bail-ins – the Problematic Tool

Thomas F. Huertas*

The Case for Bail-ins

The case for bail-ins is simple. Bail-ins are superior to bail-outs, and bail-ins are superior to insolvency and liquidation. Bail-ins are potentially a powerful resolution tool, that can help make banks, even the largest and most complex banks, 'safe to fail'. Bail-ins can potentially help assure that investors, not taxpayers, bear the cost of bank failure. And bail-ins can materially help reduce both the social cost and the disruption to markets that insolvency and liquidation could cause. So bail-ins deserve a place in the resolution tool kit that should be at authorities' disposal, if a bank fails to meet threshold conditions and needs to be resolved. But for bail-ins to be effective, they will need to be combined with other tools, and both banks and authorities will need to take preparatory measures.

Bail-ins are superior to bail-outs

Too big to fail is too costly to continue. Bail-outs strain the public finances.[1] Bail-outs distort competition. Bail-outs undermine market discipline. Bail-outs are therefore not an option.

Accordingly, G-20 leaders asked the Financial Stability Board[2] to develop a policy framework that would "address the systemic and moral hazard risks associated with systemically important financial institutions (SIFIs)". One of the cornerstones of this policy framework is to develop a resolution regime that would make banks, including SIFIs, 'safe to fail' in the sense that they could be resolved without taxpayer support to the bank's solvency and without causing significant

---

* A preliminary version was presented in May 2012 at a conference at the Institute of Law and Finance, Johann Wolfgang von Goethe University, Frankfurt. The opinions expressed here are those of the author and do not necessarily represent the position of Ernst & Young.

1 As *Tucker* (2012) writes "if the risk of banking is not incorporated into the yields of bonds issued by the banks themselves, then it will be reflected in higher sovereign borrowing costs." In this regard Ireland is Exhibit A. In 2008 it bailed out its banks by guaranteeing banks' liabilities (including bonds issued by the banks). This caused the government budget deficit to soar and sovereign debt to rise to the point where Ireland had to seek restructuring assistance from the EU and the IMF.

2 FSB 2011a

disruption to the financial system.[3] In October 2011 the Financial Stability Board set out the key attributes for such a resolution framework. This included a recommendation that countries establish special resolution regimes for banks and that such resolution regimes include bail-in as one of the stabilisation options available to the resolution authority.[4] The EU Commission has followed the recommendation of the FSB, and its proposed Crisis Management Directive (EC 2012) has included bail-in as one of the tools that resolution authorities should have at their disposal, so that investors, not taxpayers, can pay for bank failures. In the United States, the FDIC is developing proposals for resolution under its Orderly Liquidation Authority that envision what amounts to bail-in of investors at a bank's parent holding company (Gruenberg, 2012).

Bail-ins are superior to liquidation

Bankruptcy doesn't work for banks. The very essence of banking is making commitments to pay – depositors at maturity, sellers of securities due to settle, borrowers who wish to draw on lending commitments, derivative counterparties who contracted with the financial institution for protection from interest rate, exchange rate or credit risks. Putting a stay on payments to such creditors is equivalent to stopping the institution's operating business. Unlike airlines, retailers or automobile companies, banks cannot readily operate in bankruptcy. So bankruptcy for a bank is tantamount to liquidation.[5]

But liquidation destroys value. It diminishes the recovery that creditors can make. More importantly, liquidation increases contagion and assures that stress will spread from the failed institution to financial markets and to the economy as a whole. These effects are particularly grave, if the institution is large and/or complex. Indeed, avoiding such immediately adverse systemic effects is the principal reason that authorities have decided in the past to bail out systemic institutions.[6]

---

3 Other elements of the policy framework include requirements for resolvability assessments, for recovery and resolution plans, for increased capital (the so-called SIFI surcharge) and for more intensive supervision of SIFIs. For details see (FSB 2011a). For a general discussion of the issues relating to resolution see (Huertas 2011a), (International Institute of Finance, 2012) and (Randell, 2012).

4 FSB 2011b

5 *Huertas* 2011a

6 FSB 2011a; *Guynn* 2012, pp. 123–4

Bail-ins promise to be superior to liquidation. Essentially, they amount to a pre-pack recapitalisation of the bank that the authorities can invoke at the point of intervention. This reorders and stabilises the capital structure of the bank and offers the prospect (provided other complementary tools are utilised as well) that the authorities can resolve the bank in an orderly fashion as a going concern. That reduces losses to creditors of the failed bank and reduces disruption to financial markets and the economy as a whole.

Bail-ins in concept

In concept, bail-ins are straightforward. If a bank fails, the resolution authority would write down or convert into equity some or all of the instruments subject to bail in without putting the bank into formal insolvency or administration. That increases the immediate loss-bearing capacity of the bank and enables the resolution authority to conduct an orderly wind-down of the institution. Following the bail-in the resolution authority would decide how to wind down the institution as a going concern. This could lead to a rehabilitation of the institution, the sale of all or part of the institution to a third party, a wind down of one or more its business lines, the creation of a bridge bank or the transfer of its deposits (along with a matching amount of good assets) to a third party (see Figure 1).

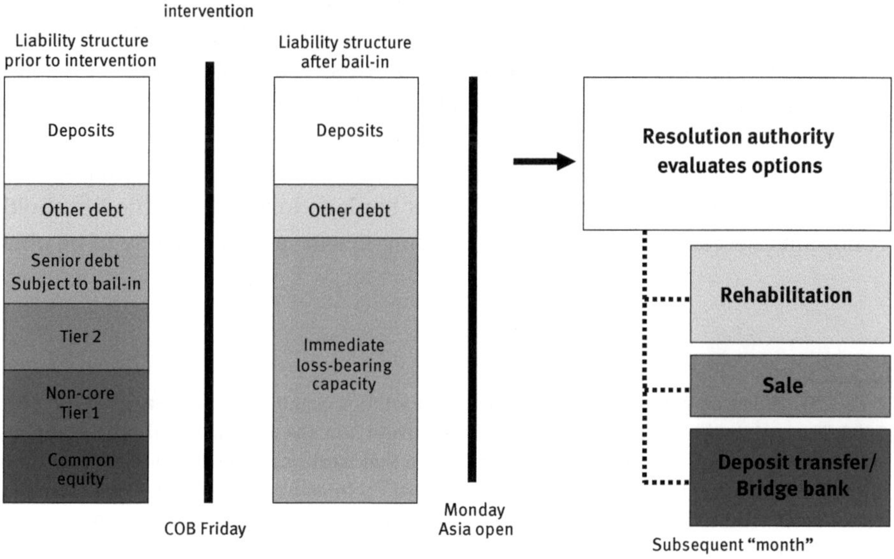

Figure 1: How bail-in could work

In fact, banks have employed much the same approach to resolution in the securitisation structures that they have developed. These are designed to go into orderly wind-down, if cash flows or asset quality criteria breach certain triggers. Cash flows are allocated to liability holders in order of strict seniority, and losses are taken in reverse order. If losses exhaust the amount of stub outstanding, then losses are allocated to progressively more senior tranches. In effect, tranches are progressively bailed-in. Importantly, the super-senior tranche continues to perform as long as the assets generate sufficient cash to pay those obligations.

The securitisation structure avoids bankruptcy costs and allows the structure to execute an orderly wind-down without fire sales of the assets. Holders of subordinated and mezzanine tranches do not receive the right to accelerate their claims if the structure breaches its triggers and goes into wind down. They must stand still. They will receive cash if and only if the structure's assets generate enough cash to pay super senior and senior obligations in full.

What is needed to make bail-ins work?

Bail-in for banks attempts to bring the approach employed in securitization to the resolution of the bank itself. However, several things are needed in order to make bail-ins work.

The first is a special resolution regime for banks.[7] The jurisdiction must have one, and this special resolution regime must give the resolution authority statutory power to impose bail-in.[8] A special resolution regime empowers the resolution authority to initiate resolution and to direct the affairs of the failed bank in much the same manner as an insolvency practitioner would be able to direct the affairs of a company in administration.[9] The trigger for that intervention is generally a finding by the bank's supervisor that bank no longer meets the threshold conditions necessary to maintain its banking license and is unlikely to be able

7 FSB 2011b; For an explanation of why special resolution regimes are necessary see *Huepkes* 2003. The regime should include provisions that govern how the resolution authority would resolve the failed bank as well as provision to assure that banks can only be resolved under the special resolution regime. For example, the proposed EU Directive (Art. 79) states that "Member States shall ensure that normal insolvency proceedings under national law may not be commenced" for banks.

8 See for example EC 2012, specifically Articles 31 and 37–50.

9 See for example EC 2012 Article 56.

to meet such conditions in the future.[10] This is effectively the point at which the bank is no longer viable in private markets, or as *Paul Tucker* (2012) put it, a bank "should go into resolution when its time is up".

The special resolution regime sets out the "tool kit" that the resolution authority may employ to resolve the failed bank. This generally includes liquidation, deposit transfer, sale of the failed institution, the authority to create a bridge bank and, in some cases the authority to take the bank into temporary public ownership. If bail-in is to be workable, the special resolution regime must include bail-in in the tool kit that the statute gives to the resolution authority. This can and should be supplemented by contractual provisions in the instruments subject to bail-in [see below], but contractual bail-in alone will not make bail-ins work.

The second precondition for bail-ins to work is obvious. There must be an amount outstanding of instruments subjects to bail-in that is sufficient to recapitalise the institution.[11] Collectively, instruments subject to bail-in should be sufficient to recapitalise the bank, even if the bank's entire common equity had to be written off. This suggests that the *minimum* amount of instruments subject to bail-in should be on the order of 7% to 10% of the bank's risk weighted assets. That would be enough to restore the bank's common equity Tier 1 capital to its minimum level. However, a higher amount (perhaps 7 to 10% of the bank's total assets) would be necessary if bail-in is to restore confidence in the bank.

Instruments subject to bail-in should include any instrument that counts as capital for the bank. In particular, it would include non-core Tier 1 capital instruments such as preferred stock as well as Tier 2 capital instruments such as subordinated debt. Indeed, under Basel III such instruments should be subject to

---

10 EC 2012 Article 27 (1) states

Member States shall ensure that resolution authorities shall take a resolution action ... only if all of the following conditions are met:

a) the competent authority or resolution authority determines that the institution is failing or is likely to fail;

b) having regard to timing and other relevant circumstances, there is no reasonable prospect that any alternative private sector or supervisory action, other than a resolution action taken in respect of the institution, would prevent the failure of the institution within a reasonable time frame;

c) a resolution action is necessary in the public interest [could not be achieved through the use of normal insolvency proceedings]

11 The IMF (IMF 2012) recommended that banks be required to have a minimum amount of instruments subject to bail-in outstanding, and the EU has adopted this recommendation (see EC 2012 Article 39). See also (DG Internal Market, 2012).

write-down or conversion at the point of non-viability (in other words subject to bail-in), if they are to continue to count as capital.[12]

Extending bail-in beyond capital instruments poses challenges. There are two approaches. One is what might be called a 'waterfall' approach. This creates a further class of instruments subject to bail-in (write-down or conversion) at the point of intervention.[13] The further class of instruments subject to bail-in would be senior to subordinated debt but junior to deposits and other customer obligations such as derivatives. The write down or conversion of such instruments at the point of non-viability would not trigger cross default with customer obligations. This would effectively amount to Tier 3 capital for the bank.[14]

If coupled with depositor preference (see below) such a step would go a long way toward creating two distinct classes of liabilities: investor capital (instruments subject to bail-in) and customer obligations (instruments that enjoy preference over investor capital and which can be expected to continue to be serviced even if the bank goes into resolution). With a sufficient buffer of investor capital, such customer obligations would enjoy the AAAA certainty that customers seek.[15]

The alternative is a 'carve-out' approach. This extends bail-in throughout the entire liability structure of the bank but creates carve-outs for certain obligations. However, carve-outs from bail-in are problematic unless they formally confer some type of preference on the instrument afforded the carve-out privilege.[16] The carve-out from bail-in confers economic (but not legal) preference. So creditors in the same class will receive different treatment. Those subject to bail-in will fare worse than those carved out from bail-in. Unless some outside party assumes the

---

12 BCBS 2011; EC 2012 Articles 51 and 52 requires the Member States to enact these provisions into national law.

13 Under this approach the requirement to maintain outstanding a minimum amount of instruments would also have to be integrated with the criteria for threshold conditions. See *Randell* 2012, p. 27.

14 The UK is proposing that UK deposit-taking institutions be required to maintain "primary loss-absorbing capacity" equivalent to 17 to 20% of the institution's risk weighted assets (HMT 2012). To the extent that the institution's equity and non-equity capital fell short of this level, the balance would have to be made up of unsecured debt with a remaining maturity of at least 12 months. This debt would be subject to a primary bail-in power. See *Randell* 2012, p. 27.

15 *Merton and Perold* 1993

16 The proposed EU crisis management directive takes the carve-out approach and suggests that debt with a maturity of less than one month should be exempt from bail-in. However, the proposed directive does not give such debt preference (nor does it propose to give deposits preference). See EC 2012 Article 38. As *Randell* (2012, p. 26) remarks, "defining the seniority of debt by reference to is tenor would be a novel departure from the creditor hierarchies of most jurisdictions".

losses that would otherwise have accrued to the carved out liabilities, the carve out will increase the probability that creditors subject to bail-in but pari passu to the carved-out liabilities will fare worse than they would have done under normal insolvency procedures. This raises the likelihood that compensation will be due to such creditors from the resolution fund under the "no creditor worse off clause".

Depositor preference represents a way to strengthen each of the two approaches. It effectively gives priority to the bank's primary customer obligation and increases the certainty and continuity of such obligations. Depositor preference also simplifies the application of other resolution tools, such as deposit transfer, that the resolution authority may wish to employ subsequent to bail-in. Depositor preference also materially reduces the risk to the deposit guarantee scheme.

Whatever approach is adopted, the issuing bank should be able to make clear to investors the risk that the instrument entails.[17] The prospectus and other information provided to investors should make clear to investors that the bank is subject to a special resolution regime, state whether or not the instrument is subject to bail-in and make clear that all instruments, even those not subject to bail-in, are subject to loss in the event that a bank goes into resolution. Exemption from bail-in does not imply any form of guarantee. Unless explicitly guaranteed (e.g. via a deposit guarantee scheme), the only entitlement that a liability holder has is the amount that s/he would have received had the bank been put into liquidation. This is the basis for the "no creditor worse off" provision included in special resolution regimes.[18]

A third precondition for bail-ins to work is the provision of liquidity to the firm in resolution.[19] Although bail-in may recapitalise the firm, it will not produce a 'Lazarus effect'. The bank in resolution is likely to require liquidity, akin to a debtor in possession financing in a corporate bankruptcy. Funding will need to be provided to the parent bank as well as its branches and subsidiaries if the bank in resolution is to remain in operation and continue to meet customer obligations. As a practical matter, this can only come from central bank(s) or the resolution authority itself, and the special resolution regime will need to make provision for such liquidity facilities.

---

17 IIF 2012

18 See EC 2012 Art. 67. If the creditor is worse off, the EC Directive envisions that industry-financed resolution funds (Art. 91) would be used to pay the compensation due to the disadvantaged creditor. For a discussion of the "no creditor worse off provision see IIF (2012, pp. 23–28).

19 IIF 2012, pp. 38–41

The framework for such a liquidity facility needs to be put in place well in advance of the bank being put into resolution. The framework should cover four factors:

(i) the priority of the liquidity facility relative to other liabilities on the bank in resolution. As a practical matter, liquidity facilities to the bank in resolution will need to be on a super-senior basis so that they would have priority in liquidation over all other unsecured creditors.
(ii) the pool of collateral backing the facility. As a practical matter this should be a charge over the unencumbered assets of the bank in resolution, including without limitation the investments of the parent bank in its subsidiaries. Any proceeds from asset sales should go toward repaying the facility.
(iii) the allocation of loss, should the bank in resolution fail to repay the facility and the liquidation of the collateral prove insufficient to repay the facility. Provision may need to be made to recoup from the industry any loss that the resolution authority/central bank might suffer.
(iv) how and where the bank in resolution might draw on such a liquidity facility.

For the framework to be practical, measures must be taken to assure that the bank in resolution will actually have unencumbered assets that might serve as collateral for such a liquidity facility. As a result of resolution planning, it can be anticipated that authorities will place an increasing emphasis on controlling asset encumbrance at banks. Measures should also be taken to assure that the central banks providing liquidity to the bank in resolution are able to smoothly and immediately replace private lenders, should it become necessary to do so. This involves not only providing funds to the bank in resolution so that it can repay private lenders, but also arranging for the central banks to take control of the collateral that the bank in resolution had previously pledged to private lenders.

With a minimum amount of investor capital (instruments subject to bail-in) and provision of liquidity to the bank in resolution, the bank in resolution (but not in insolvency/liquidation) would be in a position to continue to service its customer obligations (instruments not subject to bail-in). This will help assure continuity of critical functions and avoid excessive disruption to markets or the economy at large.

How can such continuity of customer obligations be assured? There should be a clear dividing line between instruments subject to bail-in upon initiation of resolution and those who would only be subject to loss, if the bank went into formal liquidation or insolvency. The instruments subject to immediate bail-in amount to investor capital and should be subordinated to customer obligations. Customer obligations should continue, and the bank in resolution should meet these obligations as they fall due. That will protect depositors and limit disruption to markets and to the economy as a whole.

As customer obligations continue, they should not be subject to acceleration upon the bank's entering resolution. Specifically, derivative obligations should not be subject to close out (unless there is a payment default on a maturing obligation), and repo counterparties should not be able to sell the collateral pledged by the bank in resolution unless the bank in resolution fails to repurchase the securities as scheduled.[20] This reduces the need for fire sales of the failed bank's assets and limits the contagion from the failed bank to other participants in the financial markets.

Fifth, measures will have to be taken to assure that the bank in resolution does not disrupt financial market infrastructures. This requires steps on the part of the infrastructures themselves as well as the authorities dealing with the bank in resolution. Infrastructures need to become robust, in the sense that they could withstand the simultaneous failure of two of their largest participants. CPSS-IOSCO (2012) has set out the conditions that infrastructures will need to meet in order to accomplish that objective. But infrastructures, banks and the resolution authorities also need to think through how the infrastructure will treat the bank in resolution. If one of the aims of bail-in is to assure continuity of critical economic functions and continuity of customer obligations, some measures will have to be taken to assure that the bank in resolution continues to have access to payment, settlement and clearing infrastructures, not only to clear and settle transactions initiated prior to the date the bank entered resolution but also to assure that the bank in resolution can continue to send and receive payments, settle transactions and process collateral.

Sixth and perhaps most fundamentally, for bail-ins to work banks and the authorities will have to establish reliable parameters with respect to how investors will be treated in resolution.[21] Investors will need to have some idea of the range of possible outcomes and the process that the resolution authority will follow, if they are to invest in instruments subject to bail-in. If banks are to issue instruments subject to bail-in, should the bank go into resolution, a prospective investor should want to estimate both the probability that the bank will enter resolution (fail to meet threshold conditions) and the expected loss given resolution to which the instrument will be exposed.

20 Note that this approach goes much further than the temporary stay on contracts envisaged in many special resolution regimes. It posits that instruments subject to bail-in do not trigger cross-default with derivatives contracts or repurchase agreements. This can potentially be accomplished where the special resolution regime takes a waterfall approach to bail-in, but is unlikely to be realisable under a carve-out approach.

21 For a discussion of investors views see IIF 2012, pp. 55–59.

To determine the latter, investors in instruments subject to bail-in will want some indication of the level of assets that the banks might have at the point at which it is put into resolution as well as a good sense of the priority of their particular claim on the assets of the bank in resolution. Although special resolution regimes generally call for an independent valuation of the bank to be conducted as a basis for making resolution decisions,[22] this is only a first step toward providing the assurance that investors seek. Such a valuation at the point of resolution merely establishes the extent of the losses that need to be incurred. It contains no assurance that the intervention will actually occur at a point where the bank still has positive net worth.

That assurance can only come, if the supervisor fulfils its function as monitor[23] and initiates resolution in a timely manner, i.e. at a point where the institution has fallen below minimum capital requirements but still has positive net worth. This will help assure investors in instruments subject to bail-in that they may receive positive proceeds from the bank in resolution so that their loss given resolution will be less than 100% of the amount of their investment.

In addition, investors will want to know how the resolution authority will treat each element in the bank's capital stack during resolution. As indicated above, the resolution authority will need to commit to the principle that no creditor should be worse off in resolution than it would have been if the bank had been liquidated.[24] Given the large losses in value that liquidation causes, this criterion should be relatively straightforward. The resolution authority should also commit to the principle of strict seniority, or conversely commit to imposing losses in reverse order of strict seniority. This may require the resolution authority to spell out in advance how it would actually implement bail-in.

Finally, all of the above needs to be accomplished at great speed. If the supervisor places the bank into resolution at the close of the business day, bail-in and the arrangements to assure continuity of customer obligations have to be in place by the start of the next business day. That generally leaves the authorities with at most 36 to 48 hours (elapsed time between close of business on Friday and opening of business on Monday) to complete all the tasks required to make resolution successful.[25] To do so requires considerable advance planning and preparation, and resolution plans are an important step in this direction.

---

22 See for example EC 2012 Article 30.

23 For a description of the role of the supervisor as monitor and minder see *Huertas* 2012. Disclosure to the market as well as to the supervisor should help assure that the supervisor does in fact initiate resolution in a timely manner.

24 See for example EC 2012, Article 67.

25 Although special resolution regimes limit the requirement for the resolution authorities to seek prior judicial approval of their actions [see for example EC 2012, Article 78], the regimes impose

Bail-in via stay on investor capital

Broadly speaking, there are two alternative methods to implementing bail-in. The first imposes a stay on investor capital; the second converts bail-in instruments into common equity. Both have the effect of raising the amount of capital that is immediately available to bear loss, and that is the key to stabilising the bank in resolution so that it can continue to operate its critical economic functions and continue to meet customer obligations.

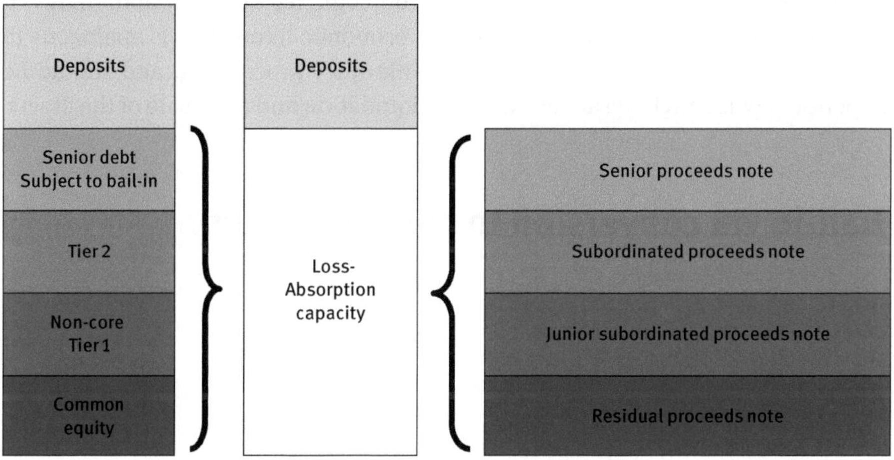

Figure 2: Bail-in via stay on investor capital

Broadly speaking, bail-in via a stay on investor capital would work as follows (see Figure 2). Upon a finding by the supervisor that the bank failed to meet threshold conditions, the resolution authority would impose a stay on all payments to all instruments subject to bail-in, including at a minimum common stock, non-core

---

various requirements that may impede the ability of resolution authorities to complete their actions within a 36 to 48 hour time frame. Such requirements in the EU include the need to consult the 'resolution college' and for the European Banking Authority to mediate possible objections to the group resolution plan proposed by the home country authority [see EC 2012 Article 83]. In the United States such requirements include a determination that the institution should not be resolved under Title I of the Dodd Frank Act (this envisages the use of normal corporate bankruptcy proceedings) but under the Orderly Liquidation Authority of Title II. The Secretary of the Treasury may make such a determination "in consultation with the President of the United States" and with the concurrence of 2/3 of the Federal Reserve Board and 2/3 of the Board of the Federal Deposit Insurance Corporation. In addition, the Secretary of the Treasury must obtain an order from the US District Court of the District of Columbia before appointing the FDIC as receiver under Title II.

Tier 1 capital (e.g. preferred stock) and Tier 2 capital (e.g. subordinated debt). Contractual payments on such instruments would be cancelled and such instruments would be fully available for loss absorption.

The resolution authority would continue to operate the bank in resolution as a going concern and continue to service customer obligations. Holders of instruments subject to bail-in would receive certificates entitling them to proceeds from the wind down/run-off of the bank in resolution. These proceeds would be distributed according to strict seniority, with senior debt being subject to bail-in being paid first, then Tier 2 capital, then non-core Tier 1 capital, and, finally, if any proceeds remained, common stock. In economic terms, this is analogous to what might be achieved in a corporate bankruptcy proceeding, and should be superior to what might be achieved under liquidation and a fire sale of the assets.

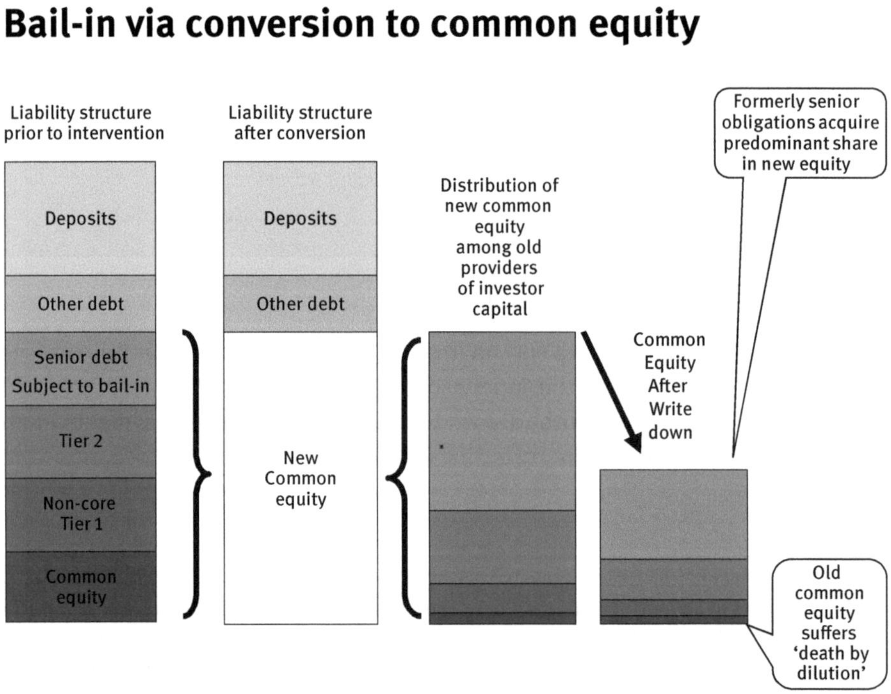

Figure 3: Bail-in via conversion

Bail-ins can also be implemented via converting the instruments subject to bail-in to common equity (see Figure 3). Under this method, at the intervention point the resolution authority would convert non-core Tier 1 capital, Tier 2 capital and senior debt subject to bail-in (Tier 3) into common equity. This would increase the total loss-bearing capacity of the bank. The resolution authority would then order the bank to realise losses from bad assets. This would cleanse the balance sheet and reduce the value of the equity to a lower but credible level.

The conversion should be conducted in a manner consistent with strict seniority. Each euro of preferred stock (non-core Tier 1 capital) should receive a lower number of common shares than a euro of subordinated debt (Tier 2 capital), and each euro of subordinated debt should receive a lower number of common shares than a euro of senior debt subject to bail-in. If instruments subject to bail-in had specified to investors the conversion ratio that would be used if the bank were to go into resolution, the resolution authority should agree to utilise the ratios specified in the prospectus for the issue in question.[26]

Bail-in under different bank structures

The structure of a bank may affect the ability of the authorities to execute bail-in and/or the steps that firms would have to take to make bail-in feasible.

Banks predominantly employ two structures. In the first, a bank is the top-level or parent organisation and this bank has subsidiaries and branches. In the second, a holding company is the top level or parent organisation. This has no direct operating business, but owns one or more bank subsidiaries, each of which may have branches or subsidiaries. For the moment assume that the bank under each of these structures operates entirely within one country.

Bail-in where the bank is the parent entity. The principal issue with respect to bail-in where the bank is the parent entity lies in avoiding the bail-in triggering the default of customer obligations. Such a default would potentially push the bank into liquidation, cause loss of value to creditors, disrupt financial markets and harm the economy at large – exactly the result that a special resolution regime should seek to avoid.

One possible approach is to distinguish more clearly between customer obligations and investor capital, make the former senior to the latter and require the bank to have a minimum amount of the latter outstanding. Investor capital would clearly be on notice that it would be bailed in, if the bank were to go into resolution, and the resolution authority should make clear to investors that it would

26 Provision should also be made to assure that the bank has sufficient authorised share capital to accommodate the number of new shares that might be issued, if conversion were to occur under resolution. See EC 2012, Article 49 (1).

implement bail-in in a manner consistent with strict seniority. To accomplish the above, the statute should make clear that the resolution authority has the ability to bail-in the instrument and the contract for the instrument should make clear to investors that the instrument is subject to bail-in. Additionally, language in customer obligations would have to be revised to exclude bail-in on an instrument subject to bail-in as an event of default so that bail-in would not trigger cross default on such customer obligations. Finally, either the resolution authority or the central bank will have to provide a liquidity facility to the bank in resolution secured by the unencumbered assets of the bank.

With such a liability structure in place, it should be possible for the resolution authority to conduct bail-in over a weekend. This would stabilise the institution and allow the resolution authority to work out – possibly in conjunction with the investors in the instruments subject to bail-in – the future course that the institution should take.

Bail-in where the parent entity is a holding company. Different issues arise where the parent entity is a holding company. Start with the case where the parent organisation is a pure holding company that owns 100% of the equity of the bank subsidiary. Where should bail-in occur – at the bank level or at the level of the parent holding company?

If it is to occur at the holding company level, the special resolution regime must give the resolution authority the right to include the parent holding company and the right to impose bail-in on the liabilities of the parent holding company. Under the assumptions given, all such liabilities would be investor capital and all such liabilities would be structurally subordinated to obligations at the bank subsidiary level. So bail-in at the parent holding company would not necessarily trigger cross-default clauses on the liabilities issued at the bank level. Theoretically, bail-in at the parent holding company need not trigger the insolvency or administration of the bank subsidiary.

In practice, however, the loss that causes the group to fail is likely to occur at the bank subsidiary level, not at the parent holding company. Bail-in at the parent does not itself recapitalise the bank subsidiary (see Table 1). Provision has to be made to accomplish this.[27]

To examine more closely why this is the case, look at the parent only balance sheet (see Table 1). On the asset side it contains equity in the bank subsidiary as well as investments in the preferred stock, subordinated debt and senior debt of the bank subsidiary. It also contains investments in third-party assets, such as

27 Steps also have to be taken to provide liquidity to the operating bank subsidiary as outlined above.

marketable securities. On the liability side, it includes equity, preferred stock, subordinated debt and senior debt, all of which is held by third party investors.

Table 1: Bail-in at parent does not necessarily recapitalise the bank subsidiary

	Parent holding company		
Assets	Prior to intervention	At Intervention	After Bail-in at parent
Marketable securities	100	100	100
Senior debt at bank subsidiary	50	50	50
Subordinated debt at bank subsidiary	25	25	25
Preferred stock at bank subsidiary	25	25	25
Common equity in bank subsidiary	100	0	0
Total	300	200	200
Liabilities			
Senior debt	100	100	0
Subordinated debt	25	25	0
Preferred stock	25	25	0
Common equity	150	50	200
Total	300	200	200
	Bank subsidiary		
Assets			
Loans	700	600	600
Other assets	300	300	300
Total	1000	900	900
Liabilities			
Deposits	650	650	650
Senior debt	200	200	200
Subordinated debt	25	25	25
Preferred stock	25	25	25
Common equity	100	0	0
Total	1000	900	900

Take the case where the bank subsidiary suffers a loss that wipes out the equity capital of the bank subsidiary.[28] The parent must write off its investment in the common equity of the bank subsidiary. This need not wipe out the parent's own equity, but it will certainly reduce it.

Bail-in at the parent level will effectively enable the parent's non-equity liabilities (preferred stock, subordinated debt and senior debt) to bear additional loss immediately. But bail-in at the parent does nothing to recapitalise the bank subsidiary. For this to occur, the resolution authority must also be empowered to direct the holding company to inject additional equity into the bank subsidiary. This can be done either in kind (e.g. through the transfer of the parent's marketable securities at conservative values into the bank subsidiary in exchange for new equity in the bank subsidiary), through write down or conversion of the parent's holdings in non-equity instruments in the bank subsidiary or in cash (if the parent holding company can borrow such cash from the resolution fund). Any recapitalisation facility has to be consistent with the liquidity facilities that are provided to the operating subsidiaries.[29]

From the standpoint of the creditors of the operating bank it is imperative that such a recapitalisation of the operating bank be highly certain to occur (i.e. that the resolution authority not only be empowered to direct the holding company to make the investment necessary to recapitalise the bank but that such an investment would actually be made). It is also important that such a recapitalisation investment be made quickly.

To this end, it is worthwhile asking whether bail-in at the parent level should be accompanied by bail-in at the level of the operating bank subsidiary. This would seem relatively straightforward for instruments that qualify as regulatory capital at the bank level, as these should be subject to conversion or write down at the point of non-viability, particularly where all such instruments issued by the subsidiary bank are held by the parent holding company. It could be more prob-

---

28 It is not clear how the FDIC proposes to handle the recapitalisation of a bank subsidiary that suffers losses which cause the bank subsidiary to fail to meet threshold conditions. In his description of the so-called single point of entry approach, *Martin Gruenberg* (Acting Chairman FDIC) stated in May 2012 that the FDIC intended to put the parent holding company into receivership and transfer the parent's equity in solvent subsidiaries to a bridge holding company. This would allow the operating subsidiaries so transferred to continue in operation. But Gruenberg was mute on how an insolvent or undercapitalised subsidiary would be treated. See *Gruenberg* 2012.

29 The recapitalisation facility should be subordinated to the liquidity facility. This will structurally be the case, if the liquidity facilities are extended at the level of the operating subsidiaries and the recapitalisation facility is extended at the holding company level.

lematic, if the bank subsidiary had issued capital instruments to third parties as well as to the parent holding company. It would also be more difficult to bail-in the parent's holdings of senior debt issued by the bank subsidiary unless the parent were willing (or forced) to accept a subordinated status relative to third party holders of senior debt issued by the bank subsidiary.[30] Finally, if bail-in at the parent holding company is to be accompanied by bail-in at the bank subsidiary, does this imply that the bank subsidiary should have issued to the parent in advance amounts of investor capital sufficient to effect a recapitalisation of the bank, if it failed to meet threshold conditions?

The situation is considerably more complicated, if the parent holding company owns less than 100% of the common equity in the bank subsidiary. Where the parent owns 100% of the common equity of the bank subsidiary, it can be argued that the creditors of the parent holding company can be held responsible for losses at the subsidiary bank (via write down or conversion of their own claims on the parent holding company and the infusion of new equity into the bank subsidiary as described above). However, where the bank subsidiary has third party shareholders the procedure outlined above potentially breaks down. Compelling the parent holding company to make an investment in the subsidiary bank sufficient to recapitalise the bank may run afoul of the "no creditor worse off" provision that the creditors of the parent holding company should receive under the special resolution regime.

Resolution of G-SIFIs

The discussion to this point has referred to a banking group that operates in a single jurisdiction. But the most important financial institutions – the so-called G-SIFIs (globally systemically important financial institutions) – are both global and complex. Although they are headquartered in one jurisdiction, they are active in fifty or more, and they run their different businesses through a variety of subsidiaries and branches. What complications arise, when an institution operates in two or more jurisdictions? Can these be overcome, so that bail-in can be become an effective resolution tool for global organisations? The following highlights some key issues that the home-host cooperation agreements mandated by the FSB will have to address.

---

30 See International Institute of Finance, 2012, pp. 25; 55–57 for a discussion of the importance of creating clarity with respect to how intra-group exposures would be treated in resolution.

Issuance of instruments to foreign investors and/or issuance of instruments under foreign law. Even if a bank has no branches or subsidiaries outside its home country, it may issue instruments subject to bail in to foreign investors and/or issue such instruments under foreign law. To assure that such investors in such instruments cannot challenge the bail-in executed by the home country resolution authority, the statutory basis for bail-in (as reflected in the home country's legislation that establishes the special resolution regime) should be reinforced by disclosure to investors and incorporation into the contracts for such instruments.[31] If possible, host countries should amend their own legislation to give recognition to bail-in.[32]

Foreign branches of the bank. If a bank has foreign branches, it is important that the host country authority refrain from seizing the bank's branch in that country and putting it into liquidation.[33] The declaration by the home country regulator that the bank fails to meet threshold conditions should not automatically trigger the host country putting the parent bank's branch in that country into liquidation. Such restraint by the host country will allow the home country resolution authority to run the resolution of the bank on a global basis. This should maximise the value of the assets and retain the franchise value of the bank in resolution. As a practical matter, however, the host country is only likely to agree to such restraint if it has the legal authority to do so and if the home country takes responsibility for providing liquidity to the bank in resolution and has made arrangements in advance with the host country that would assure that liquidity could be provided to the branch in the host country if needed to meet the obligations of the bank that mature in the host country.[34]

---

31 See for example EC 2012 Article 50 (1).

32 IMF2012, pp. 17–18

33 For example, under US law the US authorities would be entitled to take control of the US branch of a foreign bank upon entry of the foreign bank into resolution. The US authorities would then liquidate the branch as if it were a subsidiary incorporated in the US. This amounts to ex post ring fencing (see *Randell* 2012). The proceeds of the liquidation would be used first to pay the creditors of the US branch of the foreign bank. If these proceeds were insufficient, the US authorities would place a claim on behalf of the creditors of the US branch on the estate of the failed foreign bank. Such a territorial approach to resolution practically forces the entire bank into liquidation. For bail-in at the parent bank level to work, the host country authority must refrain from invoking its right to implement such ex post ring fencing, at least where the home country resolution authority sees the possibility of implementing a group resolution.

34 For example such a liquidity facility might be on a global basis with a single collateral pool with the home country central bank responsible for any credit loss that might be realised if the bank in resolution could not repay the facility and the liquidation of the collateral proved insufficient. The host country central banks would act as agents for the home country central bank.

Foreign subsidiaries within the group. If there are foreign subsidiaries in the group, either as direct subsidiaries of the parent bank or direct subsidiaries of the parent holding company, two issues stand out. First, how bail-in at the parent affects the subsidiary in the host country, and second, how liquidity would be provided to the subsidiary whilst the group is in resolution.

As outlined above, bail-in at the parent holding company does not necessarily result in the recapitalisation of any subsidiary. Viewed solely from the perspective of the home country, the home country resolution authority might like to assure that it retains control over solvent and viable foreign subsidiaries whilst retaining its option to walk away from an insolvent foreign subsidiary. Such an approach is hardly likely to appeal to host country supervisors and resolution authorities. The host country authorities could react by refusing to approve the change in control of the subsidiary to the home country resolution authority or asserting their right to initiate local resolution proceedings the moment the parent went into resolution.[35] Prior to resolution, the host country authorities could insist that subsidiaries under their jurisdiction issue to their parent (or third parties) an amount of investor capital (instruments subject to bail-in) that would be sufficient to recapitalise the subsidiary. That would allow the host country to trigger bail-in at the subsidiary level and the host country would be responsible for assuring that the subsidiary in resolution had access to adequate liquidity (this would have to be provided by the resolution authority and/or central bank of the host country). Such an approach amounts to what might be called a dissolution model, and this may be practical, if the banking organisation is in fact structured as a series of separately capitalised, separately funded subsidiaries.

But few groups are actually structured that way. Many if not most global SIFIs operate as integrated global enterprises with business lines that span several different legal vehicles in many different jurisdictions. Such institutions are global in life, and this enables them to serve clients more effectively and to improve the efficiency of global trade, global investment and global markets.

The question arises as to whether such institutions can be global in resolution as well. Note that this can redound to the benefit of the creditors in the home country, if such a global approach creates greater assurance that the home country resolution authority will continue to be able to control and derive value from solvent subsidiaries in host countries.

If such a global approach is to be attempted, the home country resolution authority will have to act together with its central bank as the leader of what

---

35 In an extreme case the host country could seize even a healthy subsidiary without immediate compensation to the home country.

might be called a resolution syndicate. This should make clear to host country authorities that the home country resolution authority will cause the parent holding company in resolution to act as a source of strength to subsidiaries in the host country and that the home country will arrange a global liquidity facility for the group in resolution. The framework under which the parent holding company in resolution would inject capital into the host country subsidiary should be specified in advance at least for material subsidiaries as should the basis on which the host country resolution authority/central bank would participate in any global liquidity facility. Ideally, the relevant authorities would establish such a framework as part of the institution-specific cooperation agreements that they are developing for the FSB rather than attempt to negotiate this on the weekend following the entry of the bank into resolution. A convention, such as the one proposed by the International institute of Finance[36] could provide a further underpinning to such institution-specific cooperation agreements.

Conclusion

In sum, bail-in is potentially an extremely useful tool for a resolution authority to have in its tool kit. It can effect what amounts to a pre-pack recapitalisation of the bank and contribute to the stabilisation of the bank. This helps assure that investors not taxpayers bear the cost of resolving the bank. If combined with provision of liquidity facilities to the bank in resolution by the central bank, bail-in can allow the resolution authority to resolve the bank in an orderly manner, maintain the continuity of customer obligations and critical functions and minimise losses to creditors, disruption to markets and damage to the overall economy.

However, to achieve these benefits several pre-conditions need to be fulfilled. First, the bank's home country must have a special resolution regime and this must include bail-in as one of the tools in the kit given to the resolution authority. Second, for instruments subject to bail-in documentation and other communications with investors should reinforce that instruments are subject to loss (unless explicitly guaranteed under a deposit guarantee scheme) and subject to bail-in. Third, the amount of instruments subject to bail-in should be sufficient to recapitalise the bank if they were written down or converted to equity at the point of non-viability (intervention). Fourth, bail-in needs to be supplemented by liquidity to support the bank in resolution, akin to debtor in possession financ-

36 International Institute of Finance, 2012

ing. This can only come from the resolution authority and central banks. Fifth, measures need to be taken to assure that bail-in does not trigger events such as cross-default clauses, close-out of derivative contracts, sale of collateral provided to repo counterparties and closure of access to financial market infrastructures that would obstruct the ability of the bank in resolution to continue meeting its customer obligations. Finally, for banks that operate in more than one jurisdiction all of the above has to be done in coordination and with the agreement of host country authorities. And, it all has to be so well prepared that it could be executed within 48 hours.

That is a tall order. Filling it is the objective of resolution plans and firm-specific cooperation agreements.

References

Basel Committee on Banking Supervision. (2011). Basel Committee Issues Final Elements of the Reforms to Raise the Quality of Regulatory Capital. Retrieved from http://www.bis.or/press/p110113.pdf

Committee on Payment and Settlement Systems and Technical Committee of the International Organisation of Securities Commissions. (2012, April). Principles for Financial Market Infrastructures. Retrieved from http://www.bis.org/publ/cpss101a.pdf

DG Internal Market. (2012, March 30). Discussion paper on the debt write-down tool – bail-in. Retrieved from http://ec.europa.eu/internal_market/consultations/docs/2011/crisis_management?consultation_paper_en.pdf

European Commission. (2012, June 6). Proposal for a Directive of the European Parliament and of the Council establishing a framework for the recovery and resolution of credit institutions and investment firms COM(2012) 280/3. Retrieved July 4, 2012, from http://ec.europa.eu/internal_market/bank/docs/crisis-management/2012_eu_framework/COM_2012_280_en.pdf

FSB 2011a. Financial Stability Board. Policy Measures to Address Systemically Important Financial Institutions. Retrieved from http://www.financialstabilityboard.org/publications/r_111104bb.pdf

FSB 2011b. Financial Stability Board. Key Attributes of Effective Resolution Regimes for Financial Institutions. Retrieved from http://www.financialstabilityboard.org/publications/r_111104cc.pdf

Gruenberg, M. J. (2012). Remarks to the Federal Reserve Bank of Chicago Bank Structure Conference. May 10, 2012. Retrieved from http://www.fdic.gov/news/news/speeches/chairman/spmay1012.html

Guynn, R. D. (2012). Are Bailoouts Inevitable? Yale Journal on Regulation , 29 (Winter), 121–154.

HM Treasury and Department of Business, Iinnovation and Skills (UK). (2012). Banking reform: delivering stabilty and supporting a sustainable economy. Retrieved from http://www.hm-treasury.gov.uk/d/whitepaper_banking_reform_140512.pdf

Huepkes, E. H. (2003). Insolvency – Why a Special Regime for Banks? Current Developments in Monetary and Financial Law, 3.

Huertas, T. F. (2011a). Barriers to Resolution. Retrieved from http://www2.lse.ac.uk/fmg/events/conferences/2011/DBWorkshop_14Mar2011/11-ThomasHuertas.pdf

Huertas, T. F. (2011b). Crisis: Cause, Containment and Cure (2nd ed.). London: Palgrave Macmillan.

Huertas, T. F. (2012). A Race to the Top? Retrieved from http://www2.lse.ac.uk/fmg/workingPapers/specialPapers/PDF/SP208.pdf

International Institute of Finance. (2012). Making Resolution Robust – Completing the Legal and Institutional Frameworks for Effective Cross-Border Resolution of Financial Institutions.

IMF 2012. Zhou, J., Rutledge, V., Wouter, B., Marc, D., Nadege, J., & Michael, M. (2012) From Bail-Out to Bail-In: Mandatory Debt Restructuring of Systemic Financial institutions. Retrieved from IMF Staff Discussion Note: http://www.imf.org/external/pubs/ft/sdn/2012/sdn1203.pdf

Merton, R.C. and Perold, A. (1993) Theory of Risk Capital in Financial Firms, Journal of Applied Corporate Finance 6 (3): 16–32.

Randell, C. (2012). The FSB's "Key Attributes": The Road to Cross-Border Resolution of Financial Institutions.

Tucker, P. (2012). Resolution: a progress report. Retrieved from http://www.bankofengland.co.uk/publications/Documents/speeches/2012/speech568.pdf.

Dirk H. Bliesener*

Legal Problems of Bail-ins under the EU's proposed Recovery and Resolution Directive

Table of Contents

* I am indebted to *Alexander von Jeinsen*, Rechtsreferendar in Frankfurt am Main, who contributed to this paper. Errors remain mine. Unless otherwise specified, this paper is current as of 31 December 2012.

A. Introduction: The European Commission's proposal

On 6 June 2012, the European Commission published its proposal for a directive "establishing a framework for the recovery and resolution of credit institutions and investment firms", commonly known as the "Recovery and Resolution Directive" proposal (RRD).[1] The proposal is the result of an extensive discussion that was initiated in October 2010 with the European Commission's communication setting out plans of an EU framework for crisis management in the financial sector.[2] The RRD proposal reflects major efforts undertaken on the G20 level to agree on guidelines for resolution regimes that permit an orderly wind-down of large and complex cross-border financial institutions.[3] Some of the resolution tools such as asset or share transfer orders or bridge bank platforms proposed to be introduced across the European Union are already part of national law in

1 Proposal for a Directive of the European Parliament and the Council "establishing a framework for the recovery and resolution of credit institutions and investment firms and amending Council Directives 77/91/EEC and 82/891/EC, Directives 2001/24/EC, 2002/47/EC, 2004/25/EC, 2007/36/EC and 2011/35/EC and Regulation (EU) No 1093/2010", COM (2012) 280/3, http://ec.europa.eu/internal_market/bank/docs/crisis-management/2012_eu_framework/COM_2012_280_en.pdf. In this paper, references to "RRD proposal" or "RRD" are to the proposal of the directive published on 6 June 2012.

2 *European Commission* "An EU Framework for Crisis Management in the Financial Sector" (2010), COM (2010) 579 final. The contributions authorised for publication are available at: https://circabc.europa.eu/faces/jsp/extension/wai/navigation/container.jsp?FormPrincipal:_idcl=Form-Principal:_id3&FormPrincipal_SUBMIT=1&id=3e98fc27-19f5-424f-8a8c-feff3a8a148b&javax.faces.ViewState=rO0ABXVyABNbTGphdmEubGFuZy5PYmplY3Q7kM5YnxBzKWwCAAB4cAAAAAN0AAExcHQAKy9qc3AvZXh0ZW5zaW9uL3dhaS9uYXZpZ2F0aW9uL2NvbnRhaW5lci5qc3A=.

3 *Financial Stability Board* "Reducing the Moral Hazard Posed by Systemically Important Financial Institutions" (2010), p. 4; *Financial Stability Board* "Consultative Document – Effective Resolution of Systemically Important Financial Institutions" (2011); *Financial Stability Board* "Key Attributes of Effective Resolution Regimes for Financial Institutions" (2011); *International Monetary Fund* "Crisis Management and Resolution for a European Banking System" (2010); *International Monetary Fund* "An EU Framework for Cross-border Crisis Management in the Banking Sector" (2010).

a number of jurisdictions including the UK,[4] Germany,[5] and Denmark[6]. Given its untested novelty, the "bail-in" tool has emerged as the most controversial weapon among the guns in the RRD arsenal.[7] In contrast to the public "bail-out" support granted to financial institutions in the aftermath of the Lehman bankruptcy through guarantees, capital injections, subsidized transfers to bad bank structures and the like,[8] "bail-in" is shorthand for loss absorption by unsecured creditors through write-down of liabilities and/or conversion of debt to equity by way of governmental order.[9] Under traditional banking law, debt can only be used to absorb losses in liquidation or insolvency proceedings when liabilities are settled and any residual debt is found irrecoverable or written off. As insolvency proceedings destabilize the financial system and create contagion risk with respect to other institutions and markets, the bail-in tool provides a mechanism to impose losses on shareholders and creditors in a going-concern scenario. The bail-in simulates the distribution of losses among shareholders and creditors without winding-down the debtor institution, but in accordance with a ranking borrowed from insolvency laws.

Statutory bail-in as proposed by the European Commission is an alternative or supplement to traditional subordinated capital instruments which provide for loss absorption in insolvency or liquidation of the institution[10] as well as to the more novel contingent convertible capital instruments ("CoCos"). CoCos are designed to recapitalize a bank once a contractually agreed trigger point is

4 Banking Act 2009, last amended in July 2009.

5 Gesetz zur Restrukturierung und geordneten Abwicklung von Kreditinstituten, zur Errichtung eines Restrukturierungsfonds für Kreditinstitute und zur Verlängerung der Verjährungsfrist der aktienrechtlichen Organhaftung (Restrukturierungsgesetz), BGBl. I 2010, p. 1900, implementing especially Sections 48a et seqq. KWG.

6 A special resolution regime for banks was introduced with the Bank Package (2008) and amended with the Credit Package (2009), the Exit Package (2010) and the Consolidation Package (2011).

7 The main characteristics have been outlined by *European Commission* "Discussion paper on the debt write-down tool – bail-in" (2012).

8 *Bliesener* "Interventionsmechanismen nach dem deutschen Restrukturierungsgesetz", in Too Big To Fail – Brauchen wir ein Sonderinsolvenzrecht für Banken? *Kenadjian* (Ed.), (2012), p. 129 (131).

9 *Calello/Erwin* "From Bail-out to Bail-in", The Economist, 28 January 2010; *European Commission* "Explanatory Memorandum" to the RRD proposal, COM (2012) 280/3, p. 13.

10 Under Art. 51 of the proposed RRD, Tier 2 and other capital instruments would have to be written off before the institution becomes subject to resolution measures, see Part D.IV below.

reached.[11] So far mandatory write-down or conversion features have been used in capital instruments by British and Swiss banks in particular.[12] Recent issues of CoCos reflect the "minimum requirements for going-concern contingent capital" proposed in 2011 by the Basel Committee.[13] As a minimum, CoCos result in automatic conversion or write-down of debt instruments upon reaching an objective trigger such as a specific Common Equity Tier 1 ratio. However, based on guidance by Basel Committee on non-common Tier 1 and Tier 2 instruments[14], trigger events include a determination by the relevant authority that a write-off of the instruments is necessary or the institution requires a public sector injection of capital or equivalent support, without which it would become non-viable. These discretionary elements have become the focus of the recent discussion on "designated" bail-in instruments that would combine public intervention powers with triggers to be included in the bond documentation.[15]

As part of a statutory resolution regime, the loss absorption through bail-in is not an automatic mechanism activated by contractual triggers but provides the government with a discretionary intervention power to impose losses on creditors which is not limited to specific instruments.[16] Both timing and degree of bail-in

---

11 In March 2012, the German government proposed an amendment of Sections 221(1) and 192 of the German Stock Corporation Act (Aktiengesetz) to clarify that institutions may issue mandatory convertible bonds and convertible bonds providing for the right to conversion on part of the issuer and that it is permissible to create the necessary contingent capital, see *Bundesregierung* "Entwurf eines Gesetzes zur Änderung des Aktiengesetzes (Aktienrechtsnovelle 2012)" (2012), BT-Drucks. 17/8989. For a discussion of issues concerning the legislation currently in force see *Seiler* in *Spindler/Stilz* "Aktiengesetz" (2012), § 221 notes 150 et seqq.

12 Visible issuers included Lloyds (2009, contingent convertible bonds), Credit Suisse (2011/2012, contingent convertible bonds), UBS (2012, contingent write-down bonds) and Barclays (2012, contingent convertible bonds).

13 *Basel Committee on Banking Supervision* "Global systemically important banks: assessment methodology and the additional loss absorbency requirement, Rules text" (2011), Annex 3, including a trigger for permanent write-off or conversion to common shares when the Common Equity Tier 1 ratio falls below 7% of risk-weighted assets. On the discussion in Switzerland in particular see *Eidgenössisches Finanzdepartment*, "Kommentar zur Änderung der Bankenverordnung und der Eigenmittelverordnung" (2012); *Bösch/Leisinger* "Contingent Convertible Bonds – CoCos, Umsetzung in der Schweiz", SZW/RSDA (2012), p. 2.

14 *Basel Committee on Banking Supervision* "Minimum requirements to ensure loss absorbency at the point of non-viability", Annex to press release "Basel Committee issues final elements of the reforms to raise the quality of regulatory capital" (2011), www.bis.org/press/p110113.pdf.

15 *Liikanen* et al. "High-level Expert Group on reforming the structure of the EU banking sector, Final Report" (2012), pp. viii, 103 et seq.; see also e.g. *Gleeson* "Legal Aspects of Bank Bail-ins", Special Paper (2012), LSE Financial Markets Group Paper Series, p. 18.

16 The UK's Vickers Commission endorsed a two-step approach whereby based on a primary bail-in power only long-term senior unsecured bonds would be bailed-in followed by a second

measures can be adapted to the individual circumstances. The flexibility of the bail-in measures and the resulting uncertainty of the concrete effects of such measures are inevitable features of governmental bail-in. Where the bail-in tool is applied, it can be expected that the immediate reduction of the embattled institution's liabilities will neutralise losses on the asset side of its balance sheet and avoid fire sales of assets and disorderly break-down. The extent to which a reduction on the liability side of the balance sheet is required to avert contagion in the financial system must be assessed in each individual case in the then prevailing market environment. This discretionary design of bail-ins, however, raises serious concerns both as to how the authorities will use or forbear from using their powers and how the bail-in tool is perceived by market participants in "good weather" and what its economic impact will be on the funding market for financial institutions and the stability of the financial system generally. Clearly, market participants including other financial institutions invested in the "bail-in eligible" liabilities over the interbank market would absorb the losses on their balance sheets, potentially causing bank runs on other institutions and infecting vital parts of the financial system.[17] The risks associated with bail-in eligible debt raise the question who should[18], and would be prepared to, invest in such debt at what price. Efficient pricing of bail-in eligible debt requires transparent triggers, legally reliable rules and predictable effects on shareholders and creditors.

Subject to severe conditionality, the bail-in tool as presented by the RRD offers the possibility to recapitalize a failing institution and thereby rescue business activities outside of formal insolvency proceedings and without having to split the institution in good bank and bad bank which can be particularly challenging for large multinational institutions involved in global cross-border activities.[19] Like all resolution tools, the bail-in tool ultimately aims at enhancing

bail-in phase affecting all other unsecured liabilities, *Independent Commission on Banking* "Final Report, Recommendations" (2011), pp. 13, 100 et seqq. The European Central Bank takes a similar approach, see *European Central Bank* "Opinion of the European Central Bank on a proposal for a directive establishing a framework for recovery and resolution of credit institutions and investment firms" (2012) (CON/2012/99).

17 *Armour* "Resolution Powers and Coordination" in "The Challenges of Cross-border Resolution" (2012), p. 9.

18 According to the Liikanen Report, bail-in instruments should not be held within the banking sector, *Liikanen* et al. "High-level Expert Group on reforming the structure of the EU banking sector, Final Report" (2012), pp. viii, 104.

19 *Institute of International Finance* "Making Resolution Robust – Completing the Legal and Institutional Frameworks for Effective Cross-Border Resolution of Financial Institutions" (2012), p. 22; similarly *Lastra* "From Bail-Out to an Adequate Resolution Framework" in "The Challenges of Cross-border Resolution" (2012), p. 12.

financial stability as well as reducing moral hazard while protecting depositors and the continuity of systemically critical financial services.[20] However, bail-in is and remains a resolution tool used in lieu of insolvency proceedings and does not necessarily pave the way to continued operation of the failing institution in its previous setup. Rather, bail-in requires the replacement of senior management and a full-fledged business reorganisation. Similar to the conditions imposed by the European Commission in state aid cases in the banking sector, bail-in may be accompanied by severe measures leading to a miniaturisation of the viable banking nucleus with the vast majority of activities being sold in one or more lots to competitors or slowly wound down in a separate vehicle. In combination with other tools, bail-in may lead to a "cold" wind-down of the main part of the institution's business.[21]

Various questions regarding the efficient structure and implementation of a statutory bail-in tool are still in discussion among the various member states' governments. During the expected transposition period, there will be ample opportunity to clarify and discuss the features of bail-in resolution action although it may be even more instructive to test the tool in practice. More like a telescope, this paper looks into some more practical legal issues of the bail-in tool.[22]

B. Objectives and triggers of bail-in

As the bail-in tool is one of the resolution instruments introduced by the proposed RRD, both the general objectives and conditions for resolution action in relation to an institution under Art. 26 and 27(a) RRD and the specific objectives and additional conditions under Art. 37 RRD have to be taken into account.

---

20 See also *European Commission* "An EU Framework for Crisis Management in the Financial Sector" (2010), COM (2010) 579 final, p. 4; *European Commission* "Technical Details of a Possible EU Framework for Bank Recovery and Resolution" (2010), p. 48 et seq.; *Financial Stability Board* "Consultative Document – Effective Resolution of Systemically Important Financial Institutions" (2011), p. 35; *Lastra* "From Bail-Out to an Adequate Resolution Framework" in "The Challenges of Cross-border Resolution" (2012), p. 10.

21 Cf. *Independent Commission on Banking* "Final Report, Recommendations" (2011), p. 103 (para. 4.73).

22 This paper can, however, not describe and discuss the background, scope, triggers, functioning and shortcomings of the resolution tools under the RRD generally. For a discussion of the policy debate on bail-in in various forms prior to the publication of the RRD proposal, see *Kenadjian* (in this volume, p. 231 et seqq).

The RRD's general resolution objectives provide guidance for resolution action to be undertaken by resolution authorities. These objectives mirror the guidelines set forth in the preamble and Section 2.3 of the FSB's Key Attributes. The resolution objectives are necessarily broad and succinct, affording an enormous amount of discretion to the authorities called to pursue them when implementing any of the new crisis management tools. In principle of equal importance and reflecting a general consensus on the lessons learned from bail-out measures taken at the peak of the global financial crisis in 2008–2009, the resolution objectives combine the protection of both public interests and individual property rights. The major concerns of genuine public interest are

(i) the financial stability including the continuity of critical, systemically important functions in the financial industry, the prevention of contagion and maintenance of market discipline (Art. 26(2) (a)–(b) RRD), and
(ii) the protection of taxpayer funds by minimizing the reliance on public bail-out action (Art. 26(2) (c) RRD). In addition, the objectives include
(iii) the protection of deposits and investor assets as well as other client funds and assets (Art. 26(2) (e)–(f) RRD) and
(iv) the protection of bank creditors from unnecessary losses, thereby minimizing the overall economic cost of resolution (Art. 26(2) (d) RRD).

In addition to these general objectives, the bail-in tool may only be applied for the purpose of

(v) either (a) recapitalization of the embattled institution to restore its ability to carry on business activities in compliance with CRD and MiFID or (b) capitalization of a bridge bank to which claims or debt instruments of the institution have been transferred (Art. 37(2) RRD).

On this basis, the competent resolution authority may apply the bail-in tool when the general conditions for resolution are satisfied (items (1) through (3) below, see Art. 27(1) RRD). Where the institution's business is to be transferred, in whole or in part, to a bridge bank, there are no additional conditions to be met. If, however, the institution is to be recapitalized to continue its business activities, further specific bail-in conditions must be satisfied (item (4) below, see Art. 37(2) and (3) RRD). Overall, the bail-in triggers are as follows. All of them must be reached before bail-in action can be taken.

(1) *Failure*: The resolution authority determines that the institution is failing or likely to fail.[23]

23 This condition is further specified in Art. 27(2) RRD. An institution is deemed to be failing if it is (a) in breach of the capital requirements for continuing authorisation, (b) its assets are less

(2) *Ultima ratio*: There is no reasonable prospect that private sector or supervisory action would prevent the institution's failure within a reasonable timeframe.
(3) *Public interest*: Bail-in is necessary in the public interest, i.e. achieving one or more of the aforementioned general resolution objectives which cannot be achieved through normal insolvency proceedings.
(4) *Viability prospects*: In the case of recapitalization of an institution: There is a realistic prospect that the bail-in (together with any other resolution tool) will restore the institution's financial soundness and long-term viability in accordance with a business reorganization plan to be submitted, within one month after the application of the bail-in tool, to the resolution authority by an administrator appointed for the institution, setting out measures to restore the long-term viability of the institution or parts of its business within a timeframe of no more than two years.

In light of both general and specific triggers, two consecutive decisions must be taken to implement a bail-in order: As a first step, the resolution authority must decide to put the institution under resolution. The second step is to choose the bail-in tool from its toolbox. The combination of these decisions affords an enormous power to the resolution authority.[24] Within the limits of the proportionality principle which applies to the use of government intervention powers generally[25], the resolution authority is granted an unfettered margin of judgement (*Beurteilungsspielraum*) in determining and applying the vague and indefinite legal concepts underlying the "conditions for resolution". In addition, discretion (*Ermessensspielraum*) is vested in the resolution authority to select the nature and timing of its response to the actual or imminent failure of the institution under resolution. For purposes of this analysis, the resolution authority has to evaluate numerous elements of information and consider a multitude of criteria. As the concrete situation and related market environment cannot be foreseen, there is little guidance which could narrow the resolution authority's discretion and render the outcome

---

than its obligations, (c) the institution is unable to pay its obligations as they fall due, or (d) the institution requires extraordinary financial support. In all of these scenarios it is sufficient if there are "objective elements" to support a determination by the competent authority that the institution will meet one of the aforementioned criteria in the near future.

24 The RRD does not contain an obligation for the resolution authority to act which bears the risk of regulatory forbearance; see for a discussion of the forbearance risk *Randell* "Triggers for Bank Resolution" in Too Big To Fail – Brauchen wir ein Sonderinsolvenzrecht für Banken? *Kenadjian* (Ed.) (2012), p. 103 (117 et seqq.).

25 For the German constitutional perspective see *Grzeszick* in *Maunz/Dürig* "Grundgesetz-Kommentar" (66th suppl. 2012), Art. 20 notes 107 et seqq.

of an exercise of the bail-in tool more predictable to institutions, their counterparties, lenders and shareholders as well as potential new investors in managing their exposures and estimating the impact of the institution's failure on their positions.

C. Scope of bail-in

I. Who may be subject to bail-in?

In principle, the scope of the RRD proposal is identical to that of the Capital Requirements Directive (CRD)[26] and would make the bail-in tool applicable to any credit institution or investment firm[27], regardless of its size or the scope of activities. Needless to say that the implementation of resolution measures including bail-in is less complex in the case of institutions with comparatively small balance sheets, simple business models and limited international activities. In addition, the general introduction of the bail-in option does not contradict mutual support regimes developed for small or medium-sized institutions such as *Volksbanken* or *Sparkassen* in the German co-operative and public banking sectors[28].

As a basis for the zero risk weighting of intra-sector exposures, the *Verbund* regimes are the backbone of the competitive position of their member institutions. To the extent a member of one of the relevant sectors experiences severe problems or faces insolvency, the sector's mutual support organizations may agree on joint action to rescue, merge or resolve the institution as a matter of "family solidarity" and to demonstrate the sector's integrity and robustness to the markets. If support is available on a timely basis from sources within the sector, such support would be treated as alternative private action preventing the institution's breakdown and insolvency. As a result, when checking the resolution conditions, the institution would fail the *ultima ratio* test (Art. 27(1)(b) RRD) and would not be subject to bail-in or any other resolution measures. However, the experience with *Landesbanken* in the German public banking sector has shown that, while institutions may be members of the mutual support regime, the sector may not be universally willing to make available the resources necessary for their resolution but rely on external support. In the past, substantial taxpayers' funds were

---

26 *European Commission* "Explanatory Memorandum" to the RRD proposal, COM (2012) 280/3, p. 8.

27 Credit institutions and investment firms are referred to as "institutions" in the RRD proposal.

28 E.g. Sicherungsreserve der Landesbanken und Girozentralen.

used to inject equity capital or support stabilization measures under the German financial markets stabilization legislation. As resolution tools such as bail-in are designed to replace the use of public bail-out monies to the greatest extent possible, co-operative and public sector banks will be able to rely on bail-in and other resolution tools as remedies of last resort once the resources of their sector-wide protection regime (*Verbundsicherung*) are exhausted.

Bail-in and other resolution tools also apply to financial institutions (*Finanzunternehmen* under Section 1(3) of the German Banking Act – KWG) that are part of a group supervised on a consolidated basis and financial holding companies as well as fully licensed branches of non-EU institutions. The proposed breadth in scope of the bail-in regime draws a lesson from experience during the financial crisis where relatively small banks posed a substantial risk to financial stability, domestically and internationally.[29] It is therefore appropriate to expand the scope beyond the FSB Key Attributes which deal only with global systemically important financial institutions (G-SIFIs).[30]

II. Which liabilities may be subject to bail-in?

The objective of the bail-in tool is to restructure the liability side of the balance sheet of a failing institution. However, reduction or conversion of all liabilities to equity may exacerbate contagion risk and spread losses to other systemically relevant market participants. Conversely, the bail-in tool would be useless if its scope were restricted to a narrow class of eligible liabilities and the volume for extraordinary loss absorption were too modest to create new or additional equity sufficient to restore market confidence in the institution. Therefore, the key question is which liabilities are to be bailed-in. Within the RRD framework the bail-in tool is available to be applied to all of the failing institution's liabilities according to a creditor hierarchy modelled on typical rankings of creditors in the distribution of proceeds in connection with insolvency proceedings, ensuring that basically no creditor incurs greater losses that would be incurred under normal insolvency proceedings.[31] However, the bail-in proposal of the European Commis-

---

29 See also *European Commission* "Explanatory Memorandum" to the RRD (2012), COM (2012) 280/3, p. 5.

30 See *Financial Stability Board* "Key Attributes of Effective Resolution Regimes for Financial Institutions" (2011), p. 5.

31 *Financial Stability Board* "Consultative Document – Effective Resolution of Systemically Important Financial Institutions" (2011), p. 38; *Zhou/Rutledge/Bossu/Dobler/Jassaud/Moore* "From

sion is guided by the principle that creditors of the same class are treated in an equitable manner[32].

Exemptions from the scope of bail-in eligible liabilities which result in deviations from that principle must be justified by significant public interests that require preferential treatment. There are essentially three distinct rationales for excluding liabilities from bail-in. First, as bail-in is a loss absorption regime designed to allocate losses according to insolvency principles but without the devastating impact of insolvency on vital business activities of the institution, liabilities that are protected in insolvency should also be exempted from bail-in. This rationale is consistent with the aforementioned principle that no affected creditor should be worse off as a result of bail-in than under normal insolvency proceedings. The second reason for excluding liabilities from bail-in is based on practical wisdom from the liquidity management of an embattled bank and understanding of market reactions and related contagion risk for the financial system. In a crisis scenario there will be many different opinions as to whether or not and to what extent a risk of contagion towards other market participants exists or a bank run is imminent. As proposed in June 2012, the RRD clearly limits the types of liabilities where bail-in is not justified due to presumed contagion risk, subject to exceptions for derivatives and covered bonds. A more discretionary approach is, however, being considered by member states' governments in the ongoing debate. In the interest of legal predictability for investors and the market, the Commission merits support for restricting the exclusions from bail-in to specifically defined types of liabilities. Finally, the third reason for excluding liabilities from bail-in is the need to continue all of the business or (in the case of a bridge bank assuming only part but not all of the institution's activities) only some business lines of the institution for which a reasonable viability prospect exists or which are vital to the day-to-day operation of the bank.

1. Liabilities protected in insolvency

The RRD proposal excludes from bail-in secured liabilities (Art. 38(2)(b)), trust liabilities (Art. 38(2)(c)) and, to the extent preferred under applicable insolvency law, tax and social security liabilities (Art. 38(2)(e)(iii)).

Bail-out to Bail-in: Mandatory Debt Restructuring of Systemic Financial Institutions" (2012), p. 12.

32 Art. 29(1) (e) RRD, see *European Commission* "Technical Details of a Possible EU Framework for Bank Recovery and Resolution" (2010), p. 49; also *Lastra* "From Bail-Out to an Adequate Resolution Framework" in "The Challenges of Cross-border Resolution" (2012), p. 12.

(a) Secured liabilities

According to their definition in Art. 2(58) RRD, secured liabilities are liabilities where the right of the creditor to payment is secured by a charge over assets, a pledge or lien, or collateral arrangements including liabilities arising from repurchase transactions and other title transfer collateral arrangements. This definition is very broad and includes all types of "security collateral arrangements" where the full ownership remains with the collateral provider and "title transfer collateral arrangements" where the full ownership is transferred to the beneficiary including repurchase agreements. The secured creditor would in each case benefit from a preferential treatment in insolvency, in German law either in the form of a right to separation (*Absonderungsrecht*) or as a right to segregation (*Aussonderungsrecht*). The definition does not limit the eligible security to contractual collateral arrangements but would also include security interests arising by operation of law or in enforcement proceedings.

Secured liabilities are excluded from the scope of the bail-in at least up to the value of the underlying security.[33] It is, however, possible to write down the portion of the liability that exceeds the value of the collateral (Art. 38(2) RRD) because that portion would not benefit from preferential treatment in normal insolvency proceedings. The bail-in of the unsecured part of secured liabilities requires a valuation of the collateral and an assessment of the redemption amount plus accrued interest of the relevant liability which may not be trivial, in particular in the case of structured or zero coupon bonds. The valuation should assess the market value according to the valuation guidelines under Art. 30 RRD. Where the markets in the assets subject to the collateral arrangements do not function properly, the "long-term economic value" would have to be determined.

Depending on the contractual or statutory structure of covered bonds[34] under applicable law, those bonds may be technically secured by cover assets or not. For example, under the German Pfandbrief Act, Pfandbriefe may not qualify as secured liabilities within the meaning of RRD. However, they constitute payment claims that are covered by a specific pool of registered assets reserved for all bonds issued against that pool.[35] The pool is separated from the insolvency estate

---

33 *European Commission* "Impact Assessment" accompanying the RRD (SWD (2012) 166), p. 44; see also *European Savings Banks Group* "ESBG response to the consultation on the debt write-down bail-in tool" (2012) available at http://www.esbg.eu/uploadedFiles/Position_papers/0499%281%29.pdf, p. 5.

34 As defined in Article 22(4) of Council Directive 86/611/EEC.

35 See *Bliesener/Schneider* in *Benteux/Van Gallebaert/Bliesener/Schneider/Wagner/Péporté/Scheltema/Mercer/Black* "Regulated Covered Bonds: A Comparative Review", Capital Markets Law Journal 4 (2009), p. 349 et seqq.

and, together with the Pfandbrief liabilities, is managed by one or two administrators (*Sachwalter*) as an independent bank in the event of insolvency proceedings being instituted over the issuing institution. Given the special ring-fencing of Pfandbriefe and related asset pools and their separate treatment in insolvency proceedings, it would not be appropriate to commingle the resolution of the bank and the resolution of the separate asset cover pools of Pfandbriefe. To this end, the RRD proposal stipulates that member states may exempt covered bonds completely from the scope of the bail-in tool (Art. 38 (2), 3rd sentence RRD). To protect market confidence in the regulatory supervision of covered bonds, member states should use this exemption option established by the RRD.

(b) Trust liabilities

Liabilities that arise from the institution's holding client funds or assets on the basis of a trust relationship are excluded from the scope of bail-in. This exemption is in line with the status of trust claims of creditors in insolvency proceedings. Under German law, it is generally recognized that the creditor who is the beneficiary under a trust relationship holds a right to segregate (*Aussonderungsrecht*) the trust assets from the insolvency estate of the trustee (*Treuhänder*).[36] On this basis, it is justified to track the preferential treatment of claims to trust property under normal insolvency proceedings for purposes of the bail-in tool.

2. Liabilities subject to contagion risk

As mentioned above, insured deposits and qualified short-term liabilities are exempted from bail-in under the RRD proposal (Art. 37(a) and (d)).

(a) Deposits

In some jurisdictions, bank deposits benefit from a preferential treatment in insolvency proceedings. Unlike with respect to secured liabilities, however, depositor preference is not a universally recognized principle of bank insolvency. Under German law, for example, as depositors are unsecured creditors, depositor protection is understood to be achieved by the statutory depositor insurance scheme under the Directive/94/19/EC (implemented in Germany by the Depositor

---

36 Section 47 of the German Insolvency Code, see *Brinkmann* in *Uhlenbruck* "Insolvenzordnung" (13th ed. 2010), § 47 note 33.

Insurance and Investor Compensation Act (EAEG) of 1998[37]) and industry protection schemes such as the Deposit Protection Fund (*Einlagensicherungsfonds*) of the private banking industry.[38] Despite the expectation of indemnification by deposit protection schemes under elaborate rules developed over the years both for the statutory deposit insurance regime and the German private Deposit Protection Fund, it can be expected that defaults on bank deposits by an institution will create a bank run risk for the institution and collateral damage for the entire banking system in the relevant region or country. On this basis, it is justified to exclude deposits from the scope of the bail-in.

Exclusion of insured deposits

The RRD proposal excludes deposits that are insured under EAEG in Germany or similar legislation implementing Directive 94/19/EC in other EU member states. Deposits under these statutes are amounts credited to accounts, regardless of their certification, but excluding debt securities in bearer form or made to order, covered bonds under Directive 85/611/EEC and bills of exchange. However, as the exclusion of depositors from bail-in is not designed to protect the fund designated to support the deposit insurance scheme that would otherwise have to compensate eligible deposits up to the statutory limit of 100,000 euros, Art. 99(2) RRD requires the deposit insurance scheme to contribute in cash to the institution an amount up to the loss the scheme would have absorbed in normal insolvency proceedings. If the deposit insurance scheme were activated in the case of a default of the institution, the scheme would acquire, by operation of law[39], the customers' deposit claims against payment of the indemnification to the customer. The mandatory contribution under Art. 99(2) RRD is essentially a short-cut for bailing-in the liabilities that the institution owes to the deposit insurance scheme after the customer has been indemnified.

The German Deposit Protection Fund

Subject to certain restrictions and exclusions, the German Deposit Protection Fund (*Einlagensicherungsfonds*) covers liabilities owed to non-banks up to 30%

37 Einlagensicherungs- und Anlegerentschädigungsgesetz (EAEG) of 16 July 1998, BGBl. I p. 1842.

38 The Einlagensicherungsfonds is a separate fund within the federal association of the German private banks, Bundesverband deutscher Banken e.V. (BdB).

39 See Section 6(5) EAEG (*cessio legis*).

of the institution's equity capital[40] to the extent they are not insured by the statutory deposit insurance scheme. Neither the institution nor any customer has a legal right to require payments from the fund. The Deposit Protection Fund may also provide assistance to the institution itself to avert insolvency proceedings or resolution action under the RRD.

Pursuant to the current RRD proposal, in contrast to the bail-in of the statutory deposit insurance scheme, any uninsured portion of deposits that are covered by the Deposit Protection Fund may be subject to bail-in.[41] There is no assurance that the Deposit Protection Fund would reimburse bank creditors for claims written off and/or converted to equity in the institution. According to its statute, the Deposit Protection Fund's objective is to avoid adverse effects on the confidence in the German private banking sector. To this end, the Deposit Protection Fund can provide relief to depositors in the form of direct payments or by way of other measures, if a member bank faces imminent or actual difficulties. Even if the Deposit Protection Fund provides assistance to bailed-in creditors after resolution action including bail-in measures have been taken with respect to a member bank, it can be expected that the bail-in of retail deposits above 100,000 euros, Schuldschein investments of the German Mittelstand and other deposits covered by the fund would have severe adverse knock-on effects on the depositor confidence which would be very similar to the negative impact expected by a bail-in of deposits insured under the statutory deposit guarantee regime. Testing the efficiency of the Deposit Protection Fund makes no more sense than requiring the statutory scheme to indemnify insured depositors in connection with a bail-in.

However, under the statute of the Deposit Protection Fund there is no obligation to provide any assistance in a crisis scenario. Rather, any and all assistance granted is discretionary and does not give rise to a legal right of the customer or the member bank. If the Deposit Protection Fund indemnifies depositors upon bail-in of their claims in accordance with a resolution package under the RRD, the institution and its majority shareholder(s) would be obliged to compensate the Deposit Protection Fund for any payments made to customers as part of the assistance granted to the institution under the statute.[42]

---

40 See the statute of the Deposit Protection Fund (*Statut des Einlagensicherungsfonds*) (2012), Section 6. The coverage will be sequentially reduced to 8.75% of equity capital until 2025.
41 Art. 38(2) RRD, 4th sentence explicitly states that the exemption of client trust monies from bail-in does not prevent the resolution authorities to exercise the bail-in power in relation to any amount of deposits that exceeds the coverage under Directive 94/19/EC.
42 See Section 5(19), (12) of the statute (*Statut des Einlagensicherungsfonds*).

In the absence of a legal obligation to make payments to customers of a defaulting institution, the Deposit Protection Fund cannot, unlike the statutory deposit insurance scheme, be required to make a contribution equal to a hypothetical amount that it would have been required to pay had the resolution action not been taken and the bank been liquidated under normal insolvency proceedings. Deposits protected by a voluntary deposit guarantee regime will therefore not be excluded from bail-in in the same manner as insured deposits. This raises the question whether the compensation claim arising from subsequent assistance by the Deposit Protection Fund will become subject to bail-in. At the time the initial bail-in order is issued by the resolution authority, the compensation liability towards the Deposit Protection Fund does not constitute a liability of the institution as it is still uncertain whether there will be any assistance of the fund at all. However, decision-makers at German private banks backing the Deposit Protection Fund will take into account that, if the fund makes payments to depositors bailed-in above the statutory EUR 100,000 threshold, it will have a compensation claim vis-à-vis the institution for all amounts so paid out but, in turn, this compensation claim may also be bailed-in by a second, subsequent bail-in order. Depending on whether the Deposit Protection Fund can successfully claim reimbursement from other parties such as controlling shareholders with deep pockets, the possibility of a second bail-in order may influence the decision on providing assistance in the first place. It may be questionable in a given situation whether adverse effects on German private banks can be effectively prevented when the bail-in tool is used with respect to one of the fund's member institutions in connection with a full-fledged resolution procedure. As the deposits guaranteed by the Deposit Protection Fund are not excluded from bail-in, arguably any action taken by the Deposit Protection Fund *after* the bail-in may result in an undesirable test for the regime and cause public attention to its limitations that would damage the private banking sector as a whole. Overall, the Deposit Protection Fund may have an incentive to avert the resolution action in its entirety by taking alternative measures with respect to the institution *prior* to any bail-in order.

(b) Short-term liabilities

The RRD proposal excludes liabilities with an original maturity of less than one month from the scope of bail-in. Traditionally, short-term funding is perceived to include all funding liabilities with a tenor of less than one year. It is debatable if preferred short-term liabilities should be limited to liabilities of a tenor of less than one month.

3. Other liabilities

(a) Operational continuity

The RRD proposal further excludes from bail-in liabilities owed to providers of goods and services that are essential to the daily function of the going-concern operation of the institution's business (including IT services, utilities, rental, servicing and maintenance of the premises on which the institution operates) and accrued salaries and other remuneration (excluding variable compensation) and pension benefits of the institution's employees. This privilege is not known in insolvency proceedings under German law but is justified as part of the bail-in procedure to ensure the uninterrupted operation of the institution following the recapitalization which requires a reasonable prospect of long-term viability of at least part of the bank's business.

(b) Derivatives

Since the bail-in mechanism has first been suggested, there is a debate whether liabilities arising from derivatives transactions should be affected by write-down and/or conversion in a bail-in scenario. Article 38(3) of the RRD proposal leaves it up to the resolution authority in each individual case to decide whether derivatives liabilities should be excluded from bail-in to the extent they are not already excluded as short-term liabilities or secured liabilities and if their exclusion appears necessary or appropriate to ensure the continuity of critical functions or to avoid significant adverse effects on financial stability, including risks of contagion and for the maintenance of market discipline (Art. 26 (2)(a)–(b) RRD). More detailed specification of the necessity and adequacy of excluding derivatives from bail-in is expected from further legislative action delegated to the European Commission in view of the systemic impact of close-out in connection with bail-in, the effects on central counterparties and the effects on risk management of other market participants (Art. 38(4)(b) RRD). If the resolution authority, however, decides to apply the bail-in in respect of liabilities arising from derivatives transactions that are subject to a netting agreement, the liability will have to be determined on a net basis in accordance with the terms of the agreement (Art. 44(2) RRD). Additionally, the EBA will develop technical standards specifying methodologies and principles on the valuation of liabilities arising from derivatives (Art. 44(4) RRD).

The European Commission recognizes that liabilities arising from derivatives transactions might be too complex to be bailed-in.[43] According to ISDA, derivatives exposures are not an appropriate form of debt to be made subject to bail-in.[44] On the one hand, there would be severe valuation and operational difficulties to apply the bail-in to on-going derivatives transactions. Derivatives transactions are contingent in nature and there is a wide variety of possible product types[45] and the broad range of possible underlying assets and methods of valuation[46]. In addition, due to their complexity, it would be difficult if not impossible to value all transactions within a "resolution weekend".[47]

In principle, where the resolution authority applies the bail-in tool with respect to a failing institution, derivatives transactions cannot be terminated on account of the bail-in action in itself, whether based on any event of default, termination option or otherwise (Art. 57(5) RRD), and even after the expiry of a one-day suspension period under Art. 63(4), termination rights may not be exercised by the counterparty to derivatives contracts if the bail-in is ordered for the purpose of recapitalizing an institution (other than in a bridge bank scenario).[48] However broadly defined, the events of default or termination provisions included in market standard master agreements such as the ISDA master agreement, the European Banking Federation's European Master Agreement (EMA) or the German master agreement (*Deutscher Rahmenvertrag* für *Finanztermingeschäfte* – DRV) will not be triggered by a bail-in order. Against this background, derivatives transactions should be treated according to a two-pronged approach:

---

43 *European Commission* "Impact Assessment" accompanying the RRD (SWD (2012) 166), p. 44.
44 The reaction of the ISDA in respect to the FSB Key Principles is available at: http://www.financialstabilityboard.org/press/c_110909ll.pdf; the reaction of the ISDA in respect to the European Commission's discussion paper on the debt write-down tool is available at: http://www2.isda.org/functional-areas/public-policy/financial-law-reform/. See also the summary of arguments in the ISDA response to the European Commission's discussion paper (2012), p. 2 et seqq.
45 Swap, forward, option, cap, collar, floor and many variations and sub-variants of these product types, see ISDA response to the FSB Key Principles (2011), p. 7.
46 Including rates, prices and indices relating to interest rates, foreign exchange rates, equities, debt securities, credit risk, commodities, bullion, emissions allowances, inflation and other economic and monetary statistics, meteorological data, freight forward rates, bandwidth and so on, see ISDA response to the FSB Key Principles (2011), p. 7.
47 ISDA response to the European Commission's discussion paper (2012), p. 2.
48 Arg. Art. 63(4)(b) RRD.

Bail-in of closed-out derivatives transactions

Where the resolution authority orders the institution to discontinue on-going derivatives transactions, based on its control right under Art. 64(1) RRD and subject to the terms of the underlying agreements and applicable law, the counterparty's final claim against the institution (if any) will be bailed-in. In practice, this may be the case for trading positions that do not serve a relevant business purpose on the basis of the adjusted strategy according to the institution's business reorganization plan. Where derivatives transactions are subject to a netting arrangement, the liability of the institution (or the counterparty, as relevant) will be determined on a net basis in accordance with the terms of the underlying agreement (Art. 44(2) RRD). To this end, the close-out netting provisions included in market standard documentation will be recognized in the case of a termination initiated by the institution or the resolution authority, or where the counterparty exercises a termination right on any basis other than by virtue of the bail-in alone. In such case, the institution would not necessarily be the debtor of the net amount.[49] Unless any bail-in exemption applies, any net liability of the institution under the derivatives transactions towards a particular counterparty will be reduced and/or converted in accordance with the bail-in order.

No bail-in of on-going derivatives transactions

However, while it may be possible and appropriate in certain circumstances to terminate some or all of the institution's derivatives transactions and write down the net close-out liability upon such termination, it will not be the universal objective of the resolution authority in the case of a recapitalization by bail-in action to terminate all hedging relationships and other derivatives transactions of the institution that has by definition a reasonable prospect to continue at least part of its business operations for a foreseeable time. Where the derivatives transactions are carried on according to their terms and tenor, the net positive or negative exposure vis-à-vis each derivatives counterparty is determined on a daily basis for regulatory purposes and/or for purposes of assessing the collateral amount to be posted under credit support arrangements. To the extent collateral arrangements have been made under the ISDA credit support documents or other collateral arrangements, as is the case for a vast majority of derivatives transactions in

---

49 ISDA response to the FSB Key Principles (2011), p. 7: Even if the net close-out amount were owed to the institution, "the benefit of realising that asset may be outweighed by the disadvantage of losing the on-going risk protection offered by the transactions under the master agreement".

the market, the derivatives will fall within the category of secured liabilities[50] in accordance with Art. 2(58) RRD and will be exempt from bail-in. However, even where no such collateral arrangements exist, current derivatives transactions do not constitute liabilities that may be subject to bail-in. The gross exposures and the net exposure change on a daily basis. Even if the institution had a net exposure vis-à-vis a counterparty at the time of bail-in that would crystallise as a net claim upon close-out, the reduction of that claim would require crystallisation by way of close-out and re-entry into a new derivatives master agreement on the same terms. There is, however, no basis for forcing derivatives counterparties to novate their master agreements at the order of the resolution authority.

The European Commission was well aware of the specificities of derivatives transactions and therefore the RRD proposal vests a power in the resolution authorities to exclude derivatives transactions from bail-in in accordance with Art. 38(3) RRD. With respect to micro or macro hedges against interest rate, currency exchange or other risks in particular, the exclusion from bail-in may be justified as those derivatives are arguably similar in nature to service or supply agreements which are vital to the continued operation of the institution and therefore excluded from bail-in under Art. 38(2)(e)(ii) RRD. In addition, as OTC-traded derivatives transactions generally increase the interconnectedness of banks, their abrupt termination may be a major source of contagion,[51] and their continued performance may be in the interest of financial stability. It should be noted that where both vital hedging positions and pure trading engagements are bundled together under one single, inseparable derivatives master agreement, one group of transactions cannot be terminated alone and the continuance of the hedging transactions will require the continued performance of the transactions entered for trading purposes only.

(c) No extension to other types of liabilities

In view of the precise definition of liabilities that are exempted from bail-in for operational reasons, the resolution authority has no discretionary power to expand the list of privileged creditors whose liabilities are to be excluded from bail-in. In particular, there is no super-senior privilege or other form of exclusion from bail-in for financing liabilities incurred in connection with restructuring measures taken prior to the resolution procedures. Such a privilege is currently

---

50 See also ISDA response to the FSB Key Principles (2011), p. 6; ISDA response to the European Commission's discussion paper (2012), p. 6.

51 *European Commission* "Impact Assessment" accompanying the RRD (SWD (2012) 166), p. 89.

included in the German regime of the rehabilitation proceeding (*Sanierungsverfahren*) under the Credit Institution Reorganisation Act of 2010.[52] Previous experience of bank failures and restructurings have shown that the effectiveness of resolution measures greatly depend on the availability of additional short-term funding. Notwithstanding the role of central banks in providing liquidity to the financial system even in times of stress, the RRD proposal aims to set up a funding system financed by the financial industry itself.[53] Instead of giving super-senior priority to new funding facilities, Art. 90–99 RRD require the establishment of resolution financing arrangements which can be used to ensure the effective application of the resolution tools and powers by the resolution authority.

III. Minimum requirement of bail-in eligible liabilities

In order to limit the institution's options to circumvent or avoid bail-in action, the resolution authority shall require institutions to maintain a minimum amount of own funds and bail-in eligible liabilities, measured as a percentage of total liabilities (other than regulatory capital). The percentage will be set according to the individual needs of an institution but based on general guidelines and criteria (Art. 39(3) RRD) which are to be further specified by the European Commission regarding categories of institutions and ranges of percentages. While the European Commission suggested that the minimum level could be about 10% of total liabilities (excluding regulatory capital),[54] the various stress analyses presented by the impact assessment accompanying the RRD proposal[55] show that high volumes of loss absorbing liabilities may be required in a banking crisis depending on the severity of the crisis.

---

52 Section 2(2), 3rd sentence of the Act on the Reorganisation of Credit Institutions (*Gesetz zur Reorganisation von Kreditinstituten* – KredReorgG) of 9 December 2010, BGBl. I p. 1900. See *Bliesener* "Interventionsmechanismen nach dem deutschen Restrukturierungsgesetz", in Too Big To Fail – Brauchen wir ein Sonderinsolvenzrecht für Banken? *Kenadjian* (Ed.), (2012), p. 129 (131).
53 RRD Recital No. 68.
54 *European Commission* "Explanatory Memorandum" to the RRD proposal, COM (2012) 280/3, p. 13.
55 *European Commission* "Impact Assessment" accompanying the RRD (SWD (2012) 166), Annex XIII, pp. 124 et seqq.

IV. Transitional provisions

Under Art. 115(1) of the RRD proposal, the bail-in provisions would have to be implemented by EU member states under domestic law by 1 January 2018 at the latest whereas the transition period for most other provisions of the proposed directive would end on 1 January 2015. If adopted as proposed in June 2012, the bail-in powers would apply to liabilities irrespective of their terms and tenor and regardless of the disclosure made in prospectuses or other offering documents with respect to the possibilities of the occurrence of bail-in action.

During the consultation process regarding the RRD proposal, it was discussed whether there should be a long implementation period for the bail-in tool or instead grandfathering provisions excluding from bail-in any debt issued prior to a specific cut-off date.[56] The European Commission's impact assessment indicates that a broad consensus existed in favour of the delayed transposition of the bail-in tool to reflect relevant "maturity cycles" of existing debt,[57] and only little support was given to grandfathering provisions by member states and industry experts.[58] As a result, there are no grandfathering rules in the RRD proposal regarding the application to liabilities issued or otherwise established before 2018. It can be expected that the bail-in tool will be applied to all liabilities regardless of their issue date including liabilities issued prior to the publication of the RRD proposal.

Under German law in particular, grandfathering provisions are rare, including in connection with financial restructuring legislation.[59] As an unusual example, limited grandfathering protection from statutory pay and pension caps was granted to the existing remuneration claims of bank managers in institutions subject to public support under the German Financial Market Stabilisation Fund

---

56 *European Commission* "Discussion paper on the debt write-down tool – bail in" (2012), p. 23.
57 On this issue see *Dohrn* "Der Richtlinienvorschlag zur Festlegung eines Rahmens für die Sanierung und Abwicklung von Kreditinstituten und Wertpapierfirmen", WM 2012, pp. 2033 (2038).
58 See *European Commission* "Impact Assessment" accompanying the RRD" (SWD (2012) 166), p. 241.
59 Tax laws regularly insert specific reference dates and, for example, Section 8a of the German Financial Markets Stabilisation Fund Act (FMStFG) also refers to assets acquired prior to a specific cut-off date. However, none of these provisions is intended to grandfather existing debt. Under Section 8a FMStFG, stabilisation measures should not be available with respect to assets acquired for speculative reasons after the introduction of the legislation, see the reasoning for the draft Second Financial Market Stabilisation Act (*Zweites Finanzmarktstabilisierungsgesetz*), BT-Drucks. 17/8343, pp. 12 et seq.

Act (FMStFG).[60] However, recent legislation on debt equity swaps in restructuring and insolvency situations[61] do not include any grandfathering rules in favour of existing shareholders and debtors. Irrespective of the German legislator's limited powers to supplement European law when implementing a directive in national law, it is unlikely that the German legislator would consider exemptions for existing debt.

Finally, it is also unlikely that the application of bail-in rules vis-à-vis existing debt would raise serious constitutional concerns. The principle of legal certainty restricts the discretion of the legislator if the addressee of the legislation relied upon existing law and such reliance is legitimate and deserves legal protection.[62] In general, the principle of affording protection to legitimate expectations (*Vertrauensschutzprinzip*) precludes legislation from taking effect at any point in time before its publication, but a retroactive legislation is possible where the purpose to be achieved so demands and where the legitimate expectations of those concerned are duly respected.[63] An overriding public interest may even preclude the requirement of transitional measures.[64] As the losses for the creditor under the bail-in tool are limited to the position the creditor would be in under insolvency proceedings leading to the liquidation of the institution and the bail-in tool is designed to avert risks to the financial market at large, it appears unlikely that the European Court of Justice would limit the legislator's discretion regarding the bail-in tool.

Notwithstanding the uncertainties with respect to the introduction, design and timing of the bail-in tool for the financial sector, it is to be considered by issuers, arrangers and managers if the disclosure documentation for new issues of Tier 1 or Tier 2 capital instruments as well as unsecured bonds of institutions launched after the publication of the RRD should reflect the risks associated with the potential future bail-in powers.[65]

---

60 Section 10a (2c), 5th sentence, of the German Financial Market Stabilisation Fund Act (FMStFG).

61 Section 9 of the German Bank Reorganisation Act (KredReorgG) and Section 225a of the German Insolvency Code (InsO).

62 See *Jarass* in *Jarass*, Charta EU-Grundrechte, Einleitung para. 39.

63 ECJ (Crispoltoni), Case C-368/89, para. 17.

64 ECJ (Affish), Case C-183/95, para. 57.

65 See, e.g., the related risk factors in the prospectus dated 12 September 2012 of Rabobank Nederlands' GBP 500 million 5.25% subordinated notes due 2027, pp. 11 et seq.

D. Write-down and conversion

Once the decision to exercise the bail-in tool has been taken, the resolution authority will initiate the necessary steps to restructure the institution's liabilities. It is crucial that this process can be effected within a weekend when markets are closed in all relevant time zones.[66] During the resolution weekend, there will be no time to carry out complex asset valuations[67] or seek the approval of creditors.[68] Building on preparatory work documented in recovery and resolution plans, the resolution authority will have to select and apply all necessary powers within this timeframe (Art. 56(1)(j)) and (k) RRD).[69]

Pursuant to Art. 56(1) RRD, the resolution authority is vested with a number of specific powers to implement the bail-in. It may take one or more of the following measures:

(i) write down or convert capital instruments into shares or other instruments of ownership of the institution or a relevant parent institution under resolution (Art. 56(1), 2nd sentence, (f));

(ii) reduce (including to zero) the principal or outstanding amount due under bail-in eligible liabilities (Art. 56(1), 2nd sentence, (g));

(iii) convert bail-in eligible liabilities into ordinary shares or other ownership instruments of the institution, a relevant parent institution under resolution or a bridge institution (Art. 56(1), 2nd sentence, (h));

(iv) cancel debt instruments issued by an institution under resolution (Art. 56(1), 2nd sentence, (i));

(v) cancel shares or other ownership instruments of an institution under resolution (Art. 56(1), 2nd sentence, (j));

(vi) require an institution under resolution to issue new shares or other instruments of ownership or capital instruments including preference shares and contingent convertible instruments (Art. 56(1), 2nd sentence, (k));

---

66 *Huertas* "The Road to Better Resolution – From Bail Out to Bail In" (2010), p. 12, published in *Beblavý/Cobham*/Ódor (Eds.), The Euro Area and the Financial Crisis Editors, p. 243 et seqq.

67 Regarding valuation requirements see Part E below.

68 *Zhou/Rutledge/Bossu/Dobler/Jassaud/Moore* "From Bail-out to Bail-in: Mandatory Debt Restructuring of Systemic Financial Institutions" (2012), p. 12.

69 See also *Financial Stability Board* "Consultative Document – Effective Resolution of Systemically Important Financial Institutions" (2011), p. 36; *Zhou/Rutledge/Bossu/Dobler/Jassaud/Moore* "From Bail-out to Bail-in: Mandatory Debt Restructuring of Systemic Financial Institutions" (2012), p. 14.

(vii) require the conversion of debt instruments which contain a contractual term for conversion, subject to certain circumstances (Art. 56(1), 2nd sentence, (l));
(viii) amend the maturity or interest payable under debt instruments including by temporary suspension of payment (Art. 56(1), 2nd sentence, (m)).

Any liability reduced by order of the resolution authority will be treated as discharged to the extent reduced (Art. 48(3) and (4)(a) RRD).

As an initial step, the institution's losses and resulting level of regulatory capital gap or even over-indebtedness (*Passivüberhang*) must be determined. To this end, the resolution authority will establish, or cause to be established, a valuation[70] of the institution's assets and liabilities and assess on that basis the aggregate amount by which bail-in eligible liabilities must be converted to equity or reduced to restructure the regulatory capital position and/or the balance sheet of the institution and thereby to restore it viability.

In the case of recapitalization of a failing institution, the bail-in may either be limited to a conversion of eligible liabilities to equity capital instruments or include both the write-down of liabilities and subsequent conversion.

I. Conversion only

To the extent losses are incurred on assets of the institution that reduce the outstanding amount of ownership or capital instruments in accordance with their terms, an additional reduction of shares or other bail-in eligible liabilities may not be necessary. Instead, the regulatory capital position of the institution may no longer be in compliance with CRD/CRR and/or may require the injection of additional equity to restore its viability and investor confidence in the institution. In this situation, the resolution authority will select the class or classes of creditors according to the bail-in hierarchy of claims set out in Art. 43(1) RRD and convert their claims into equity.[71] According to Art. 45(2) RRD, the conversion rate must reflect the loss absorbed by the relevant creditors and its rank in the bail-in hierarchy (Art. 45(2) RRD). Technically, the conversion is ordered to restore the equity position of the institution but not to cover losses. Where only the conversion tool is used, losses have been absorbed by existing capital instruments. The same is true if bail-in eligible liabilities are converted to equity positions after a write-

70 See below Part E.
71 See below Part D. III.

down that was imposed on creditors to cover losses incurred by the institution (see II. below).

If appropriate to reflect the priority of senior liabilities, the resolution authority will establish a higher conversion rate for senior liabilities than for subordinated liabilities (Art. 45(3) RRD). As a result, creditors of a more junior class whose claims have to be diluted to some extent may receive less than what they would have received in insolvency. In such event, they are entitled to compensation equal to such difference.

II. Write-down and conversion

Where losses cannot be absorbed by hybrid capital or other capital instruments and the institution is or would be over-indebted as a result of realizing losses on its assets, the institution may only be recapitalized by a combination of (i) reducing and/or cancelling eligible liabilities and (ii) converting eligible liabilities into shares or other equity instruments.

The allocation of losses by sequential write-down follows the waterfall established by the hierarchy of claims according to Art. 43(1) (a)–(d) RRD. Following the write-down, the institution shows a balance sheet where assets match liabilities. The conversion of further eligible liabilities into Common Equity Tier 1 (CET1), Additional Tier 1 or Tier 2 instruments is a further step of the bail-in action undertaken to restore the institution's CET1 ratio and overall regulatory capital position to applicable supervisory standards and to increase the equity capital to a level that is required, in the view of the resolution authority, to rebuild business viability and market confidence in the institution. The conversion of the bail-in eligible liabilities is guided by the hierarchy of claims. Where more than one class of creditors in the hierarchy of claims is affected by the conversion, multiple conversion rates may be necessary.

III. Inter-creditor regime

The hierarchy of claims within the RRD framework constitutes a strict order of priority of bail-in eligible equity positions and debt liabilities. The European Commission refrained from giving the resolution authority any discretion as to the sequence according to which eligible liabilities should be written down or converted.[72] Art. 43(1) (a)–(d) RRD establish a strict "waterfall" where CET1 instruments are the first to absorb losses, followed by Additional Tier 1 instruments that are liabilities and Tier 2 instruments. Subordinated debt is in the next class, followed by the remainder of bail-in eligible liabilities. Each class has to be written down in its entirety before the next following, more senior class absorbs any loss. The creditors within each class are treated *pari passu*. Accordingly, the creditors of the class which does not need to be written down entirely to absorb the last portion of losses will be subject to a *pro rata* haircut to their respective claims.

As a policy matter, the approach taken by the European Commission has great merit as it enhances the bail-in's predictability for investors and strengthens legal certainty. The RRD differentiates between clearly defined creditor classes and applies a strictly sequential approach to inter-creditor treatment. The current German legislation, instead, takes a more flexible and less transparent approach: In the case of a partial transfer of assets and liabilities of a failing bank to a bridge institution in accordance with a transfer order (*Übertragungsanordnung*), BaFin is required to select the creditors or creditor groups whose liabilities are transferred to the bridge institution primarily based on its opinion of the "systemic relevance" of every single liability and creditor[73] instead of a clear overall hierarchy of classes. In addition, the current legislation allows for cherry picking of creditors and tranches of bonds within one single bond issue in connection with the selection of liabilities to be transferred to the bridge bank, resulting in practical legal problems of splitting a uniform bond issue among two legal entities in connection with resolution action.[74] In contrast, the RRD proposal provides for equal treatment of liabilities within a class of debt, equity or hybrid capital regardless of its holder at the time of resolution.

IV. Special provisions on write-down of capital instruments

Chapter IV of the RRD contains additional provisions on the write-down of capital instruments. According to these provisions, Additional Tier 1 instruments and

---

72 Discretionary creditor selection had been suggested at an earlier stage and should have been based on the systemic risks associated with writing down certain creditors, see *European Commission* "Overview of the results of the public consultation on technical details of a possible EU framework for bank resolution and recovery" (2011), p. 87.

73 Section 48k(2), 4th sentence, in conjunction with Section 48j(3), 3rd sentence KWG.

74 *Bliesener* "Interventionsmechanismen nach dem deutschen Restrukturierungsgesetz", in Too Big To Fail – Brauchen wir ein Sonderinsolvenzrecht für Banken? *Kenadjian* (Ed.), (2012), p. 129 (149 et seq.).

Tier 2 instruments[75] have to be written down by the resolution authority before any resolution action is taken (Art. 51 (1) RRD). These provisions shall ensure that capital instruments fully absorb losses at the point of non-viability of the issuing institution.[76] If the bail-in tool is applied, the bail-in waterfall ensures that Tier 1 and Tier 2 instruments are the first classes of liabilities to absorb any losses. In this situation, the rules on implementing the bail-in (Art. 41 et seqq. RRD) will achieve the objectives underlying Chapter IV[77]. However, there may be situations where resolution action is taken or public bail-out funds are used to support the failing institution. Pursuant to Art. 51(4) RRD, the write-down of capital instruments must be implemented by the resolution authority, irrespective of whether the bail-in tool is used or not, wherever the institution is found to meet the resolution conditions or to be no longer viable without such write-down or without public support that it is granted or where the capital instruments are recognised as regulatory capital on an individual or consolidated basis and the consolidated group is found to be no longer viable without such write-down. In essence, this rule is to prevent that hybrid investors can get away from the crisis without significant losses.

V. Suitability of converted equity investors

Where the conversion power is used by the resolution authority, debt investors will receive shares or other equity instruments in the institution under resolution. Depending on the distribution of debt exposures among investors, a concentration of few investors in bail-in eligible debt instruments would result in a similar concentration of new shareholders. To the extent debt investors would become significant shareholders with holdings of at least 10%, their suitability would be subject to the scrutiny of the banking regulator. Clearly, if the banking regulator were to examine the suitability in its own right[78] and the consummation of the bail-in were subject to waiting periods of approximately 3–5 months,

---

75 Art. 2(65) RRD defines relevant capital instruments "for the purposes of Sections 5 and 6 of Chapter III of Title IV" as Additional Tier 1 instruments and Tier 2 instruments. Chapter III Section 5 is followed by Chapter IV "Write Down of Capital Instruments" which indicates that the aforementioned definition is applicable to Art. 51 et seqq.

76 RRD Recital No. 51.

77 According to Art. 42(2) (b), shareholders that became shareholders as a result of such conversion under Art. 52, are not treated differently from other shareholders.

78 In Germany, a significant shareholder's suitability must be examined by BaFin upon notification under Section 2c of the Banking Act (KWG).

a swift implementation of the bail-in would be compromised and the success of an urgently needed resolution endangered. As suitability proceedings are similar to approval requirements of public authorities that prejudice the effectiveness of resolution action, member states must ensure that resolution measures such as bail-in are not subject to those obstacles.[79] It can be expected that, in implementing RRD in national law, there will be an exemption for the pre-consummation suitability proceeding. Once the shareholdings have been acquired, the banking regulator may check *ex post* if any new significant shareholder fails the suitability test. Under German law, the banking regulator (BaFin) may order that the voting rights of unsuitable investors be exercised and transferred to a court-appointed trustee who can also be mandated to sell the shares to other market participants.[80]

E. Valuation

The European Commission proposes that two distinct valuations be undertaken in connection with the application of the bail-in tool.

I. Preliminary valuation

Prior to the implementation of the bail-in, a first, "preliminary" valuation of the institution's assets and liabilities shall be carried out by an independent expert (in urgent cases by the resolution authority) to help the resolution authority assess the quantum (the "aggregate amount" under Art. 41 RRD) of bail-in eligible liabilities that are required to be reduced and/or converted in order to recapitalize the institution or generate equity capital for the bridge bank to which the liabilities are transferred. In a recapitalization scenario in particular, the resolution authority is required to set the amount of liabilities to be reduced or converted at a level that is both (i) suitable to reinstate the institution's CET1 capital ratio at the minimum standard under CRD/CRR and (ii) required in the opinion of the resolution authority to uphold or restore "sufficient market confidence" in the institution and enable it to continue its business activities in compliance with CRD and MiFID. While the definition of this recapitalization target level implies a fair amount of discretion for the resolution authority, the underlying valuation

79 Art. 56(2), 1st sentence, (a) RRD.
80 Section 2c (2), 2nd sentence et seqq. KWG.

will have to follow the general criteria established for all resolution tools under Art. 30 RRD. The valuation must assess the market value of assets and liabilities at the time of the implementation of the resolution action (Art. 30(2) RRD) based on "prudent and realistic assumptions" including as to default rates and loss severity, and irrespective of any (actual or potential) public support. Only where the market for any asset or liability is dysfunctional, the European Commission suggets to establish the long-term economic value instead of the market value. The EBA will publish technical standards which will specify the methodology for assessing the market value as well as the long term economic value of assets, but pending these publications the European Commission's 2009 Impaired Assets Communication[81] may provide some initial guidance as it had first developed the distinction between these two concepts.[82]

According to the principles provided in Annex IV of the Impaired Assets Communication, the long-term economic value or "real economic value" may be based on market input and realistic and prudent assumptions regarding future cash flows. Simple reverse auction procedures could be used in the case of assets where market values are reasonably certain. More sophisticated auction procedures would be better suited to the valuation of more complex assets if there is less certainty about market values and a more exact method of price discovery of each asset is needed. If the valuation were to become so complex that a reliable forecast of developments in the foreseeable future would appear impracticable, the European Commission is likely to consider uniform haircuts to approximate the real economic value.[83]

The European Commission suggested in its Impaired Assets Communication to base the valuation process and the assessment of the likely future losses on rigorous stress-testing against a scenario of protracted global recession to render the valuation more solid. Absent more specific regulation, this principle could also be adopted for purposes of the valuation under the RRD. Regardless of whether the valuation would be based on different models for approximating the real economic value or uniform haircuts, it should be complemented by stress tests of these values against a systemic crisis, presumably resulting in an additional safety haircut.

---

81 *European Commission* "Communication from the European Commission on the treatment of impaired assets in the Community banking sector" (2009/C 72/01).
82 *European Commission* "Communication from the European Commission on the treatment of impaired assets in the Community banking sector" (2009/C 72/01), para. 39 et seq.
83 *European Commission* "Communication from the European Commission on the treatment of impaired assets in the Community banking sector" (2009/C 72/01), para. 40.

However, irrespective of whether the market value or the long term economic value is to be determined, the valuer should not give credit to the existing but embattled franchise of a failing institution but assume a gone-concern scenario for its valuation. Otherwise the "aggregate amount" of the contribution by creditors based on asset valuations at a going concern level would risk to be insufficient to restore the long-term viability of the restructured institution, and no safety buffer would be available to correct errors and neutralise unforeseen events having an adverse impact on the value of assets. These arguments have resurfaced in the ongoing debate on the valuation concept. Even if markets are dysfunctional, optimistic valuations may endanger the effectiveness of bail-ins because the tool will be used only in situations where hybrid capital and other capital buffers have not been sufficient to ensure the viability of the institution.

In addition to the (preliminary) valuation as such, if time permits, the valuer shall make available certain accounting information (Art. 30(3) RRD) and an analysis of the treatment expected for all classes of creditors according to their priority level in normal insolvency proceedings (Art. 30(4) RRD). The valuation is not definitive (but only provisional) as long as the additional information under Art. 30 (3) and (4) RRD has not been furnished.

II. Ex post valuation

After the bail-in has been implemented, a second, *ex post* valuation shall be made by an independent expert to determine whether shareholders and creditors whose claims were reduced and/or converted through bail-in have been treated in at least the same way as they would have been treated in normal insolvency proceedings (Art. 66 RRD). If the bail-in action was based on a provisional valuation only, the definitive valuation may be made separately or together with the ex post valuation required under Art. 66 RRD.

As the decision to take bail-in action may be challenged and annulled in court but its enforcement may not be suspended or reversed, (arg. Art. 76(2)(d) RRD), the purpose of the first ("preliminary") valuation, whether provisional or definitive, is to ensure that the bail-in's definitive interference with shareholders' and creditors' property rights is kept to a level proportionate to the resolution objectives. The intrusion into shareholders' and creditors' rights must not put them into a worse position than they would be in under normal insolvency proceedings. According to the RRD's concept, the "no creditor worse off" requirement is tested twice, at least in principle, on the basis of the second valuation under Art. 66 RRD. In practice, only a single full valuation may be made if the first valuation was provisional and the second valuation is combined with the definitive first valuation. If any creditor or other person affected by the bail-in action challenges the resolution authority's decision based on the inadequacy of the compensation (if any) granted to it (Art. 78(2)(c) RRD), the court will have to review the underlying valuations.

F. Compensation

The constitutional framework of the European Union[84] requires the payment of compensation where a person is deprived of his or her property.[85] Even though the European Convention on Human Rights (ECHR) does not require compensation of the full market value of the property under all circumstances,[86] payment that is not reasonably related to the property value will constitute a disproportionate interference with the property right.[87]

Under the RRD framework, safeguards set out in Art. 65 and 66 RRD provide for compensation based on the treatment that shareholders and creditors would have received if the institution had entered normal insolvency proceedings immediately before the bail-in was effected (Art. 66(2)(a) RRD).

If the valuation under Art. 66 RRD[88] reveals that the reduction and/or conversion of liabilities pursuant to the bail-in action does not meet the test that "no creditor shall be worse off than in insolvency", the resolution authority will be required to pay the difference. Creditors will be entitled to compensation where

---

84 The German constitution (*Grundgesetz*, Art. 1–Art. 19) neither applies to the RRD itself nor to German national legislation implementing the EU directive in domestic law, see *BVerfG*, 2 BvR 197/83 ("Solange II").

85 While Art. 17(1) of the Charter of Fundamental Rights of the European Union (CFREU) explicitly requires a fair compensation being paid in good time, Protocol 1 to the ECHR refers to the conditions provided for by law and by the general principles of international law. Nevertheless, according to the ECHR, "*compensation terms under the relevant legislation are material to the assessment of whether the contested measure respects the requisite fair balance and, notably, whether it does not impose a disproportionate burden on the applicants.*" ECHR (Grainger and others v. UK), No. 34940/10, para. 37.

86 See also *Jarass* in *Jarass*, Charta EU-Grundrechte, Art. 17 para. 24.

87 ECHR (Grainger and others v. UK), No. 34940/10, para. 37.

88 An independent person has to determine the gone concern value of the respective claims, assuming no resolution action would have been taken and disregarding any extraordinary public support (Art. 66(3) RRD). In the assessment of the Northern Rock nationalisation the ECHR approved that the UK laws required the valuation to reflect a situation that disregarded extraordinary public support as this allows determining the "realities of the situation". ECHR (Grainger and others v. UK), No. 34940/10, para. 40.

the preliminary valuation proves to be erroneous because the asset market values had been set too low resulting in a higher bail-in reduction amount and hence higher losses to shareholders and creditors than they would have suffered in a normal insolvency proceeding. Alternatively, if the bail-in was used to restore the institution's CET1 ratio to the statutory minimum and such minimum is higher than its actual CET1 ratio immediately prior to the bail-in, a bailed-in creditor may suffer a loss that is higher than in insolvency proceedings because the CET1 ratio would not be respected in the case of a wind-down of the institution in connection with an insolvency proceeding. In such case, the creditor may claim compensation for the difference.

Further, even if the preliminary valuation was adequate and irrespective of the institution's current CET1 ratio, the resolution authority may, based on its view of the level of support required to uphold or rebuild market confidence in the institution, order a reduction of liabilities that is higher than would be required on the basis of an adequate preliminary valuation. In addition, in order to reduce contagious effects, there are some types of liabilities which are excluded from bail-in which receive preferential treatment.[89] As a result of such preferential treatment which deviates from the ranking of liabilities in normal insolvency proceedings, the losses incurred by creditors that are not excluded will be higher than in normal insolvency proceedings.

The right to adequate compensation should ensure that bail-in carries the same effects as normal insolvency proceedings for creditors and therefore meets the constitutional standards for the protection of creditors' property rights. However, as mentioned above, the resolution authority may also trigger a bail-in before the institution is balance-sheet insolvent. Even though the effectiveness of the bail-in cannot be challenged as such (Art. 78(2)(d) RRD), the valuation on which the compensation would be based must assume that the institution would have entered normal insolvency proceedings immediately after the bail-in has been effected (Art. 66(3)(a) RRD). In other words, the value of the claim may be determined assuming a liquidation which might turn out to not have been necessary. Based on considerations of financial stability, bail-in should still be considered proportionate even if the bail-in decision proves to be premature. If bail-in occurs prior to an insolvency situation, it may be argued that affected creditors should be entitled to additional damages based on the going-concern enterprise value immediately before the bail-in order, in addition to the compensation based on the liquidation value. As the RRD is silent on this issue, member states may address this issue by providing for governmental liability for erroneous resolution

---

89 See above Part C.

decisions. Under existing German restructuring law, however, resolution decisions of BaFin are privileged and exempted from liability under Section 48a(2), 2nd sentence KWG.

G. Cross-border effects

Systemically important and many other financial institutions operate beyond national borders. To establish an effective resolution toolbox, the European Commission's proposal also had to embrace rules and principles for a cross-border implementation of the resolution measures including the bail-in tool. This is also necessary to improve the predictability of the outcome for market participants.[90] From the European perspective, two levels have to be addressed separately.

First, resolution action must be coordinated among member states. When the European Commission published the RRD on 6 June 2012, the process towards a supervisory banking union had just been initiated, but in the meantime it has been suggested to shift the supervision of banks to the European level. According to the European Commission's proposal for a new directive, the supervision of credit institutions would be conferred on the European Central Bank (ECB).[91] Under this single supervisory mechanism, the ECB will be responsible for supervising all banks within the banking union.[92] Such a single supervisory mechanism would simplify cross-border resolution as it reduces informational deficits in a cross-border context.

In addition, the European Commission has emphasized that a banking union should also include a more centralised management of banking crises. As soon as an agreement on the recovery and resolution proposal[93] is achieved, the European Commission intends to publish a proposal "for a single resolution mechanism which would govern the resolution of banks and coordinate in particular the application of resolution tools to banks within the banking union."[94]

Before a more efficient cooperation framework among national resolution authorities has developed, the RRD would facilitate cross-border resolution in

90 *Hüpkes* "Allocation Costs of Failure Resolution" in Cross Border Bank Insolvency *Lastra* (Ed.) (2010), para. 5.57.
91 COM(2012) 511 final.
92 *European Commission* "A Roadmap towards a Banking Union" (COM (2012) 510), p. 7.
93 With respect to an additional proposal on deposit guarantee schemes, see http://ec.europa.eu/internal_market/bank/guarantee/index_en.htm.
94 *European Commission* "A Roadmap towards a Banking Union" (COM (2012) 510), p. 9.

two ways. It harmonizes the tools available to the national resolution authorities and provides tools for the coordination of resolution activities. Designated "group level resolution authorities"[95] are to establish resolution colleges that coordinate resolution action at the level of banking groups (Art. 80 RRD). The primary responsibility, however, for the resolution of a group lies with the group level resolution authority. If applicable, it proposes a group resolution scheme outlining, *inter alia*, the resolution action that should be taken by the relevant resolution authority. According to Art. 83(9) RRD, the relevant authority has to perform all actions without delay and with due regard to the urgency of the situation. The only option for a national authority to challenge a proposed group resolution action is to refer the matter within 24 hours to the EBA. The EBA will have to decide within another 24 hours with its decision being binding for the resolution authority (Art. 83(6) and (7) RRD). In addition to these provisions addressing the complexity of group resolutions, the European Commission suggests amending Directive 2001/24/EC[96] which provides for the mutual recognition and enforcement of decisions concerning the reorganization or liquidation of credit institutions in all member states. Its scope would be expanded to resolution action.[97]

On a second level, resolution action with respect to international activities of a failing institution need to be coordinated with the competent authorities of third countries outside of the European Union. The European Commission's proposal ultimately aims at concluding agreements with third countries to govern the cooperation and recognition of resolution proceedings. Until such agreements have been concluded, the EBA is responsible to decide on the recognition of third country resolution proceedings (Art. 85 et seqq. RRD). To date, the implementation of FSB's "Key Attributes" across different jurisdictions should harmonize the resolution regimes to a certain minimum degree. However, there is still no approach requiring national authorities to cooperate efficiently.[98]

In addition to general issues of cross-border resolution, there are some challenges that are peculiar to the exercise of the bail-in tool in a cross-border context. The bail-in order is issued by the resolution authority located in the institution's

---

95 Group level resolution authority means the resolution authority in the Member State in which the consolidating supervisor (the competent authority responsible for supervision on a consolidated basis as defined in Article 4(48) of Directive 2006/48/EC) is situated. Art. 2(31), (38) RRD.

96 Directive 2001/24/EC of the European Parliament and of the Council on the reorganisation and winding up of credit institutions OJ L 125, 5.5.2011, p. 15.

97 RRD Recital no. 86.

98 See also *Institute of International Finance* "Making Resolution Robust – Completing the Legal and Institutional Frameworks for Effective Cross-Border Resolution of Financial Institutions" (2012), p. II.

home jurisdiction. Where the bailed-in debt instruments provide for jurisdiction in other countries[99] or the institution has significant assets in other countries making legal action and subsequent enforcement attempts worthwhile, the success of the resolution action depends on whether the bail-in is recognized by the laws in those countries. As debt instruments of the institution will most likely be governed by the laws of relatively few jurisdictions, the number of countries where relevant court disputes may be located will be limited. Consequently, bail-in could be more effective than other resolution tools in a cross-border context,[100] provided that the write-down is recognized in each jurisdiction in which legal action or enforcement action on assets of the institution can legitimately occur. Furthermore, it will be very complex to observe the principles governing the bail-in in a group resolution scenario where all group creditors of the same rank have to be treated in an equitable manner, regardless of their counterparty. If doubts were to arise as to whether no group creditor is worse off than in liquidation, it would be necessary to determine the hypothetical liquidation value of each single member of the group.[101]

H. Judicial review

The RRD limits the judicial review by creditors and shareholders to an *ex post* assessment of the adequacy of their compensation, leaving the legal effect of the resolution order untouched. Consequently, affected shareholders and creditors have no veto or rescission rights.[102]

---

99 Typically, debt instruments of an issuer governed by non-domestic law will provide for jurisdiction in the country whose law governs the relevant instrument (e.g., English courts for bonds governed by English law).

100 *Zhou/Rutledge/Bossu/Dobler/Jassaud/Moore* "From Bail-out to Bail-in: Mandatory Debt Restructuring of Systemic Financial Institutions" (2012), p. 19; *Gifford* "Balancing the Impact of Bail-in" in "The Challenges of Cross-border Resolution" (2012), p. 7.

101 See *Institute of International Finance* "Making Resolution Robust – Completing the Legal and Institutional Frameworks for Effective Cross-Border Resolution of Financial Institutions" (2012), p. 6

102 See e.g. *Financial Stability Board* "Consultative Document – Effective Resolution of Systemically Important Financial Institutions" (2011), p. 39: "Judicial review should be ex post and not result in the reversal of the bail-in measures taken by resolution authorities acting within their legal powers." Also European Commission "Technical Details of a Possible EU Framework for Bank Recovery and Resolution" (2010), p. 66; *Hüpkes* "Allocation Costs of Failure Resolution" in Cross Border Bank Insolvency *Lastra* (Ed.) (2010), para. 5.43.

According to Art. 78(2) RRD, the right to challenge the resolution action in court does not lead to an automatic suspension of the effects of the challenged decision. Rather, the decision of the resolution authority is immediately enforceable and may not subject to a suspension order by any court (Art. 78(2)(a) and (b) RRD). Remedies for a wrongful decision or action by the resolution authorities are limited to compensation for the loss suffered by the plaintiff as a result of the decision or act (Art. 78(2)(d) RRD). Additionally, normal insolvency proceedings under national laws may not be commenced with respect to an institution under resolution or even an institution in relation to which it has been determined that the conditions for resolution are satisfied (Art. 79(1) RRD).

Although each shareholder or creditor subject to bail-in is entitled by constitutional law to effective remedy by judicial review (Art. 47 CFREU), there is broad consensus[103] on these limitations amongst legal commentators. As timing is critical in resolution proceedings, any *ex ante* judicial review would limit the effectiveness of the bail-in.[104] Further, even the possibility to rescind the bail-in order *ex post* would limit the credibility of the resolution action and undermine the institution's access to funding markets after the bail-in has been implemented.[105]

I. Conclusion

The main challenge to the designers of an efficient bail-in regime is to resolve the tension between predictability and flexibility of the scheme.[106] Predictability and transparency are necessary to facilitate the valuation and efficient pricing of bail-in eligible financial instruments and to ensure legal certainty for partici-

---

103 A more critical view is expressed by *Institute of International Finance* "Addressing Priority Issues in Cross-Border Resolution" (2011), p. 23 et seq.

104 *Lastra* "From Bail-Out to an Adequate Resolution Framework" in "The Challenges of Cross-border Resolution" (2012), p. 12; also *Zhou/Rutledge/Bossu/Dobler/Jassaud/Moore* "From Bail-out to Bail-in: Mandatory Debt Restructuring of Systemic Financial Institutions" (2012), p. 12; *Randell* "Triggers for Bank Resolution" in Too Big To Fail – Brauchen wir ein Sonderinsolvenzrecht für Banken? *Kenadjian* (Ed.) (2012), p. 103 (123) considers an ex ante review to be "illusory".

105 *Gleeson* "Legal Aspects of Bank Bail-ins" (2012), Special Paper (2012), LSE Financial Markets Group Paper Series, p. 16.

106 *Hüpkes* "Allocation Costs of Failure Resolution" in Cross Border Bank Insolvency *Lastra* (Ed.) (2010), para. 5.64. See also the Annex "Investors' Perspective" in *Institute of International Finance* "Making Resolution Robust – Completing the Legal and Institutional Frameworks for Effective Cross-Border Resolution of Financial Institutions" (2012), p. 55 et seqq. and *European Commission* "Explanatory Memorandum" to the RRD (2012), COM (2012) 280/3, p. 5.

pants in active debt and equity capital markets. Flexibility undermines legal certainty but is essential to respond to an unexpected bank failure or an unforeseen magnitude of losses and thereby to prevent contagion.

The RRD's bail-in tool ensures a high level of flexibility in granting discretion to the competent resolution authority to assess numerous variable and uncertain institution- and/or market-specific factors and criteria enshrined in the conditions to resolution, to set the timing of the bail-in order, with or without other appropriate resolution tool(s), and to establish the volume of write-down and conversion based on a valuation of assets and liabilities which will in itself include estimates and expectations, regardless of whether the market value or the long-term economic value is appraised. In addition, the right to set conversion rates for distinct classes of creditors is vested in the resolution authority to ensure that no creditor is worse off than in liquidation under insolvency proceedings.

However, the regime of sequential allocation of losses to creditors is determined by the RRD's strict waterfall which is largely based on the hierarchy of claims in insolvency proceedings similar in many jurisdictions, subject only to limited exceptions. The RRD's creditor ranking relies on few but clear-cut categories of liabilities or creditors and contributes to the high degree of predictability of the loss absorption process. Unlike in the existing German resolution regime for partial asset transfer orders (*Übertragungsanordnung*)[107], the distribution of losses among the creditor community does not depend on yet another discretionary decision on the systemic relevance of those creditors that are treated more favourably than others in the resolution although they received the same risk premium on their investment. Rather, even if more discretionary exemptions from the scope of the bail-in tool were to become available to the resolution authority, all affected liabilities within one class, whether shareholder, hybrid capital, subordinated or senior unsecured, are treated equally where a bail-in order is issued. Any creditor who proves to be worse off as a result of the bail-in than he had been under a normal insolvency proceeding will be entitled to adequate compensation. The compensation determined by the resolution authority and eventually by the courts may be imprecise but this residual uncertainty is the price of removing the "too big to fail" subsidy for systemically important financial institutions.[108]

107 See Section 48j(3), 3rd sentence of the German Banking Act (KWG).
108 See *Ueda/Weder di Mauro* IMF Working Paper WP12/128 (2012) "Quantifying Structural Subsidy Values for Systemically Important Financial Institutions", p. 4.

It is tempting to limit the bail-in to a separate category of designated debt instruments.[109] While such a focused bail-in tool would only create another layer of loss-absorbing capital, it would be based on contractual arrangements and thus enhance market predictability and discipline. In contrast, a discretionary bail-in power granted to resolution authorities may be exercised with respect to all unsecured, unprivileged funding liabilities regardless of their contractual terms and would, at least theoretically, allow for an unlimited scope of loss absorption, subject to potential regulatory forbearance by the resolution authorities, pricing uncertainty and resulting moral hazard in the marketplace.[110] In any event, one should recall that the bail-in tool can only be used effectively if the institution has sufficient bail-inable liabilities held by non-banks.[111] Given the far-reaching exceptions from the bail-in tool under the RRD proposal, it remains uncertain whether unlimited discretionary bail-in powers would avoid the use of public funds when unexpected losses exceed the existing level of bail-inable liabilities. Bridging this gap, however, is one of the key objectives of establishing a special resolution regime for financial institutions.

109 *Liikanen* et al. "High Level Expert Group on reforming the structure of the EU banking sector, Final Report" (2012), p. 103 et seq.
110 See for an economic analysis *Brown/Dinç* "Too Many to Fail? Evidence of Regulatory Forbearance when the Banking Sector is Weak", Review of Financial Studies (2011), p. 24. These issues have also been mentioned by the Liikanen report, see *Liikanen* et al. "High Level Expert Group on reforming the structure of the EU banking sector, Final Report" (2012), p. 96.
111 See *Krahnen/Siekmann* "Stellungnahme zum Gesetz zur Restrukturierung und geordneten Abwicklung von Kreditinstituten, zur Errichtung eines Restrukturierungsfonds für Kreditinstitute und zur Verlängerung der Verjährungsfrist der aktienrechtlichen Organhaftung („Restrukturierungsgesetz")" (report on the draft German Bank Restructuring Act) (2010), p. 5 (http://www.bundestag.de/bundestag/ausschuesse17/a07/anhoerungen/2010/029/Stellungnahmen/22_Prof_Krahnen.pdf).

Patrick S. Kenadjian*

CoCos and Bail-Ins

Introduction: An Alternative to Bail-Ins

My friend *Tom Huertas* has made a very cogent case for the need for bail-ins. I agree with him entirely that we are far better with them than without them. I would like to complement his work by making the case for the usefulness of contingent convertible debt, popularly referred to as "CoCos". Convertible or write-down CoCos are a way for financial institutions to contract in advance with investors willing to buy their debt that, for a higher coupon than the institution normally pays on its unsecured subordinated debt, these investors will grant the issuer the right to put specified amounts of its equity to them in exchange for this debt or to cut its debt to them at a point in time when the issuer's financial position has deteriorated and it might otherwise be unable to raise equity in the market or otherwise reduce its debt without serious contagion effects.

In bank regulatory parlance contingent convertible debt should be viewed as a loss-absorbing capital instrument, which means it serves to increase the issuer's equity capital or reduce its debt upon the occurrence of specified "trigger" events and it can be designed to do this, depending on how the trigger events are designed, sufficiently early that this occurs on a "going concern" basis, *i.e.* at a time when that conversion or write-down can contribute to the continued viability of the institution. This is important because financial institutions, especially banks, operate with a very thin equity capital layer of a few percent, one that would be inconceivably thin outside the financial sector, which can be eaten through every quickly by losses and which, as we saw in the 2008/2009 crisis, can be very hard to replace, especially in the midst of a crisis.

Bail-ins and CoCos are often seen as complementary instruments or procedures which operate in similar ways, but at different times. Because bail-ins involve a decision by a public authority to interfere with contractually agreed property rights, the general consensus is that they should really only be used at a point where a danger to the financial system as a whole is sufficiently great that it justifies this interference with private property rights, which many see as akin to expropriation. This means that – to use the phraseology favored by the European Commission – the "bail-in tool" is only proposed to be used at the point of non-viability of a financial institution. This is, however, the point at which the tool

* The opinions expressed herein are the author's own.

may be least effective and the cost of its use the greatest, in the sense that more debt may have to be converted or written off to achieve the goal of returning the institution to viability. In contrast CoCos, which are a contractual instrument, can be designed by the parties, the debtor and its creditors, to be triggered either early or late, with a high or a low trigger. They may thus be more effective at a lower cost than the bail-in tool.

The two instruments or procedures have thus often been viewed as complementary and, in an ideal world we would like to have both available. The problem at least within the European Union, is that, we do not currently have either. On the one hand, the European Commission's proposal for a "Directive of the European Parliament and the Council establishing a framework for the recovery and resolution of credit institutions and investment firms" of June 2012 (the "Resolution Directive" or "RRD") would not require the bail-in tool to be available until 2018. On the other hand, in part, I believe, as a result of decisions by the Basel Committee on Banking Supervision ("BCBS") and the European Banking Authority ("EBA") in late 2011 which questioned the place CoCos should have in the regulatory capital of European Union financial institutions, especially systematically relevant ones, development of a market for CoCos has been slowed considerably, although it appears to be slowly returning.

I am sure neither set of decisions was taken lightly or without consideration of many important factors and I am not suggesting that either could or should be reversed lightly. Nonetheless, their conjunction effectively leaves the European Union as a whole[1] without a way to recapitalize its banks in a crisis when capital markets are effectively closed to them. The effective date for the bail-in tool relates in part of the structure of bank debt maturities within the European Union[2] and the difficult question to how enforceable "grandfathering" (*i.e.* the application of the tool to debt outstanding prior to the publication of the Directive) would be. These are non-trivial considerations outside the ability of public authorities to control.

On the other hand, the decision on the place of CoCos in bank capital structures was a by-product of a laudable preference for common equity over hybrids

---

1 Individual Member States can of course adopt bail-in laws into national legislation in advance of the effective date provided for by the RRD. Spain adopted such a law in September 2012 pursuant to its June 2012 MOU with the European Council relating to the bail-out of its banks. The problem is that piecemeal adoption risks sacrificing the uniformity sought by the Directive and may not be as effective if other Member States do not adopt similar laws more or less simultaneously.
2 By coincidence or calculation it occurs after the bulk of currently outstanding Eurozone bank debt, including the credits extended to Eurozone banks by the European Central Bank ("ECB") under its LTRO (long term repurchase operations) in late 2011 and early 2012 have matured.

in the buffer capital of globally systemic important banks ("G-SIBs") by the BCBS. The BCBS specifically stated it did not intend to foreclose use of CoCos, especially for supplemental capital buffers, and the EBA action (in the form of a "common term sheet"), related solely to instruments intended to qualify as Tier 1 capital. However, the fourth iteration of the European Union's Capital Requirements Directive ("CRD IV") and its companion Capital Regulation Directive ("CRR") seem now to have enshrined the exclusion of CoCos which are not perpetual instruments from both Tier 1 capital and the various capital buffers provided for in the third iteration of the Basel accords ("Basel III") into European Law, so that further development of CoCos will have to take place under the "Pillar 2" authority of national supervisors.

The 2018 effectiveness date for the bail-in tool could be amended during the adoption process of the Directive, and numerous voices, including that of my co-editor Andreas Dombret of the Bundesbank, have been raised in favor of bringing it forward. However, the balance of the RRD as a whole does not come into effect before 2015 and it is unclear to me how realistic it would be to bring that date any further forward, given the need for what may be quite a delicate translation into local law, in view of the sensitivity of the expropriation issue and the need for multiple changes in corporate law to allow the bail-in tool to function as intended.

Bail-in, the radioactive silver bullet

"Too big to fail" was the big problem left over from – some might even say created by – the financial crisis of 2008/2009 and the way public authorities reacted to it.[3] A bank resolution regime was meant to be its solution, a "third way" between disorderly insolvency as typified by the aftermath of the collapse of Lehman Brothers in September 2008, which is still playing out in courtrooms in the US, the UK and Germany almost four years later, and the costly tax payer funded bail-outs which preceded and followed it.

The initial model for financial institution resolution was the procedure which the US Federal Deposit Insurance Corporation ("FDIC") had been applying to the resolution of US deposit taking institutions for years, most recently during the

3 While actions, in the form of bail-outs, speak louder than words, in the United States at least there was also a clear declaration by all the Federal banking supervisors, on February 23, 2009, pledging to "preserve the viability of systemically important financial institutions". Joint Statement by the Treasury, FDIC, OCC, OTS and the Federal Reserve, February 23, 2009.

financial crisis. All of the “first movers” in the area, the United Kingdom in the Banking Act 2009, the United States in the Orderly Liquidation Authority provisions of the Wall Street Reform and Consumer Protection Act of 2010 (the “Dodd Frank Act”) and Germany in the Kreditinstitut-Reorganisationsgesetz of 2010 modeled themselves more or less closely on the powers and procedures found in the Federal Deposit Insurance Act (“FDIA”) as amended by the Federal Deposit Insurance Corporation Improvement Act (“FDICIA”) of 1991.

The FDIA served the FDIC and the US tolerably well because the banks to be resolved were relatively small, uncomplicated commercial banks operating predominantly in the United States, whose liabilities were made up largely (85% on average) of deposits insured by the FDIC.[4] However, an FDIA-like approach left many problems open when applied in the European context of universal banks operating across multiple borders both within and outside of Europe. In this context a key issue would be the extent to which the orders of a home country resolution authority like the FDIC would be respected in host countries.[5] In fact, the fear that these orders would be ignored or undermined by host country authorities was one factor in moving some European governments towards bail-outs during the crisis.

In searching for a tool which could be wielded by home country authorities whose effectiveness would not depend on the recognition or cooperation of host country authorities, clever minds hit upon the idea of the anti-bail-out, or bail-in, a tool which would enable a home country authority to write-off, write-down or convert into equity debt securities issued under domestic law by the financial institution in its home country. It was a brilliant insight: Orders by a home country authority to a domestic bank that required the cooperation of its foreign subsidiaries or access to its deposits located abroad could clearly be blocked by order of banking supervisors in those countries, but what authority would allow a host country supervisor to oppose actions taken under home country domestic law by a competent authority which merely rearranged the capital structure of the equity of a domestic institution? This would not involve the transfer of shares of a subsidiary located in a host country, which transfer might be subject to local approval. It also would not involve access to deposits located in a host country or require contesting the payment of debts incurred locally by a foreign branch or subsidiary, conceivably all under foreign law. The home country authority would be acting at home and under its own law. Furthermore, the action could

4 *Kenadjian* (2012).

5 *Claessens, Herring and Schoenmaker* (2010) contains an excellent description of the size and complexity of multinational financial institutions, especially European ones.

be taken quickly – over a weekend even it was said – and it solved what was a serious problem for FDIC "purchase and assumption" style resolutions when dealing with a "too big to fail" institution. These institutions were likely to be "too big to merge" as well, in the sense that the universe of potential buyers for the whole institution was likely to be small and a combination of these firms could be expected to raise serious antitrust questions, while splitting the institution up would take time and potentially leave messy bits and pieces still to be liquidated afterwards. In the heat of the crisis, some antitrust concerns had been overridden, not always with happy results. So, all in all, an internal recapitalization had much to recommend it.

Thus the bail-in concept was greeted as something akin to a silver bullet for the TBTF problem. The hopes for it are perhaps best exemplified in a passage of the European Commission Staff Impact Assessment of June 2012 (the "Impact Assessment") accompanying the Commission's draft Resolution Directive which compared Lehman's fate under the US bankruptcy and the UK insolvency regimes with what would have happened to it "under bail-in":

> "According to market estimates, Lehman's balance sheet was under pressure from perhaps $25 bn [sic] unrealized losses on illiquid assets. But bankruptcy expanded that shortfall in practice to roughly $150 bn of shareholder and creditor losses.
> With bail-in, officials could have proceeded as follows. First, the concerns over valuation could have been addressed by writing assets down by $25 billion, roughly wiping out existing shareholders. Secondly, to recapitalize the bank, preferred-stock and subordinated-debt investors could have converted their approximately $25 billion of existing holdings in return for 50% of the equity in the new Lehman. Holdingers of Lehman's $120 billion of senior unsecured debt would have converted 15% of their positions, and received the other 50% of the new equity.
> The remaining 85% of senior unsecured debt would have been unaffected, as would the bank's secured creditors and counterparties.
> The equity of this reinforced Lehman would have been $43 billion, roughly double the size of its old capital base ... A bail-in like this would have allowed Lehman to open for business on Monday." Commission Staff Impact Assessment, at 176.

The authors do note that there would also have been the need for a multi-billion dollar funding facility, but they think it could have been provided voluntarily by the private sector, providing it ranked ahead of existing senior debt, to shore up Lehman's liquidity[6], but in a nutshell that is the vision of bail-in as silver bullet.

6 Under Dodd-Frank the liquidity facility would be provided by the FDIC borrowing from the Treasury.

However, the silver bullet also turns out to be a bit radioactive. The write-off, write-down or conversion has a flavor of expropriation to it, which has led some to have their doubts about its legality. The German lawmakers in 2010 specifically elected not to give their resolution authority bail-in powers because of doubts on precisely this point. The European Commission also felt it prudent to supplement their consultations on the RRD, which were officially closed on March 3, 2012, by additional "discussions" on the bail-in tool which took place in April 2012 and delayed the publication of the proposal until June 6, 2012. Briefly put, the legal issue is whether bail-ins contravene the right of property guaranteed to both shareholders and holders of "bail-inable" debt of the institutions involved under Article 17 of the Charter of Fundamental Rights and Article 1 of the First Additional Protocol of the European Convention for the Protection of Human Rights and Fundamental Freedoms, or whether they are justified by the greater good of preserving financial stability in the European Union[7]. While many legal scholars are convinced that, in view of the magnitude of the public interest in preventing the collapse of the financial system, bail-ins should not contravene the Charter or the Convention, the answer clearly involves a balancing of important interests on both sides and cannot be given *ex ante* with absolute certainty.

Furthermore, the potential that making a large part of a bank's debt subject to bail-in might significantly raise the costs of debt financing for the affected institution and possibly even dry up its sources of senior unsecured debt was also a non-trivial concern. A large part of the April discussions appear to have centered on how the tool could be designed to accomplish its desired function of allowing a restructuring to take place over a weekend without leading to unwanted deleveraging of the financial institutions in the midst of a potential double dip recession.[8]

In the end, use of the bail-in tool in the RRD is subject to a number of restraints, best viewed as safeguards of the rights of creditors. It can only be used late in the process, at the point of non-viability of the institution. And furthermore it can only be used to recapitalize a whole institution (as opposed to capitalizing a bridge bank) if it can be expected to restore the institution to going concern status. It must be done quickly and yet requires an independent valuation of the institution's assets before it can be applied. It requires a "business restoration plan" – ostensibly different from the recovery and resolutions plans which are

---

7 Article 4.3 of the Explanatory Memorandum to the RRD says: "the use of resolution powers should be limited to the extent necessary in order to meet an objective of general interest, namely preserving financial stability in the Union."

8 Commission Staff Impact Assessment, Annex XVIII.

required as part of the institutions' living wills, but which is only to be drawn up after the tool is applied. Finally, because no-one could agree on the immediate effects that the availability of the tool would have on the debt markets for the institutions involved, its applicability was delayed until January 1, 2018, three years after the rest of the RRD enters into effect on January 1, 2015.

The CoCo Alternative

Thus, whatever the virtues of the bail-in tool, the current Commission proposal would not make it available to resolution authorities for another five years. In the meantime, what should we be doing in the bank recapitalization "space"? The alternative which comes readily to mind is contingent capital debt, popularly known as CoCos. CoCos have one key feature in common with bail-inable debt: they can be subject to write-down or conversion into equity at a given point. But they also have several decisive differences. First, the trigger point need not be set so late (the point of non-viability), or so low (the point at which the institution would lose its license). It can be set earlier, and higher, and thus at a point where there is a greater likelihood that its use would return the institution to financial health as a going concern. Second, its trigger would be set contractually and its use would be contractual in nature. Rather than a resolution authority deciding in its discretion when to trigger it, the trigger is described in the instrument and is negotiated between debtor and creditors. Thus, when the conditions of the trigger are met there should be no question of expropriation. Its use is actually quite close to the effect of a "pre-packaged" Chapter 11 case under US bankruptcy law, which can be executed swiftly because the creditors and the debtor have all agreed to the respective haircuts or conversion rates to be applied to various classes of creditors in advance of the filing (the triggering in the case of the CoCos). Advocates of bail-ins often compare their tool to a "pre-pack". In doing so they are ignoring the fact that the resolution authority's action has not been agreed to by the creditors, but only, at most, been subject to the creditors' acknowledgement that one day such a thing might occur.

Since CoCos are contractual, they also have two additional advantages: the market knows exactly what securities are subject to compulsory conversation of write down and can price them accordingly. If they are issued in sufficient quantity to effect a recapitalization, just the CoCos should bear the additional cost attributable to potential write down or conversion. In contrast, with the exception of the Liikanen Report, most proposals for bail-inable debt resist identifying it *ex ante* as a specific subset of the institutions' debt, but rather prefer to be able to bail-in any non-secured debt other than specified categories of excluded debt (such as insured deposits or customer, employee or tax-related obligations). Consequently, as discussed more fully below, the cost of a large proportion of the institution's senior debt may be subject to a conversion or uncertainty surcharge. JP Morgan in its a march 2012 research note on the topic estimates this may be as high as 345 basis points over the cost of unsecured senior debt to compensate for the instrument's contingent features.[9]

CoCos, like the bail-in tool, were also initially greeted with a degree of enthusiasm, in part because they were seen as a possible replacement for the approximately $1 trillion of hybrid instruments financial institutions had issued under Basel II as supplementary Tier 1 or Tier 2 capital which will lose that status by 2022. CoCos could clearly be designed to be loss-absorbing on a "going-concern" basis and the Basel Committee on Bank Supervision ("BCBS") had referred to them in that connection in its January 2011 Basel III paper. The US Treasury's White Paper of June 2009 which preceded the adoption of Dodd-Frank had recommended they be a required part of bank capital and Dodd-Frank commissioned a study on their use. The Swiss Financial Markets Authority ("FINMA"), made a place for both high trigger "recovery" CoCos and low trigger "resolution" CoCos as part of the "Swiss Finish", the supplementary capital buffer required for its largest banks above and beyond the requirements of Basel III. Several European financial institutions issued CoCos in early 2011 which sold well, albeit often in exchange for old hybrid instruments which the institutions had indicated they would otherwise redeem, and investment funds were organized to invest in this potential market. Then, in November 2011, in its statement on loss absorbency for G-SIBs, the Group of Governors and Heads of Supervision (GHOS) of the BCBS rejected their use as additional loss-absorbing instruments to meet the additional capital buffers required for G-SIBs, the largest global financial institutions. The GHOS did say that it would consider CoCos to meet national loss-absorbency requirements above and beyond the global minimum, meaning that the FINMA "Swiss Finish" and any similar national "gold plating" regulations could prescribe CoCos, but that they would be ineligible for the estimated €700 billion capital buffers to be required of the G-SIBs.

The practical use of CoCos even for supplemental national buffers within the EU seemed to be further reduced by two additional European initiatives. The draft of the fourth iteration of the EU Capital Requirements Directive ("CRD IV"), strongly supported by France, would narrow the scope for higher national requirements in the name of a "single rule book" and "maximum harmonization"

9 *J.P. Morgan* (2012).

to that area of discretion national authorities have under their "Pillar 2" powers under the Basel II regime. In addition, the December 2011 Common Term Sheet for Buffer Convertible Capital Securities issued by the European Banking Authority ("EBA") requires that, in order to qualify for Tier 1 treatment, these instruments should be undated (*i.e.* have a perpetual life) and subordinated, with two triggers, a core Tier 1 ratio of 7% and a viability ratio. This left open the extent to which any senior debt instrument with a fixed maturity and a high trigger could qualify for buffer treatment under Basel III, but work on the design and marketing of CoCos outside the academic world pretty much ground to a halt, except in Switzerland, in response to the supplemental buffer capital requirements of FINMA under the "Swiss Finish".

Then, in early July 2012, the possibility of CoCos playing a role in Europe resurfaced rather surprisingly in press reports that the EU's conditions for assistance to the Spanish banking sector included the issuance of CoCos by certain Spanish banks by year-end 2012. In the event, the Spanish banks issued preference shares with CoCo-like triggers, rather than CoCos, but a reference to them in an EU document is encouraging. In addition, in a much noted speech to the British Banker's Association on the future of banking regulation in the UK, delivered on October 17, 2012, Andrew Bailey, Managing Director, Prudential Business Unit of the UK's Financial Services Authority gave CoCos another welcome boost. He noted that CoCos could present an attractive alternative to additional equity in that, upon issuance, they did not effect an immediate dilution for shareholders.[10] From the context of his remarks it has been deduced that the FSA, were it to endorse CoCos, would only do so under its so-called "Pillar 2" authority under Basel II, which allows national supervisory authorities to require a limited amount of additional capital to be held. Together, the EU and FSA statements are, especially in view of the deferred availability of the bail-in tool under the RRD until 2018, an additional incentive to revisit the pros and cons of CoCos. Finally, in November 2012, Barclays PLC of the UK brought to market a CoCo, apparently after extensive consultation with the FSA, which attracted extensive demand amid speculation that the FSA would allow it to count towards the "Pillar 2" capital cushion it can require SIFIs to maintain. Barclays has since issued a second CoCo in April 2012 and Swiss banks Credit Suisse and UBS name also issued CoCos.

Another potentially useful, if for the moment still Largely misinterpreted development in this area is the recommendation contained in the Liikanen Report that there should be a separate class of debt securities, referred to as "designated bail-in instrument", with a clear position within the hierarchy of debt

10 *Bailey* (2012).

commitments in a bank's balance sheet.[11] In explaining this recommendation, Governor Liikanen has referred to "instruments with clear pre-specified contractual terms in order to create a well-functioning market for these instruments."[12] His testimony before the Joint Committee on Banking Standards of the UK Parliament makes it clear that his Group is thinking about instruments whose terms of conversion into shares and/or write down would be set in advance.[13] These arguments make clear that their bail-in instrument would work much like CoCos and are not intended to limit the scope of the bail-in tool referred to in the RRD. In any event, all the arguments the Report makes in favor of their brand of designated bail-in instrument would apply equally well to CoCos.

CoCos and Bail-Ins Compared

The idea behind CoCos and bail-in eligible debt is very similar. It is to provide a financial institution with a debt instrument which, upon the occurrence of certain triggering events, can be converted into equity or written down, either in whole or in part, in order to replenish the institution's capital. The two share many of the same advantages and the same limitation: they are a good solution for banks which have a capital adequacy problem, but they will not help separate out bad assets, so that if asset impairment is the problem, they will not be the sole solution. Both of them bring in no new cash to the enterprise, so their effect on the market remains somewhat uncertain. Both may trigger contagion effects. And finally, both will require amendments to corporate law in many European jurisdictions to facilitate their use.

The main differences between the two reside in the triggers and who pulls them. As discussed more fully below, CoCos issued to date have been designed with two kinds of triggers: high or early ones, for example when an institution falls below 7% on Tier 1 common equity; and low or late ones, for example at the 5% level. These regulatory capital related triggers have been criticized as lagging indicators, intransparent and subject to manipulation internally by the issuer, especially now that we are all focusing on how different calculations of risk weighted assets ("RWAs") can be from one bank or country to another. These are legitimate concerns. In particular, it makes little sense to use a lagging indica-

11 *Liikanen* Report at 103, 104.
12 *Liikanen* (2012).
13 *Liikanen* (2012A).

tor in a prompt corrective action context. A leading measure of financial distress clearly makes more sense and there are a number of market-related triggers, for example based on the stock market price of the institution's stock or the spread on credit default swaps ("CDSs") on its debt which can be used instead of balance sheet triggers. These would be harder for the issuers to manipulate, although manipulation by third parties in the market remains possible, but there are solutions for this concern which I will discuss below. There are, of course, limitations on the ability to use the market-related triggers in Europe, which stem from the relatively small proportion of European banks whose securities are publicly traded.[14] Thus a market-related trigger will not work in particular for many small savings and mutual banks, but since these banks are also not those which are the main targets of bail-in legislation, this should not constitute a major obstacle to their use for G-SIBs or even most SIFIs.

Both balance sheet and market-related triggers can be set sufficiently high that they would kick in before the point of non-viability and thus contribute to a recovery of the bank's fortunes before the institution became a source of dangerous externalities for the financial system. The trigger would also not require a supervisor or resolution authority to pull it, it would be sprung by a quarterly report showing capital had fallen below the trigger level or by the average price of either common equity or the CDS spread on the institution's debt having been below or above the contractually agreed level over a period of time. And then the conversion or write down would occur. Academics and others continue to tinker with the model, adding refinements to it, such as Call Option Enhanced Reverse Convertibles (whose acronym is COERC, presumably meant to be pronounced, "coerce") or dual trigger stock price models.

We have noted the brake on issuances which followed the BCBS and EBA pronouncements in November and December 2011. However, with banks under increasing pressure to raise additional capital and finding it difficult to raise common equity, CoCos may again be looking like a viable alternative, even if they can only qualify as Tier 2 capital, since they are dated instruments and limited in amount to what the national regulator can allow under its Pillar 2 powers. But are there other advantages for the institution to issue them and will a market develop for them it?

From the institution's point of view, issuing higher coupon CoCos could paradoxically result in an overall lower cost of funding on its senior debt. As noted

14 *Maria Nieto* notes that of almost 7,800 credit institutions in the EU, only 312 have shares which are stock exchange listed, 737 have debentures (which I take it to mean publicly traded debt) and 54 have traded CDSs. *Nieto* (2012) at 16.

above, the market should apply the risk premium to the CoCos on the understanding that they would be triggered first, but might well consider that the balance of the institution's senior debt was then subject to a lower probability of default or of bail-in, so that the risk premium on the balance of the institution's bail-inable debt could be lower. This is also the argument advanced in the Liikanen Report to argue that bail-inable debt should constitute a separate class of debt of financial institutions.[15] The institution would also gain a measure of self-control over the conditions of conversion or write-down of its debt, which it lacks when the decision on these matters is taken by banking or resolution authorities exercising bail-in powers. In so doing, it might also be able to forestall the use by authorities of "prompt corrective action" powers, including removal of management, by agreeing to what Haldane calls "contractual corrective action" itself.[16]

So even without a favorable capital treatment, CoCos can offer some advantages to the institutions which issue them, but the major advantage of such instruments comes from the systemic or public policy point of view, what the Bank of England calls the "social value": such instruments would have a chance of avoiding the kind of crisis in which a bail-in tool would need to be activated. Thus the chances of contagion and the attendant costs to the taxpayer could be reduced. However, realistically seen, a market for these instruments can be expended to be slow to develop, unless the right incentives are provided for the issuers to use them on a broad enough scale that they become a recognized asset class which can attract investors in sufficient quantity. And that, would be greatly enhanced by a clear place in the Basel III capital structure for European banks to replace some or all of those Basel II hybrid instruments that they are having to phase out.

I recognize fully that these are new instruments, so they raise many questions, including how susceptible market based triggers are to manipulation, but there are multiple possible solutions to this problem. One solution, suggested by John Coffee, would be a double stock price trigger, one for the issuer's stock price and the other for an index of financial stocks, which would be harder to manipulate than just the stock of one single institution.[17] Another, suggested by *Andrew Haldane* of the Bank of England, would be a ratio of market capitalization to total assets or total debt.[18] Finally, he and other commentators have suggested that

---

15 *Liikanen* Report, at 103. As noted above, that the High Level Group was thinking about a separate class of security, such as CoCos, rather than the debt potentially covered by bail-in powers in a resolution process has been widely misinterpreted.

16 *Haldane* (2011) at 6.

17 *Coffee* (2011).

18 *Haldane* (2011).

setting the conversion rate based on a sufficiently long period of trading would make manipulation through shorting much more expensive and thus much less likely. Some suggestions, for example, *Calomiris and Herring* (2011), extend to 90 days, which strike me as too long, as a practical matter, although I understand why they suggest it,[19] something on the order of 30 days would make sense.

There are also questions about the signaling effect the trigger – a high trigger may also be viewed as too early a trigger – might have both on the issuer itself and on the sector as a whole, being potentially misunderstood as a signal of a coming collapse not only of the institution concerned but also of the financial sector as a whole. There is also the concern, first raised by *Charles Goodhart* I believe, of triggering a "death spiral" in an institution's stock price through a combination of pre-conversion selling by existing equity holders to avoid the coming dilution, short selling by either CoCo holders seeking to hedge potential losses on conversion or by speculators, compounded by the actual initial dilution to existing shareholders upon conversion and subsequent dumping of the shares by the CoCo holders. These holders are generally expected to be traditional debt investors, who may not be interested in holding equity or who may even not be allowed to do so. The concern about shorting at least can be dealt with by lengthening the time period over which the stock price is calculated, as noted above, which would significantly increase the cost of carrying the short position and thus reduce the economic benefits of shorting.

In May 2012, the Bank of England published a very useful paper which summarizes the main arguments pro and con for CoCos and reviews the experience with their issuances to date as well as much of the academic literature on the subject.[20] They note that CoCos have been issued by Credit Suisse (several series in 2011, including one eleven times oversubscribed, with a double trigger, one at a 7% of common equity Tier 1 to risk weighted assets ratio, the other a regulatory trigger to be used by the Swiss regulatory authority), Bank of Ireland, Alba and Irish Life and Permanent, all also in 2011 (with features similar to the Credit Suisse issues, including a double trigger, a "capital deficiency event" based on common equity Tier 1 to risk weighted assets falling below 8.25% and a "non-viability event" if a bank would be insolvent without state support), Lloyds Banking in 2009 (with a single trigger of core Tier 1 ratio falling below 4%), Newcastle Building Society in 2010 and three issues by Rabobank in 2010 (with triggers of

19 It is related to the back-testing of various triggers against the historical stock prices of financial institutions which encountered difficulties during the crisis where, as discussed further below, a three month measuring period yielded highly predictive results.
20 *Murphy, Walsh and Willison* (2012).

7 and 8% of equity capital to risk weighted assets). The Credit Suisse CoCos were clearly intended to be high trigger recovery CoCos under the Swiss Finish. Subsequent to the publication of the paper, UBS issued low trigger contingent capital with a permanent write down feature in August 2012, intended to be low trigger "resolution" CoCos under the Swiss Finish. It is, I think, no coincidence, that the bulk of these issuances have taken place in Switzerland, where FINMA has made a place for them in the Swiss Finish capital structure, and the UK, which has traditionally tried to defend its powers to include additional capital requirements, rather than in France or elsewhere on the Continent. Andrew Haldane's work in the area may also have influenced the UK issuances.

Most interestingly, the authors cite literature and back-testing on the historical record using market capitalization based triggers which show that a formula based on a 40% decline in a bank's market capitalization over a period of three months would have triggered CoCos in six major financial institutions which failed or experienced severe problems in 2007/2008 well in advance of their failure or crisis. Three would have been triggered in December 2007, two more in March 2008 and the last in June 2008. In particular, Lehman Brothers and AIG would have hit the trigger a full six months before Lehman declared bankruptcy and AIG was bailed out. Similar results are found for European institutions. For example, RBS and UBS would have hit the trigger in January 2008, Lloyds and Dexia by June 2008 and ING by September.[21] Whatever the precise formula chosen, market based capital ratios of the "crisis banks" Haldane selects[22] started to deteriorate in April 2007, almost a year and a half before the Lehman crisis.[23]

This research does not prove that CoCos would have saved these institutions from failure or crisis. Among other things, the amount of CoCos issued by them would have had to have been sufficient to stabilize them either alone or in conjunction with other measures, so that the mere fact that the instrument would have been triggered does not necessarily guarantee a successful recapitalization. Still, what it does show is that a market based trigger can be effective in allowing a timely infusion of capital. It thus refutes the common reproach that, because most financial institutions which failed during the crises were adequately capitalized from a regulatory point of view, a CoCo instrument cannot be expected to

21 *Murphy, Walsh and Willison* citing *Claessens, Herring and Schoenmaker* (2010) which in turn relies on *D'Sousa* et al. (2009).

22 These are RBS, HBOS, Lloyds TSB, Bradford & Bingley, Alliance & Leicester, Citigroup, Washington Mutual, Wachovia, Merrill Lynch, Freddie Mac, Fannie Mae, Goldman Sachs, ING Group, Dexia and Commerzbank. *Haldane* (2011) at 14.

23 *Haldane* (2011) at 5, 14.

be effective.[24] I believe it can if it is properly designed, and that using a market capitalization based trigger (as opposed to the balance sheet based capital adequacy test which, being based on a lagging indicator as discussed above, not surprisingly failed to predict failure during the crisis) is an element of such design.

There are also other issues, of course, such as the tax deductibility of the CoCo instrument in the United States, which will significantly affect its cost to the issuer, as well as their rating. With respect to ratings, a consensus seems to be emerging that they will be about four notches under regular senior debt. This may well be more of a problem than was initially thought, since, given the recent downgrades of European banks, their CoCos may well end up firmly in high yield, or "junk" territory. Finally, CoCo holders will have to recognize that if their securities are triggered and converted into common shares, a subsequent bail-in will effect a further dilution of the value of their investment. Even if they are not triggered before the bail-in, the sequential conversion of junior and convertible instruments provided for in Article 43 of the RRD is likely to lead to much the same result.[25] It is not clear whether the market has yet focused on this sequence of events, but once it does it could well lead to an upwards repricing of CoCos.

It should therefore be clear that CoCos are not a panacea for the TBTF issue, but neither do I think it is wise for regulators to expect that the market will develop an alternative in the absence of regulatory guidance and encouragement. The BCBS, in rejecting their use as loss absorbing instruments for G-SIBs

---

24 Some of these studies go further than this and conclude that sufficiently dilutive CoCos would have led firms in distress to raise capital rather than allow the CoCos to trigger. *D'Sousa* et al (2009). *Calomiris and Herring* (2011). The back-testing conducted by *D'Sousa* et al. and *Calomiris and Herring* compare the cost to existing shareholders of dilution through a rights offering at a 15% discount from the then current market price at the points in time at which CoCos would have been triggered with the dilution brought about by their triggering and concluded that in each case it would have been cheaper for the firms involved to resort to new equity capital raising and that rational management would have chosen to raise fresh equity rather than risk the more severe dilution of the firm's existing equity holders through triggering of the CoCos. If they are right, then effectiveness of the CoCo instrument is not necessarily tied to it being issued in amounts sufficient to restore by itself the firm's capital upon conversion, but rather in the incentive it provides to management to raise capital on a timely basis. Back–testing of Bear Stearns, Lehman Brothers and AIG appear to confirm their thesis. Whether this will continue to hold in the future is of course open to question, given how infrequently banks have raised equity capital in the last two years, so that a large amount of CoCos (relative to equity) may be needed. But since bank equity in the Eurozone tends to be less than 3% of balance sheet totals, a large amount of CoCos in relation to equity still seems doable.

25 Article 43(3) which is, I think, meant to cover CoCos, is not entirely clear, but that seems to be what it aims to do. See also the discussion above of *Claessens, Herring and Schoenmaker* (2010).

in its November 2011 paper, advanced a number of non trivial grounds for their objections to CoCos, including trigger failure (will they function as designed); cost effectiveness (will they be cheaper than equity simply because they are less loss-absorbent); complexity (new products, no one knows exactly how they will function); death spiral (the downward pressure on share prices discussed above); adverse signaling (a variation on the contagion theme); and negative shareholder and management incentives (to avoid punitive dilution to shareholders management will deleverage by scaling back loans or selling assets).

With respect to cost, the experience of CoCos already issued by Lloyds, UBS and Credit Suisse indicate increased yields of between 451 and 636 basis points over these institutions' senior unsecured debt[26]. As I noted above, this may need to be revised upwards, but it does present a current benchmark for comparing the costs of CoCos with the cost of common equity or other subordinated instruments. Many of the other objections are legitimate criticisms of a trigger based on a 7% Tier 1 equity capital ratio to risk weighted assets, which the BCBS chose as the basis for their analysis in that document. They would not apply to *Haldane's* or *Calomiris* and *Herring's* proposed triggers based on market capitalization ratios. The latter also have the charm of using a metric, market capitalization, which as discussed above, had a demonstrable predictive effect during the crisis. Other parts of their objections, in particular trigger failure and cost effectiveness, would apply to bail-ins as well. And yet we are willing to back bail-ins and not CoCos. I find making bail-ins the only alternative undesirable for a number of reasons.

The first is the time point at which bail-in takes place: non-viability, which strikes me as just too late. The second is the circumstances under which bail-in takes place: the pressure cooker of the short weekend before the Asian markets open, during which a decision as to the value of the institution's assets and liabilities needs to be made with enough certainty that the resulting conversion or write-down is sufficient to ensure viability. While Article 30 of the RRD which deals with the valuation is titled "Preliminary Valuation," in Section 2 it states that its goal is "that any losses that could be derived are recognised at the moment the resolution tools are utilised". That is going to be very hard to achieve, unless one takes a very broad view of when that moment occurs and how long it lasts.[27] The third is the very idea that we are putting all our eggs in this one basket, the

26 Barclays in its research cited below comes up with an average of 500 basis points, perhaps using a weighted average.

27 I understand that in Denmark bail-ins have been accomplished over weekends, but that involves erring on the side of bailing-in more debt than may be necessary, subject to a right of subsequent write ups or reimbursement. That does not seem to be the route the RRD is taking.

exercise of discretion by fallible humans who did not prove any more adept than anyone else at discerning risks and intervening surgically during the last crisis. They were surely not any worse at it, but no better either, and they were subject to intense political pressure.

Lehman was not rescued for many reasons, one of which was precisely the difficulty in valuing its assets over a weekend in order to determine how much capital it needed, but another was the pressure from Congress on the Federal Reserve and the US Treasury after the rescue of Bear Stearns not to do it again. Today, of course, the last crisis is still fresh enough in our memories that everyone is still focused on taking prompt action to avert further risks and crises, but as John Coffee notes in a recent article promoting his brand of CoCos, there is what he calls a "regulatory sine curve" under which regulatory activism, while intense in the wake of a regulatory crisis, relaxes thereafter, as lobbying and the impact of regulatory arbitrage and capture softens the resistance of the regulators. This concern is strongly echoed in the first of the Reports of the Advisory Scientific Committee to the European Systemic Risk Board, entitled "Forbearance, Resolution and deposit insurance" (July 2012).

In the U.S., in the wake of the savings and loan crisis we tried to make sure regulators did not forbear on shutting down insolvent "zombie" banks, by prescribing in the FDICIA a specific point, determinable by a simple balance sheet test (common equity as a percentage of total assets), at which authorities were required to close a bank. The idea was a good one, but it still relied on an inherently lagging measure of balance sheet assets and the level of equity selected, 2% of assets, was too low to make it as useful a tool as it might have been. The RRD does not have a bright line trigger point. Instead it is predicated on a regulatory judgment by a national (as opposed to a European level) authority in what will inevitably be a politically charged atmosphere that, based on the criteria of Article 27 of the RRD, an institution is likely to fail in the near future. I am skeptical how well this will work. Under Article 27(4) the EBA is meant to issue guidelines to promote convergence of national supervisory and resolution practices regarding the interpretation of these circumstances, but it is clear these interpretations may vary. But if you start putting in hard criteria for intervention, you are coming close to a CoCo, only with the lowest possible trigger point, non-viability. So you may well end up in a situation similar to the US under FDICIA, with something that looks reassuring on paper, but triggers too late to be effective in a crisis. Another possibility would be that, in the course of the "European banking union" discussions, the separate national supervisors will be replaced by a central European supervisor. That would solve the consistency problem, but leave open the level of trigger.

As I noted at the beginning, it is not likely that resolution authorities will be allowed to wield the bail-in tool at an earlier point than non-viability because of the concerns that such action might involve unlawful expropriation[28], but allowing it to be used only at that point in essence makes the institution's survival turn on a single card very late in the game. I would far prefer a process that kicks in earlier and more automatically, which is realistically only achievable with a contractual instrument like CoCos.

Finally, I think there is a distinct advantage to creating a defined class of securities subject to conversion or write-down upon the occurrence of clearly defined triggers, which are then priced according to the market's evaluation of the likelihood of these events occurring. As noted above, these securities will surely be more expensive to issue than ordinary senior debt of the same institution, but that price will apply just to those designated bonds. Compare to that the situation where all the senior debt of an institution, with a few exceptions for insured deposits, secured debt, derivatives and the like are potentially subject to bail-in. This will most likely result in increasing the cost of all of the institution's unsecured debt and at the limit could make its unsecured debt close to unmarketable. If this occurs, the institution will have to rely even more on secured debt in the form of covered bonds, repos with its central bank or the ECB or the overnight repo market. At some point the institution runs out of eligible collateral or finds that its pledged collateral has declined in value or increased in volatility so that it can no longer support its outstanding debt. As we found in the last crisis, that can happen very quickly, exposing the institution to what has been called a "run on repo"[29] and thus making it more rather than less unstable.

I think we should be concerned about exacerbating this trend in the context of an already shrinking market for unsecured bank senior debt. The Wall Street Journal reported in an article on July 20, 2012 that current senior debt raising by Eurozone banks, at €112 billion through June 2012, had declined by 47% year on year and now amounted to a little over one third of the borrowing level of 2009 (€315 billion).[30] Part of this decline may be due to the substitution effects of the European Central Bank's two long term repurchase operations ("LTROs") at the

28 Article 4.3 of the Explanatory Memorandum to the CDM specifically notes this concern and says "[I]t is for this reason that the point of entry into resolution should be as close as possible to insolvency ...".

29 *Gorton and Metrick* (2010).

30 These numbers strike me as very high, but a more recent survey of reports on bank bond issuances in the Frankfurter Allgemeine Zeitung (FAZ) of August 16, 2012 cites studies by the rating agencies which point in the same direction. According to the FAZ, unsecured Eurozone bank debt issues declined by 28% to €182 billion through the end of July, while issuances of covered

end of 2011 and in early 2012, but those operations were made necessary by the inability of Eurozone banks to raise unsecured senior debt to replace maturing debt which had been guaranteed by their governments during the financial crisis. This trend is largely attributed to the growing reluctance of banks to lend to each other on an unsecured basis, rather than being the consequence of a fear that such debt would be subject to bail-in, but making that debt "bail-inable" can only contribute to reinforcing the trend, it seems to me. As David Marks of JP Morgan pointed out in his presentation at the conference, investors have other investment alternatives and do not need to buy Eurozone bank debt. So that on the way to a one card show down, the bail-in tool could end up contributing to destabilizing the institutions involved. It is of course possible to restrict the proportion of senior debt which is subject to bail-in to a percentage total liabilities but, as noted in the RRD Impact Assessment and discussed more fully below, this risks there not being enough bail-inable debt available when needed. I thus think it is unlikely that the RRD will end up with a maximum.

I fully grant to the BCBS that CoCos are largely untried and it may well be that allowing them to be used by G-SIBs to fill their supplemental capital buffers was just the wrong test case for using them. I also note that the U.S. Financial Stability Oversight Council in its July 2012 Report to Congress on CoCos for non-bank financial companies and bank holdings companies mandated by Section 115(c) of the Dodd-Frank Act was lukewarm at best on the topic, suggesting that CoCos "remain an area for private sector innovation" and encouraging regulators to continue to "study the advantages and disadvantages" of including them in regulatory capital frameworks. For the reasons outlined above, I think that it is wishful thinking for regulators to expect that private sector innovation will suffice in the absence of regulatory direction. I think we need more willingness on both sides to experiment and find the right balance in using them rather than having to rely solely on the bail-in tool to recapitalize troubled financial institutions. This tool is equally untested and potentially much more dangerous because if it fails it will do so at the point of non-viability, with no margin for error.

---

bonds increased by 4% to €209 billion, and issues of subordinated bank debt amounted to €30 billion during the same period.

The Bail-In Tool in the RRD

As noted above, the bail-in tool required an extra round of discussions before its form could be finalized in the RRD. The form it ended up in contains a number of peculiarities which I fear will make it difficult to use. According to Article 31(2) (d) RRD the bail-in tool is a resolution tool. According to Article 26(1), in applying the resolution tools resolution authorities shall have regard to the resolution objectives set out in Article 26(2), which include ensuring the continuity of critical functions, avoiding significant adverse effects on financial stability, protecting public funds, minimizing costs, protecting depositors and client funds and assets. All of these, according to Article 26(3), are of equal significance. Then, with respect to the bail-in tool in Article 37(3), the RRD provides that this one tool may only be applied to recapitalize entire institutions (as opposed to bridge banks) if there is a realistic prospect that its application, in conjunction with a business reorganization plan required by Article 47 will, in additional to achieving relevant resolution objectives, "restore the institution in question to financial soundness and long-term viability."[31]

Article 47 requires a reorganization plan to be drawn up by an administrator appointed under Article 46 within one month (the date is still in brackets in the published text) after application of the bail-in tool. This strikes me as a remarkably short time, given how long it is taking to draft the first round of recovery and resolution plans under Dodd-Frank. While the administrator will presumably have access to those plans[32], it is unclear how much overlap there will be among them. The reorganization plan sounds like it will be more than a recovery plan (since it kicks in much later in time, when the institution's situation will have deteriorated further) but different in goals from a resolution plan (since the institution is meant to survive rather than be resolved). Article 46 does not make reference to an administrator, but Article 47 makes clear that in the case of a bail-in, the resolution authorities are meant to restore the institution to financial soundness and long-term viability, although how the authorities will be able to know they can do this at the time they apply the tool if the plan must only be drawn up one month after its application remains unclear. But this is clearly meant to be

---

31 This formulation is an elaboration of Article 3.6 of the FSB's Key Attributes of Effective Resolution Regimes for Financial Institutions of October 2011.

32 This assumes that all relevant institutions will have such plans. Not all current national legislation in Europe requires financial institutions to prepare them.

an additional hurdle to using this one tool which the authorities do not have in using other tools.[33]

The timing issues become even more complex when one turns to Article 41(1) which requires that resolution authorities assess the aggregate amount by which liabilities must be reduced on the basis of a valuation that complies with the requirements of Article 30. Article 30 provides that before taking resolution action, "resolution authorities shall ensure that a fair and realistic valuation of the assets and liabilities of the institution is carried out by a person independent from any public authority, including the resolution authority, and the institution. Where independent valuation is not possible due to the urgency in the circumstances of the case, resolution authorities may carry out the valuation ..." Art. 30(1). Article 30(6) states that "[t]he valuation shall be integrant [sic] part of the decision to apply a resolution tool ..." which seems to indicate it must precede or accompany the use of the tool and in fact Article 30(2) requires that "any losses that could be derived are recognized at the moment the resolution tools are exercised". The timing here seems rather challenging, to say the least.[34] Under Article 30(7) the EBA is charged with developing standards for these valuations, which are then to be adopted by the Commission.

Article 41(2) further requires that in the case of the recapitalization of an entire institution, the use of the bail-in tool must restore the institution's Common Equity Tier 1 capital ratio plus provide an additional "amount that the authority considers necessary to sustain sufficient market confidence in the institution and enable it to continue to comply with the conditions for authorization ..." The Article does not say for how long it must be able to continue to comply, but the

33 However, this additional requirement is necessary only if the goal is to recapitalize an institution as a whole. If the tool is to be used to capitalize a bridge bank (Article 37(2)(6) and (3)) this additional requirement does not apply.

34 The famous weekends in March and September 2008 during which the assets of Bear Stearns and Lehman Brothers were evaluated in fact started before the weekend. JP Morgan's bankers had been evaluating Bear Stearns since Thursday and Lehman had been in negotiations with Merrill Lynch and Barclays before its fateful weekend as well, during in which one assumes due diligence and valuation exercises were taking place. In neither case was a formal valuation required, and in both cases the best that could be come up with by the end of the weekend was a back of the envelope calculation of how large the hole in the respective balance sheet was likely to be. Would this level of approximation suffice to wield the bail-in tool? It is interesting to note in this connection that in the "bail-in" of the Bank of Cyprus it has apparently not been possible, despite several weeks of study, to determine with precision how much of depositors' deposits above €100,000 would ultimately have to be converted to shares: 37.5% will initially be converted, but "[a]nother 20% will be held in reserve for possible future conversion." Cyprus blames E.C.B. role in bank crisis, International Herald Tribune, April 30, 2013, p. 19.

requirement clearly means that the bail-in must not only fill in the hole in the balance sheet made by the losses, but must also fully restore capital to whatever level resolution authority thinks the market will find sufficient. There is no guidance as to how national resolution authorities are to determine this.

Article 50(1) provides that Member States should require institutions which issue debt obligations eligible for bail-in ("eligible liabilities") under a law other than that of a Member State to include in the documentation for that debt a recognition by the creditors that the instrument is subject to write-down or conversion. The requirement does not apply to debt issued under the laws of Member States, although many commentators, including *Tom Huertas* in the accompanying article, advocate including such a recognition in instruments governed by Member State law as well.

Two important changes from prior drafts of the RRD relate to the broadened scope of bail-inable debt and the question of how to determine a minimum amount of debt subject to bail-in which institutions must maintain. The scope of bail-inable debt was widened in Article 38(2)(d) and (3) by exempting as short term only debt with a remaining maturity of less than one month, as compared to one year and by not automatically exempting derivatives. Resolution authorities may exempt derivatives at their own discretion if "necessary or appropriate to achieve the objectives" of ensuring the continuity of critical functions or avoiding significant adverse effects on financial stability. The Commission is charged in Article 38(4)(6) with further specifying the circumstances where such exclusion would be appropriate.

The requirement of maintaining a fixed percentage of total own funds, subordinated debt and bail-inable liabilities has been replaced with a more subjective requirement that this total be sufficient to restore an institution's Common Equity Tier 1 ratio to "a level necessary to restore sufficient market confidence in the institution" in view of the size, business model and risk profile of the institution and the extent its failure would have an adverse effect on financial stability. The Impact Assessment still uses 10% in its calculations and the Commission in its Explanatory Memorandum says "[a]s an example ... an appropriate percentage of total liabilities which could be subject to bail-in could be equal to 10% of total liabilities (excluding regulatory capital)." This suggestion is not binding on the national authorities and Article 39(6) assumes there may be national divergences and that these divergences may even be on an institution by institution basis.[35] But unlike other sections of the RRD where the EBA or the Commission

35 In fact one wonders whether this amount may not also have to vary over time, as the amount of capital the market require may well vary with the perceived severity of the overall situation of the financial sector.

are charged with setting standards to bring about uniformity, in this case the EBA is only to report to the Commission by January 1, 2018 on whether there are divergences. Since the tool does not have to become effective prior to that date under Article 115, it is unclear what the EBA will have to report. The date may simply be a holdover from prior drafts which did not yet defer applicability of the tool.

It is also important to note that a minimum is not a maximum and that the Impact Assessment makes clear that the Commission Staff believes the safest approach is "comprehensive" rather than "restrictive", meaning that any senior liabilities not specifically excluded under Article 38 may be subject to bail-in rather than just the amount required for the minimum, however that ends up being calculated, if necessary to make the use of the tool effective.[36] This is obviously a point on which the European Parliament or the Council might come to another conclusion. However, in doing so they would have to take account of Annex XIII to the Impact Assessment that contains a set of calculations which attempt to quantify whether a 10% loss-absorbing capital plus bail-inable debt (referred to as loss absorbing capital, or "LAC") formula would have sufficed to bail-in European banks during the last crisis. The staff come to the conclusion that "for the average large EU banking group ... the restricted bail-in option would not be sufficient in the two most extreme crisis scenarios" and thus that this option "presents a theoretical risk of not providing a sufficient amount of bail-inable liabilities ...". The large banking groups are the main target of the bail-in tool. Thus, a choice to make the minimum exclusive could defeat the purpose of the bail-in tool, since in a truly dire situation it might fail to provide the buffer needed for the largest institutions, those most likely to be too big to fail.[37] The Final Report of

---

36 The Staff's "comprehensive" approach is what *Tom Huertas* refers to as the "carve out" approach in his contribution to this volume. As he notes, this results in there being a distinction in practice (*de facto*) in the recovery rates among obligations which are legally (*de jure*) *pari passu* and that this in turn could well lead to a claim by the bailed-in holders under Article 67 of the RRD that they would have received more in a liquidation, to the extent that other instruments which rank equally with theirs are not actually bailed-in and receive more in the resolution. Tom contrasts this to what he calls the "waterfall" approach and the Staff refers to as the "restrictive" approach, which would result in effect in the creation of a Tier 3 category of capital instrument for the financial institutions in question.

37 While a great deal of effort has gone into the calculations, the estimate of bail-inable liabilities is based on balance sheet data going back to 2009 and 2010 which the Staff was not able to break down fully into the relevant categories (for large EU bank groups this black box accounts for 31.12% of total liabilities). The Staff then applies an internal model called SYMBOL and concludes that a restricted bail-in model would capture only 13.03% of bail-inable debt and deposits for average large EU banking groups, whereas a comprehensive bail-in model would capture 30.27%. While 13.03% is above the 10% minimum amount for bail-inable debt contained in ear-

the Liikanen Group on reforming the structure of the EU banking sector urges that the bail-in tool should be "applied explicitly to a certain category of debt instruments" to "clarify the position of bail-in instruments within the hierarchy of debt commitments in a bank's balance sheet", noting that this would "greatly increase marketability of both new bail-inable securities and other debt instruments and facilitate the valuation and pricing of these instruments."[38] These latter arguments apply both to bail-in debt and to CoCos.

Differences in both the inclusion of derivatives and the use of the restrictive versus the comprehensive approach to the amount of liabilities subject to bail-in can result in significant differences for the institutions involved. We have just noted the Staff's estimates in Table 6 of Annex XIII of the Impact Assessment of the difference between the restrictive and the comprehensive approach. A recent equity research report from Barclays tries to calculate the impact of including or excluding derivatives. They conclude that, if derivatives are excluded "Deutsche Bank would see their amount of required bail-in liabilities fall by 40%."[39] Barclays also attempts to calculate the additional cost of financing generated by debt being subject to bail-in. It assumes that such debt will pay a yield of between 150 and 300 basis points over the institution's senior unsecured debt. If this were payable only on 10% of the institution's liabilities (minus own funds and subsidiary debt) it finds that the burden on the institutions could be bearable, at 8% of 2014 estimated earnings on average, if derivatives are excluded and 15% if they are included, although the range of impacts varies widely, from virtually no additional cost at Standard Chartered to 45 and 60% (excluding and including derivatives) at Crédit Agricole.

Barclays does not consider what the cost would be if the market were to assume that 10% is a minimum, not a maximum, so that the effect of bail-in on additional elements of senior debt above the 10% LAC could be uncertain (and it would almost have to be uncertain, since the institution will not be able to choose which elements among its unsecured senior debt the resolution authority actually decides to bail-in), then the effect could be multiplied. Barclays calculates that the selection of European banks it examines have on average about two and a half to four times the required 10% LAC minimum (excluding and including derivatives). This would be consistent with the Staff's 30.27% estimate in the Impact Assessment cited above. Applying the 150 to 300 basis point surcharge to

---

lier drafts of the Directive and is still referred to in the Commission's Explanatory Memorandum, that number has been dropped from the text itself.

38 *Liikanen* (2012).

39 *Barclays* (2012).

that broad a segment of senior liabilities could do serious damage to the institutions' earnings. Of course these calculations are all quite theoretical. Barclays starts with the current premium over senior unsecured debt being paid by existing issuers of CoCos – on average 500 basis points – and then discounts it to account for the fact that CoCos convert earlier than bail-inable debt so that the latter should have a lower implied premium. But that cannot be the end of the calculation. The more debt that is subject to bail-in, the smaller the proportion of the loss upon default or bail-in any particular debt issue should have to bear, so the calculation of the corresponding premium would not necessarily be linear. Furthermore, if one assumes a class of CoCo debt which would convert or be written down before the bail-in occurs, that could also change the calculations if investors are convinced that buffer is sufficient to make a bail-in unlikely.

The final Article of the RRD relevant to our discussion is Article 115(1) which, as noted in the Introduction to this article, allows the applicability of the bail-in tool to be delayed until January 1, 2018, three years after the rest of the RRD is to go into effect on January 1, 2015. This delay presumably relates to the thorny problem of "grandfathering," *i.e.* whether the tool should apply to debt which has been issued before the Directive is published or goes into effect. As consensus was difficult to achieve, the solution was apparently to push off the effectiveness date with a keen eye towards the maturity profile of the institutions involved. The JP Morgan March 2012 research note estimates that 70% of currently outstanding European financial institutions' debt would mature prior to January 1, 2015 and the 84% prior to January, 2018. As a consequence, the vast majority of debt outstanding when the tool becomes applicable should have been issued after the publication of the Directive and thus at a time when the purchasers would have been aware that it might be subject to bail-ins. Well advised issuers can be expected to start including health warnings concerning the possibility of a bail-in in the disclosure documents for new senior unsecured debt issuances as of now, whether or not they include it in the terms and conditions of the instruments themselves. As noted above, this compromise has the effect of leaving resolution authorities without an essential tool to recapitalize failing banks with private sector, as opposed to public, funds for another five and a half years.

Conclusion

The impression I am left with after reading through the RRD and the Impact Statement is that its authors have tried to build in safeguards for investors to protect the bail-in tool from legal attack, but that these safeguards will make using the tool – once it is available – difficult, and much more time consuming than something that can just be done over a weekend.[40] The resolution authority will need an independent evaluation and a reorganization plan. Technically only the former should precede use of the tool and the June 2012 draft has provided for a preliminary valuation, but it still requires that all losses must be realized "at the moment the resolution tool [is] utilized," so that it should be technically possible to use the tool, but it risks being a long drawn out process, taking months rather than a weekend, as the Commission Staff was told during the April discussions on the tool.[41] This warning seems confirmed by the experience of the Bank of Cyprus which after several weeks was still so unsure of how much of its deposits would need to be converted into shares that it determined to hold "in reserve" an amount equal to more than 50% of the amount initially converted. See Note 34 above. There is still a lot of work to be done on how the tool will be applied. But then we have more than five years before it can be used. Given the continued fragility of the banks in the Eurozone, I question whether we can wait that long. Many of them have not yet demonstrated that their balance sheets have recuperated from the financial crisis even as they are being negatively affected by the effects of the sovereign debt crisis.[42] I think it truly is time to take another look at CoCos, both as an alternative to bail-ins (until they become available) and as a desirable complement thereafter.

40 I have always thought the idea that a bail-in could be accomplished over a weekend was optimistic, to say the least, due to the difficulties in valuing the assets of a large and complex financial institution under stress in a crisis situation and, during the additional discussions on the bail-in tool, the Staff were apparently told to expect the process to take months. See Footnote 20 *supra*.

41 Impact Assessment, Appendix XVIII, at p. 246.

42 The need for a recapitalization tool for banks is all the more urgent, given the linkages between bank balance sheets which carry significant amounts of sovereign debt and the rating and market value of that debt. At the extreme, as we have seen in the case of Greece, if a sovereign defaults or imposes a large haircut on its creditors, we must assume that most of its domestic banks will become automatically insolvent, but downgrading of sovereign debt (with the apparent exception of the United States) can also be expected to have a negative effect on the market value of its debt. That, in turn will be reflected in the balance sheet value of that debt held by banks in their trading books. Many of the losses incurred by banks in the last crisis were due to "mark to market" losses on their holdings of asset backed securities as the ratings of those securities were slashed and their market value declined. Replace "asset backed" with "sovereign debt" and the process can be repeated, except to the extent sovereign debt is accounted for as "held to maturity" by the banks, in which case only a permanent impairment, e.g. as a result of a sovereign debt restructuring, would have that effect.

Murphy, Walsh and *Wilkinson* (2012), building in part on the work of *Calomiris* and *Herring* (2011) propose a sensible model for analyzing CoCos which could serve as a useful template for such an effort. The model includes a single trigger, defined in terms of market capitalization[43] relative to book value of assets, set at a level significantly higher than that at which bank resolution measures, including bail-ins, would come into effect, with a conversion price set at time of issue, a perpetual life and tax deductible coupons. Perpetual life is suggested to prevent holders from "running" before conversion occurs. I am not convinced that this concern is well founded. Holders of dated paper cannot "run" either during the stated maturity of the paper they hold. They can only sell it, but the instrument remains outstanding and thus available to fulfill its capital buffer function. It strikes me that sufficiently long dated paper with staggered maturities would do the job too. Tax deductibility or not is an assumption to be made to test a model, but it will turn out to be what it is under national law (possible in Europe, but less likely in the US), and is not an essential element of the instrument as I see it. When and how the conversion price is set is something I believe the market should determine. Setting the price in advance facilitates modeling and follows the traditional pattern of normal convertibles, but may not be appropriate to accomplish the role of appropriately diluting the existing common at the time of conversion.[44] Lloyds Banking Group used this option in 2009, whereas Credit Suisse in 2011 opted for the higher of the average equity price over the 30 days prior to announcement of the conversion or a pre-specified floor.

However these issues are resolved, the essential point is to get back to work on these instruments before the next crisis is upon us and we find that five years on from the outbreak of the last crisis we still do not have the tools to recapitalize banks with private sector funds, but must rely again on tax payer funds. We may not have much time before the next systemic crisis and in fact may already be in it in the Eurozone, so we really have no time to lose. To quote Calomiris and Herring, "[i]f a CoCo requirement had been in place in 2007, the disruptive fail-

43 I strongly support market-related measures over balance sheet measures as the latter are lagging indicators and, among the market-related measures, I find market capitalization the most convincing predictor of future distress. The study of the determinants of changes in CDS spreads of Eurozone credit institutions by *Anneart et al.* (2010) shows the difficulties in relying on those spreads. Also, as noted above, they are available only for some 54 Eurozone credit institutions. *Nieto* (2012).

44 As *Haldane* points out, the conversion price needs to be close to the market value at the time of conversion if we are to avoid transferring value from existing equity holders and CoCo investors. *Haldane* (2011) at 8.

ures of large financial institutions, and the systemic meltdown after 2008, could have been avoided."

Bibliography

Anneart, Jan, Marc de Ceuster, Patrick van Roy and Christina Vespno What determines euro area CDS spreads? National Bank of Belgium Working Paper Research No. 190, May 2010.

Bailey, Andrew The future of banking regulation in the UK, Speech at the BBA Annual Banking Conference, London, 17 October 2012.

Barclays Research, Bondholders to the Rescue? Bail-in debt at European banks, 5 July 2012.

Basel Committee on Banking Supervision ("BCBS"), Minimum requirements to ensure loss absorbency at the point of non-viability, January 2011.

BCBS, Global systemically important banks: assessment methodology and the additional loss absorbency requirements, November 2011.

Calomiris, Charles W. and Richard J. Herring Why and How to Design a Contingent Convertible Debt Requirement, mimeo, Revised November 2011.

Claessens, S., Herring, R.J. and Schoenmaker, D. A Safer World Financial System: Improving the Resolution of Systemic Institutions, Geneva Reports on the World Economy No. 12 (2010).

Coffee, John C., Jr. Systemic Risk After Dodd-Frank: Contingent Capital and the Need for Regulatory Strategies Beyond Oversight, Columbia Law Review, Vol. 111, p. 795 (2011).

D'Sousa, A., B. Foran, G. Hafez, C. Himmelberg, Q. Main, J. Mannoia, R. Ramsden and S. Romanoff Ending "Too Big to Fail," Goldman Sachs Global Markets Institute, December 2009.

European Banking Authority, Common Term Sheet for Buffer Convertible Capital Securities, December 2011.

European Commission, Commission Staff Working Document, Impact Assessment Accompanying the Resolution Directive, SWD (2012) 166/3 (the "Impact Assessment"), June 2012.

European Commission, Discussion paper on the debt write-down tool – bail-in, 2012.

European Commission, Proposal for a Directive of the European Parliament and of the Council establishing a framework for the recovery and resolution of credit institutions and investment firms and amending Council Directives 77/91/EEC and 82/891/EC, Directives 2001/24/EC, 2004/25/EC, 2007/36/EC and 2011/35/EC and Regulation (EU) No 1093/2010, com (2012) 280/3 (the "Resolution Directive" or "RRD"), June 2012.

European Systemic Risk Board, Forbearance, resolution and deposit insurance, Reports of the Advisory Scientific Committee No. 1/July 2012.

Financial Stability Oversight Council, Report to Congress on Study of a Contingent Capital Requirement for Certain Non bank Financial Companies and Bank Holding Companies, July 2012.

FINMA, Addressing 'too big to fail': the Swiss SIFI policy, October 2010.

Frühauf, Markus Immer weniger Bankanleihen, Frankfurter Allgemeine Zeitung, 16 August, 2012.

Gorton, Gary B. and Andrew Metrick Securitized Banking and the Run on Repo, Yale ICF Working Paper No. 09–14, November 2010.

Haldane, Andrew G. Capital discipline, Bank of England, 2011.
High-level Expert Group on reforming the structure of the EU banking sector, chaired by Erki Liikanen ("Liikanen Report"), Final Report, 2 October 2012.
J.P. Morgan European Credit Research, the $2.8 Trillion Question? Assessing the Impact of EU Resolution Regimes on Senior Debt, 23 March 2012.
Kenadjian, Patrick S, editor, Too Big to Fail – Brauchen wir ein Sonderinsolvenzrecht für Banken? De Gruyter, 2012.
Liikanen, Erkki Structural Banking Reform, speech delivered at the Financial Stability and the Single Market European Commission Conference in Brussels on November 9, 2012 (Liikanen 2012).
Liikanen, Erkki Corrected Transcript of Oral Evidence to be published as HC 606-iii, Oral Evidence Taken Before the Parliamentary Commission on Banking Standards, 22 October 2012 (Liikanen 2012A).
Murphy, Gareth, Mark Walsh and Matthew Willison Precautionary contingent capital, Financial Stability Paper No. 16 – May 2012, Bank of England.
Nieto, Maria J. What role, if any, can market discipline play in supporting macro prudential policy? Documentos Occasionales No. 1202, Bank of Spain, 2012.

Bei Fragen zur Produktsicherheit wenden Sie sich bitte an:
If you have any questions regarding product safety, please contact:

Walter de Gruyter GmbH
Genthiner Straße 13
10785 Berlin
productsafety@degruyterbrill.com